THE HANDLEY PAGE
VICTOR

VOLUME ONE

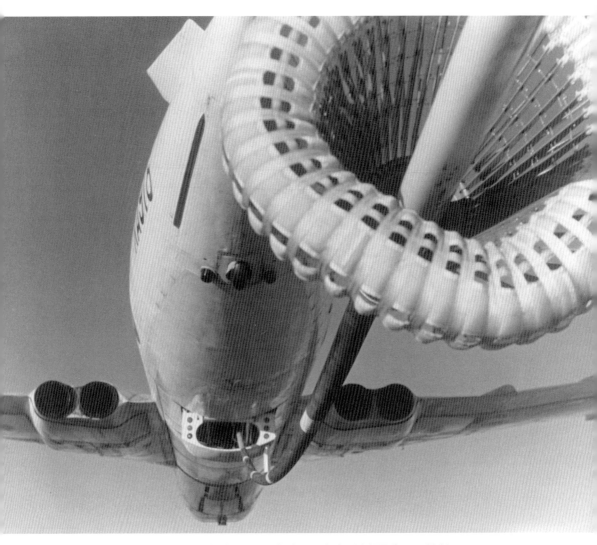

Victor BK1 XA 918 refuelling on trials duty with the A&AEE during 1964. Author's collection

THE **HANDLEY PAGE**
VICTOR

THE HISTORY & DEVELOPMENT
OF A CLASSIC JET

VOLUME ONE
THE HP 80 PROTYPE AND THE MARK 1 SERIES

ROGER R. BROOKS

ARAeS

Pen & Sword
AVIATION

Dedication

To my wife Heather, also known as 'Heater' for support and encouragement over the many years this book has been in development and compilation.

First published in Great Britain in 2007 and reprinted 2009 by
PEN & SWORD AVIATION
an imprint of
Pen & Sword Books Limited
47 Church Street
Barnsley
S. Yorkshire
S70 2AS

Copyright © Roger Brooks, 2007, 2009
Colour profiles © Dave Windle 2007, 2009

ISBN 978 1 84415 411 1

The right of Roger R. Brooks
to be identified as Author of this Work
has been asserted by him in accordance with
the Copyright, Designs and Patents Act 1988.

A CIP catalogue record for this book
is available from the British Library.

Printed and bound in Thailand
by Kyodo Nation Printing Services Co., Ltd

Pen & Sword Books Ltd incorporates the imprints of
Pen & Sword Aviation, Pen & Sword Maritime,
Pen & Sword Military, Wharncliffe Local History, Pen & Sword Select,
Pen & Sword Military Classics and Leo Cooper.

For a complete list of Pen & Sword titles please contact:
PEN & SWORD BOOKS LIMITED
47 Church Street, Barnsley, South Yorkshire, S70 2AS, England.
E-mail: enquiries@pen-and-sword.co.uk
Website: www.pen-and-sword.co.uk

CONTENTS

FOREWORD

I am honoured and delighted to have been asked to introduce this book, which is an in-depth study of an aircraft whose design and development, occupied on and off nearly half my working life from 1951. I have great affection for it, not least because it brought me into close working contact with so many highly competent people, one of the foremost being the Author. In fact, I did not meet him until long after the parent company Handley Page, went out of business, since I was an aerodynamicist by trade and (unfortunately) had little contact with the RAF people at the 'sharp end' operating and maintaining the aircraft.

Roger Brooks has some 40 years of experience of working at the 'sharp end' with the Victor and other aircraft, and has distilled some of his vast knowledge into this volume. But not only operating aspects, as he has collected a comprehensive archive covering the Victor's design and development story, mainly from those who were there – Godfrey Lee, effectively the 'Father of the Victor', Hedley Hazelden, Chief Test Pilot on the first flight, and many others, and lucidly presents it.

That valuable contribution is enhanced by reference to many Technical Manuals, Reports, Specifications and Brochure, all combining to make this a most valuable contribution to our Aviation Heritage literature.

The collection of statistical data is probably unique, and is usefully supplemented by a careful selection of illustrations.

The amount of ground covered by the Author is clear from the extensive quoted bibliography, but in fact his researches went further, and his experience as a Crew Chief for the aircraft (still continued with XL231 'Lusty Lindy' operating at Elvington) is very evident in the scope and detail in the data presented.

I feel sure this is a book which will be on most serious aviation historian's bookshelf, and will quickly get dog-eared with use, but I hope the aircraft enthusiast will also use it – at least he will know that this is the real, unassailable 'gen' compiled by someone who knows the aircraft inside out.

A.H. Fraser-Mitchell
Sometime Chief Aerodynamicist Handley Page Ltd
Vice President, Handley Page Association

January 2005

INTRODUCTION AND ACKNOWLEDGEMENTS

Over the past 40 years or so, many books have been written on the Handley Page Victor and the V Force aircraft in general. This book is not in the same vein as those. It is written as a Data File and subdivided into sections dealing with specific variations of this unique aircraft. It is intended as a reference book and you do not have to read all of it, just the relevant items that appeal to you. The accuracy of data in this book is backed up by the source material, which I have quoted the main items in the bibliography. It is by no means the definitive history of this aircraft as a considerable amount of very interesting data is not available for a variety of reasons by a few organisations for strange excuses.

I would like to produce a second edition within the next few years containing additional information on this book and the Victor in Service with the Royal Air Force from 1957-1993. Contributions for it are welcomed from all readers, no matter what they contain, and should be sent to the publisher.

I would like to thank the following for their assistance and guidance over the years in the course of developing the Data File.

The following members of the Handley Page Association:
Harry Fraser-Mitchell, Peter Cronbach, John Allam, Spud Murphy, Peter P. Baker, Jock Still, John Rudeforth, Alan Dowsett, John Harding, John Smith, Chris Scivyer, Brian Bowen, Mike Wilson, Harry Rayner, David Blades and Steve Mills. Finally, to all those members who I have spoken to over the past many years.

The following past Members of Handley Page Ltd and the Handley Page Association:
Godfrey Lee, Hedley Hazelden, Ian Bennett, Bob Williams, Gordon Roxborough, Reginald Stafford, Charles Joy, R.H. Sandifer, Dr G.V. Lachmann, W.H. MacRostie, C.O. Vernon, F.R.C. Houndsfield and John Tank. For being allowed access to the articles they wrote for the HP Bulletin nearly 50 years ago and in particular to Ray Funnell for access to his archives.

From the Royal Air Force:
Aircrew
Air Vice Marshal John Herrington, Flt Lt Pancho Painting, Flt Lt Eric Anstead, Flt Lt Alan Fisher, Air Commodore 'Spike' Milligan, Flt Lt Terry Filing, Sdn Ldr Jerry Mudford, Flt Lt Ken Norman, Air Commodore David Bywater, Flt Lt Alan Gardener, Sdn Ldr C.R. 'Pop' Miles, Sdn Ldr M Reade, Wing Commander Dave Griffiths, Flt Lt David Coleman, Group Captain Tony Ringer, Sdn Ldr Gordon Stringer, Flt Lt R.T. Hayward, Flt Lt John Bussey, Sdn Ldr Tim Mason, Sdn Ldr Al Stephenson, Sdn Ldr Bob Tuxford, Sdn Ldr Tony Cunnane, Wing Commander Barry Neal, Flt Lt Al Skelton, Wing Commander Bob Prothero, Flt Lt John Ledger. All the Victor captains and crews I flew with on the Mk 1 and Mk 2 Tanker Fleet as their Crew Chief.

Crew Chiefs
Bill Swann, David Haylett, John Kent, Sid Harding, Dave Parsons, Robbie Honnor and Brian Martin.

Ground Crew
Dennis Robinson, Gordon Stringer, Jim Jones, Jim Gosling, Paul Goss, Duncan Curtis, Mick Crooks, Dave Wynn-Jones, Don Williams (Australia), Robin Cooper, Stan Jones, Pete Claydon, Tony Regan, Rick Gill and Doug Gawley. Also, thanks go to all those whose names I have failed to remember.

Finally, my grateful thanks go to the following from many walks of like for their interest in the Victor and assisting in many ways:
Andre Tempest (Owner Victor XL231 'Lusty Lindy'), Martin Garland and BAE Systems Woodford Heritage Centre, Graeme Rodgers (NZ), Garry O'Keefe, The Victor Association, Ken Ellis, Jarrod Cotter and Duncan Cubbitt of *Fly Past*.

Cover credits:
The Front Cover: First Prototype of the HP 80 WB771 flown by Sdn/Ldr Hazelden on a test flight 1953. *Authors Collection via HPA*
The Back Cover: Top Picture: Victor B1 XA918 second production aircraft on development flying: *Authors Collection via HPA*
Second Picture: Victor B1 XH592 15 Squadron arriving at RAAF Richmond, Sydney NSW Australia on the 20/6/61 after a high speed run from England and on the last leg from Darwin beating the record time by 20 minutes. Captained by Wing Commander Tony Ringer seen here descending from the aircraft, the time from England was 19hours. *Photo and data via Graeme Rodgers New Zealand*
Third Picture: Front Cabin of Victor B1A(K2P) XH648 57 Squadron now with the IWM at Duxford. *Heather Brooks*
Fourth Picture: Victor K1A XH618 57 Squadron RAF Marham 1972. *Authors Collection*
Bottom Picture: HP 80 WB771 Banking to Port with Wheels down, Flap both nose and main down and airbrakes open. *Authors Collection HPA*

ABBREVIATIONS

AAPP	Airborne Auxiliary Power Plant
A&AEE	Aircraft and Armament Experimental Establlishment
AAR	Airborne Air Refuelling
AC	Alternating Current
ADF	Automatic Direction Finding
AEO	Air Electronics Officer (RAF Aircrew)
AMU	Air Mileage Unit
ARC 52	UHF Radio
ARI	Airborne Radio Installation
AVCAT	Aviation Jet Fuel (used by Royal Navy on Carriers)
AVTUR	Aviation Jet Fuel (Jet A1)
AVTAG	Aviation Jet Fuel JP4 Wide Cut Gasoline type fuel
AwC or AWC	Awaiting Collection
C of G	Centre of Gravity
CAT 3/Cat 3	Category 3 (Aircraft Repair Status)
CAU	Cold Air Unity
C(A)	Controller of Aircraft (Military CAA)
CL	Buffet Boundary Measurment
CRE	Central Reconnaissance Establishment
c/s	Call Sign
C/T	Continuation Training
CWP DC	Contractors Working Party (HP or HAS)
DC	Direct Current
DF	Direction Funding
DOR	Director of Operational Requirements
DTD	Directorate of Technical Development
DV	Direct Vision (small opening windows in the cabin)
EAS	Estimated Air Speed
ECM	Electronic Counter Measures
FEAF	Far East Air Force (RAF)
FI	Fatigue Index
FSII	Fuel System Icing Inhibitor
G4B	Aircraft Compass System Mk 1 Victor
GP	General Purpose
GPU	Ground Power Unit
HDU	Hose Drum Unit
HF	High Frequency
HLBSP	High Level Blue Steel Profile
HP	High Pressure/Handley Page
HZ	Hertz (frequency of electrical power)
IAS	Indicated Air Speed
IFF	Identification Friend or Foe
ILS	Instrument Landing System
IMN	Indicated Mach Number
IRT	Instrument Rating Test
JARIC	Joint Airborne Reconnaissance Intelligence Centre
JIB	Joint Intelligence Branch
JPT	Jet Pipe Temperature
JMC	Joint Maritime Control
KVA	Kilo/Volt/Amps

KW	Kilowatt
Ldg	Landing
LL	Low Level
LLBSP	Low Level Blue Steel Profile
LV	Low Voltage (24/28VDC)
M.A.P.	Ministry of Aircraft Production
Mcrit	Critical Mach Number
MF	Medium Frequency
MFS	Military Flight System (used in Mk 2 Victor/Vulcan)
Min Tech	Ministry of Technology
MOA	Ministry of Aviation
MRR	Maritime Radar Reconnaissance (H2S+ R88 Camera)
M.U.	Maintenance Unit (RAF)
MV	Medium Voltage
NBC	Navigation Bombing Computer
NBS	Navigation Bombing System (H2S+NBC)
N/F	Not Flown
NGTE	National Gas Turbine Establishment
NM	Nautical Miles
OCU	Operational Conversion Unit
ODM	Operating Data Manual
PE	Pressure Error
PFCU	Powered Flying Control Unit
PR	Photographic Reconnaissance
PSI	Pounds Per Square Inch (pressure)
PTR 175	UHF/VHF Radio
QFI	Qualified Flying Instructor
R.A.E.	Royal Aircraft Establishment
RAT	Ram Air Turbine
RATO	Rocket Assisted Take Off
RBS	Radar Bombing System
RCM	Radio Counter Measures
RE	Royal Engineers
RPM	Revolutions Per Minute
RRF	Radar Reconnaissance Flight
Rtn	Return/Returned
RWR	Radar Warning Receiver
SARAH	Search and Rescue Aircraft Homer
SARBE	Search and Rescue Beacon
SBAC	Society of British Aircraft Constructors
SOC	Struck off Charge
SOO	Special Order Only (modifications)
SSR	Secondary Surveillance Radar
TEZ	Total Exclusion Zone (South Atlantic)
Tkr	Tanker
T/O	Take Off
TRU	Transformer Rectifier Unit
Trg	Training
TTF	Tanker Training Flight
TX/RX	Transmitter/Receiver (Radio/Radar)
U/C	Undercarriage
UDF	Ultra High Frequency Direction Finding
UHF	Ultra High Frequency
U/S	Unserviceable
VHF	Very High Frequency
VISRBS	Visual Radar Bombing System
VMMU	Victor Major Maintenance Unit
ZULU	Greenwich Mean Time

BIBLIOGRAPHY

V Force, Andrew Brookes, Book Club Associates, 1982
Crash, Andrew Brookes, Ian Allan, 1991
Handley Page Victor, Andrew Brookes, Ian Allan, 1988
RAF Nuclear Deterrent Force, Humphrey Wynn, HMSO, 1994
Handley Page Aircraft, C H Barnes, Putnam, 1976
Thunder and Lightening, Chris Allen, HMSO, 1991
Tests of Character, Don Middleton, Airlife
Aim Sure 75 Years of XV Squadron, Flt Lt T W Jones, Palka Druck, 1990
Jet Adventure, Geoffrey Norris, Phoenix House, 1962
Handley Page Bulletins, nos. 213, 220, 225, 228, 229, 230, 231
Handley Page Repair Reports
Handley Page Brochures, various, HP 80, Mk 1
Handley Page Victor Servicing School Notes Mk 1
Handley Page Test Pilots Flying Log 1952-1970
Handley Page Flight Test Observers Reports
Handley Page Victor Mk 1 Tanker Final Conference Report
Handley Page Victor Low Level Role Report
Handley Page Victor Wing Tip Fuel Tanks Report
Handley Page Victor Thrust Augmentation Report
A&AEE Boscombe Down/HP Test Pilot Reports, various
Royal Aeronautical Society Transcripts of Lecture (Victor)
The following Air Publications were used for checking data accuracy only:
AP 101B-1100   Victor All Marks
AP 101B-1101   Victor B Mk 1
AP 101B-1103   Victor B Mk 1A

Bomber Command/Strike Command Victor Servicing School Notes (all Marks)
Release to Service Data
My extensive collection of a wide variety of books, magazines and other records and
    data sources collected over thirty-five years.
Interviews and discussions with Handley Page Flight Test and Ground Test Staff,
    Aerodynamicists, Production Engineers and many production staff. A&AEE Test Pilots
    and Flight Test Engineers.

PART ONE

The HP 80
From its Concept to Flight

The Requirements that lead to the HP 80 and later the Victor

This article is based on the paper by G H Lee ARCS, BSc, DIC, FRAes
Deputy Chief Designer of Handley Page in 1954 and presented to the
Royal Aeronautical Society Handley Page Memorial Lecture on 26 May 1976.

'Unassailable Aerodynamical Logic' – an enduring theme for Handley Page Ltd

As for the most of the British Aircraft History, the jet age started for Handley Page in 1945, when the war had been won and we had the chance to consider properly the implication of jet propulsion, until then used only in the fighter installations. Two events in that year should be recorded.

1. The setting up by the Ministry of Aircraft Production of the Swept Wings Advisory Committee, comprising of representatives of the official Establishments [RAE etc] and the aircraft manufacturers.
2. In September-October sent a team, to Germany to find out about the German work on tailless and swept wing aircraft.

In June 1945 Sir Frederick Handley Page was confident that a replacement for the Avro Lincoln would be needed and as the specification for the twin engine jet bomber had been issued it seemed logical to Sir Frederick that the 4 engine aircraft would be next. On the 14th June 1945 he issued a private and confidential memorandum address to R.S. Stafford, Frank Ratcliffe and Godfrey Lee in this he requested an immediate investigation of two classes of bomber one of 100,000lb all up weight with four turbojets of the size of the AJ65 (Avon) or two

The late Sir Frederick Handley Page. Author's collection

of twice that size the other a 60,000lb aircraft with two AJ65 engines and he suggested that they should have wings incorporating a 40 degree sweep.

The real start of the Victor design was in the course of the next few months actually undertaken in September-October when a visit to the German aeronautical research establishments at Gottingham and Volkenrode with a MAP fact finding team was undertaken by Godfrey Lee as the representative of Handley Page. It was, as part of this visit that the concept of the swept wing as a means of enabling an aircraft with reasonably thick wings to fly at high subsonic speeds without drag rise first became understood. From this there stemmed the realisation that by combining a swept wing with a jet engine one could have an efficient high subsonic speed aeroplane capable of carrying a good payload over a long range.

Work on this concept began at Handley Page in about November 1945

In January 1946 after work on the HP72 heavy transport had been abandoned, the designations HP72A and HP75A were used as a cover for Godfrey Lee's investigations into the possible jet propelled high-speed bomber of 90,000lb all up weight. The HP 75A with a front rider plane was quickly ruled out in favour of the 72A with 45 degree swept wings and wing tip rudders having a small swept tail plane and elevators to balance nose down pitching moments caused by either flap lowering at low speed or compressibility at high speed. With no operational requirement yet promulgated by the Air Staff to guide him, Godfrey Lee put forward an inspired proposal on the 25th February 1946, for a design of 2100sq ft, 122ft span, aspect ratio 7, wing loading 43lb/sq.ft to carry a 10,000lb bomb at 520 knots true air speed over a still air range of 5,000 statute miles; the wing root thickness/chord ratio was to be 16%, with a 9 ft diameter body accommodating a crew of four in a pressurised nose compartment. Avon (AJ65) engines were larger than the ideal size for this aircraft and Godfrey Lee suggested scaling them down to 5,600lb. Two days later Reginald Stafford approved this proposal and instructed C.F. Joy the Chief Draughtsman to prepare a brochure for submission to the Principal Director of Technical Development (Stuart Scott-Hall) by the end of March 1946; this brochure was to demonstrate the projects effectiveness as a bomber. At this stage the number HP 80 was allocated and so started the HP80/Victor project way back in March 1946.

The late Godfrey Lee, 'Father of the Victor'. Heather Brooks

The brochure was issued to the Director of Operational Requirements Group Captain Silyn-Roberts and with his deputy Group Captain Cooper they visited HP Cricklewood on the 19th July 1946 to discuss the third draft which had been issued in June 1946 of the Air Staffs requirements for a long range bomber mainly derived from the Handley Page proposal, but containing several operational innovations. These included the visual bombing facility as a back up to the possible delay and or failure of the radar bomb sight, a Flight Engineer's station, unless the engine controls could be simplified, Electronic Counter Measures operator in a separate cabin near the tail, reached by a tunnel from the main cabin and if possible a jettisonable main pressure cabin. A bomb bay load of 30,000lb was to be carried with normal tanks full, but bomb bay tanks were to be allowed to achieve maximum range with a 10,000lb bomb.

Members of the Telecomunication Research Establishment (TRE) visited HP Cricklewood on the 2nd November 1946 to discuss radar equipment, the main feature being the H2S Mk 9 Scanner 6ft long and rotating on a vertical axis within a large radome below the flight deck floor, in addition were Gee and Rebecca Mk4 for short-range navigation, IFF and ECM, the latter requiring a tail parabolic scanner of 18inch diameter facing aft, the estimated total weight of the radar equipment was 1,500lbs and all aerials would be suppressed. The TRE wanted the H2S scanner to be pressurised but this was virtually impossible and the idea was abandoned. It later came to the notice of C.F.Joy that the DOR insisted that the crew cabin being as small as possible to reduce the vulnerability, even if it were at the expense of crew comfort and that the whole pressure cabin should be jettisionable because the use of ejection seats at 50,000ft and 500mph was considered likely to be fatal. The whole cabin would be let down on large parachutes with the crew strapped in 25g seats falling nose first and relying on the nose structure to absorb the shock of impact

Two pilots were required and it was agreed that locating the ECM operator in the tail was impracticable because of the large size of the proposed nuclear weapon, which might be 6 ft in diameter and up to 30 ft long. The Air Staff intentions were made known by Stuart Scott-Hall when he visited HP Cricklewood on the 25th November 1946; they wished to replace the AVRO Lincoln in 5 years time by a four jet bomber capable of delivering a 10,000lb nuclear weapon at 500mph from a height of 45,000ft the still air range being 3,500miles; as a later development the range would have to be increased to 5,000 miles and the operational ceiling to 50,000ft these data being formally promulgated in the Air Staff Operational Requirement No. 230. Godfrey Lee estimated all up weight to be 90,000lb for 3,500 miles using a swept wing and 121,000lb for a conventional straight wing. A further meeting was held with the Principal Director of Technical Development on 14th January 1947. After Handley Page had submitted their proposal to meet OR230, the official view was that both the structure weights and drag estimates were optimistic, so that the design cruising speed would not be released. The DOR now wanted the cruising speed to be raised to 575mph which meant that the all up weight also would have to rise to 100,000lb in order to attain the 3,500 miles still air range or 120,000lb for 4,000miles. Therefore tenders would be called for to meet the revised specification B35/46 which had been finalised on 1/1/47 and approved by the Director of Aircraft Research and Development on the 24/1/47 and issued with OR 230 on 24/3/47. In view of the large wind tunnel test programme involved, the prototype HP80 could not be expected to fly until 1951. Apart from the exploration of the new problems of tip stall, high lift sections, stability and various methods of boundary layer control, a firm choice between tailed and tailless types still had to be made. Charles Joy proposed to begin the drawing office programme on the 1/10/47 allowing 21months until June 1949 for the basic layout and 30 months to March 1950 for the completion of the powered flying control system. All drawings for the first prototype would be completed by June 1951 and the extra drawings for the fully equipped prototype by March 1952. The target date for the first flight of the flying shell was March 1952 and for the fully equipped aircraft September 1952. It was a tremendous programme for the small design team but not impossible, so the HP80 tender was submitted.

On the 28th July 1947 Sir Fredrick Handley Page received a telephone call from Stuart Scott-Hall stating that the HP80 was to be ordered along with the AVRO 698 subject to the confirmation of the high-speed wind tunnel test results to approve the theoretical basis of the design.

We were started on the 'Victor'

The Basic Design Concept
Specification B35/46 called for an aircraft capable of carrying a considerable bomb load (10,000lb) over a range of 1,500 miles from a base that might be anywhere in the world. The aircraft will be required to attack targets at great distance inside enemy territory. And it must be assumed that it will be tracked by radar and other methods for a large part of its flight. It must therefore be capable of avoiding destruction by making the inevitable attack from ground and air launched weapons difficult.

To achieve this the aircraft must have the following:

1. A high cruising speed which should be such that the attacking fighters will have to

fly at a speed at which they might become unmanoeuvrable.

2. The design must be such that the aircraft can turn rapidly and without loss of height or much loss of speed when at maximum cruising height. The height being 35,000 to 50,000ft.

3.The carrying of adequate warning devices to detect the approach of ground launched weapons and the proximity of approaching aircraft.

4. The carrying of defensive equipment such as jamming devices for guided missiles.

5. The size of the pressure cabin must be as small as possible.

6. Visual and electronic bomb-aiming positions are required.

7. Maximum performance is the ultimate aim and must not be sacrificed for ease of maintenance.

8. It must be possible to operate from existing Heavy Bomber airfields at the maximum loaded weight which must, therefore, not exceed 100,000lb.

9. The aircraft must be suitable for large-scale production. It is stated in the Specification that the economic production of 500 aircraft at a maximum of 10 per month was proposed.

HP 80/Victor Specification and Design Concept

The combination of sweep and range seemed to us to lead to the need to have both high sweep (or fairly high sweep) and moderately high aspect ratio. For us combining high sweep and high aspect ratio gave rise to the tip stall problem. Therefore the Crescent wing was evolved. We came to the crescent wing by arguing that the high sweep was essential at the root for structural reasons and to provide adequate stowage for engines and undercarriage. It was then argued that if we reduced the sweep over the outer parts of the wing we would reduce at the tip where it mattered, the adverse effects from sweep that gave rise to tip stall. In particular it was expected that this would reduce the trouble from the outwardly drifting boundary layer over the rear of the wing, it being assumed that the boundary layer from the highly swept parts of the wing would stream off the wing before reaching the wing tip. We had to accept a weight penalty from the thin outer wing of about 22 degrees sweep and 6% t/c at the tip but felt that since this part of the wing is the least highly loaded the extra weight was acceptable; stowage problems did not arise in the outer wing. We decided that to go from 53 degrees to 22 degrees at one kink was too sudden so we put in an intermediate section at about 35 degrees.

The final sweep on production aircraft after further wind tunnel testing at 1/4 chord was to end up as 47.5 degrees at station 60-212 the inner wing, 40.5 degrees at station 312-330 the intermediate wing and 32 degrees at station 330-660 the outer wing.

We first intended that the HP 80 should be to all intents and purposes, tailless, since we thought we had enough sweep to do this. We had wing-tip fins and rudders and pitch control was obtained from symmetrical deflections of the elevon (we knew that tip stall was better with elevons up). To help balance the nose down pitching moment from the big Fowler flaps we introduced a small all moving swept tail plane mounted above the fuselage on a very short fin; this was to be moved so that the trailing edge up when the flaps were lowered.

However there were worries about the bad effect of tip fins on tip stall and some fears, not clearly defined that these tip fins might lead to asymmetrical conditions with objectionable yawing moments under some unspecified conditions, possibly at high Mach number

Because of this feeling it was decided to delete the tip fins and go for a conventional fin and rudder. Having got this far we also went for a 'conventional' tail plane and elevator. We put this on top of the fin primarily to get it out of the way of the jet efflux and also because we wanted to avoid the fairing and structural problems of a tail part way up the fin. We new at this time that this arrangement was bad from the tip stall point of view but we decided that we could fix this with nose flaps or something similar.

Having got a thick wing root with a maximum depth of approximately 6 ft we decided to put the engines inside the wing immediately outboard of the fuselage to save nacelle drag and to avoid any serious yawing moment from a cut engine, thus easing the design requirements for the fin and rudder. The undercarriage retracted into the wings thanks to a 4 wheeled 8 tyred bogie outboard of the engines.

Because of the way in which the engines and the undercarriage were installed the centre wing main structure was limited to a torque box ending at about 30% chord. At the fuselage side this torque box had a large kink and passed across the fuselage in a span-wise direction.

There was an important aerodynamic advantage to this centre wing box structure. Because of the high sweep, the centre wing spar structure was well forward of the C of G of the aeroplane when it crossed the fuselage. This meant that all the moveable military load (bombs or reconnaissance crates) was aft of the rear spar and thus we could mount the wing centrally on the fuselage with consequent drag and Mcrit (Critical Mach Number) advantages; further the whole fuselage cross section was available for useful load fuel at the top and military stores below thus minimising the cross sectional area diameter to 10ft.

Wing Design – High Speed

The aim was a constant critical Mach number across the span. After an arbitrary choice of taper ratio initially about 2.5 to 1 but later increased to about 4 to 1 and sweep we had at our disposal the following items by means of which we could effect the super velocities so as to get the desired critical Mach number.

1. Fairing Shape and Thickness,
2. Camber.
3. Twist

When we got our first wing designed a model was tested in the old RAE high-speed wind tunnel. (Which was no longer in use over 30 years ago) The results showed the drag rise coming in too early round about Mach 0.8 I understand. There was at that time evidence that the trouble was on the outer parts of the wing. It was a mixture of pressure plot data and indications of shock wave positions so we reduced the thickness of the outer wing by 2% chord throughout making the necessary changes to the shape of the intermediate wing, which remained unaltered at its inboard end. This fixed it and we went from there. At the wing root we got a favourable interference from the mid wing arrangement. One can I suppose, argue that if one looks at the wing fuselage intersection in plan there is an obvious wasting of the intersection line, remember it is a 6ft thick wing passing centrally through a 10ft diameter fuselage and thus there is automatically a good root fairing. We actually thought of it rather differently though the result is the same. What we said was that if you plotted, along the length of the fuselage, the cross-sectional area of the fuselage outside the wing you then had the distribution of the added area.

Low Speed

As design proceeded there was continual pressure for more wing depth at the root for stowage of engines, undercarriage etc. This led, by insidious steps to the gradual increase in the root cord until the taper ratio had increased to about 4:1 and the inner kink on the trailing edge had been eliminated: the aspect ratio was now down to about 6. When we at last got a model of this into the low speed wind tunnel the pitch-up at stall was terrible. We tried all sorts of leading edge devices with out much success.

Drastic measures were called for so we decided to increase the chord of the outer wing by a 20% forward extension: this new leading edge ran inboard to intersect the leading edge of the intermediate wing much further inboard than it formally had; the outer kink was now about half-way from the fuselage side to tip instead of $^2/_3$ as originally. This combined with a droop nose flap on the new larger outer wing gave an acceptable answer then anyway. The nose flaps were, I think, hinged at about 12.5% chord from the leading edge and went down about 45 degrees. An automatic control system was designed based on the signal provided by a pressure ratio switch which made an electrical contact when the differences in the pressure coefficient between holes on the top and bottom surfaces of the wing reached a pre-set value. The nose flap was lowered by the stored energy of a hydraulic accumulator and came down in a second. This quick action was necessary to beat the increase in Chord Line (CL) raising was slow and the hydraulic pumps had to recharge the accumulator to full pressure before the flaps retracted so that it might be ready for action again. This was later demonstrated to be acceptable by flying at high Mach numbers with nose flaps down.

Aerodynamic Controls
We started the design in 1946 and had to design the biggest aeroplane that we had ever done, with swept wings and a flight envelope going up to a pretty high subsonic Mach number. In these circumstances we decided that manual controls were ìoutî so we went for duplicated power operated controls with no manual reversion. The aileron jacks were independent, i.e. not connected across the wing from port to starboard, so we put in a fixed upwardly deflected tab to cut down bo and b.; to reduce b2 we also had a geared tab. Rolling power on the Victor is very high because when we changed over from elevons to ailerons and elevator we did not reduce the size of the ailerons and so they are larger than normal. The rudder had a geared tab. We gave up the idea of an all moving tailplane for mainly structural reasons (the HP 88 had such an item) and went instead for a very small fixed tail-plane just something to hold the hinge brackets with a very large elevator. The elevator had an enormous horn balance (the outer 60% of the span I should guess) and was deliberately overbalanced for all normal flight conditions. We did this so as to reduce the hinge movement (so saving size and weight of the jack.) at maximum flight M; positive and negative movements were about equal in magnitude and it seemed to work all right. Service experienced seems to justify our decisions as the Victor has flown at Mach numbers in excess of 1.0 on a few occasions. Although the prototype did a lot of flying without auto stabilisation, we ultimately added first a yaw damper and then a Mach trimmer. These were more important on the B2 versions with the Conway and the greater altitude capability.

Fuselage
There is not much more to add to what has already been said in connection with the wing design. We made a very smooth pointed nose with the windscreen faired into the lines without the usual step. This kept down the local shock waves and gave a very quiet cockpit. The bulge or chin below the nose resulted from putting the radome under the bomb aimer.

Engine Air Intake
Right from the start we knew that swept wing leading edge intake was going to be difficult but we went ahead with it because of the very encouraging results obtained from A.V.A. Gottingham with such an arrangement. We had the wind tunnel test report by a man called Scheerer I think or else A. Walz.
    For the Mk 1 with the Sapphire engines we just sliced off the nose section of the wing section and contrived to keep the engine air intake entirely within the original profile. The problems were to get good efficiency throughout the large range of inlet velocity/flight velocity ratios and to avoid shock waves at high Mach numbers through a fairly large range of incidence. There was the tendency under static conditions for the air to be concentrated in

the outer corner of the intake; it came out as a long thin triangle, with rounded corners, due to the high thickness taper on the inner wing. The need to supply two engines added more complications. We decided on a single inlet with division into the two separate trunks well back in the wing when we had got the air behaving nicely. The absence of a central division on the leading edge reduced the length of the intake; if we had to push the intake for the outer engine still further outboard we would have been in real trouble with the extreme outer corner, for the wing depth would have been very small indeed.

Starting with the German results and with much wind tunnel testing (many pressure plots on the lips) we got it acceptable, including the engine out cases. Later it was discovered that during the take off run there was quite a large supersonic patch at the outer corner of the intake; the tolerant Sapphire did no more than lose a bit of thrust under those conditions.

Dive Brakes (later called Air Brakes)

These were formed from sections of the fuselage near the rear on each side of a roughly trapezoidal plate swung forward and outwards leaving a gap between the leading edge of the air brake and the fuselage side. At full deflection it had moved out about 60 degrees. Since the above arrangement resulted in a convex face of the air brake facing forward we put strakes on the top and bottom edge to increase drag. At first the strakes were of equal depth but there was a pitching moment when the brakes were deployed; we cured this by making the top strake a lot bigger than the lower one.

These air brakes worked very well; they gave good braking without pitch or undo buffet at all Mach numbers up to the maximum. The pilots liked it so much that they used them for speed control on the final approach; they set up a reasonable thrust and adjusted the speed /angle of descent with the air brakes as one would on a glider since this was more precise than operation of the throttles.

Structural Design

We are committed to a thin wing (or relatively thin) and this lead to quite a high bending end loads. Because of high flight Mach number we imposed a quite stringent waviness criterion to avoid the risk of local areas having little shock waves.

We decided quite early to use sandwich construction which, because of its bending stiffness and strength, could carry end load (the main bending end-load) without the elastic in-flight buckling typical of conventional skin/stringer construction and which could also take internal (fuel tank) and external pressure loads without significant distortion. (*For a complete description of the structural design of the Victor by the then Assistant Chief Designer (Structures) R H Sandifer*)

Flutter on the Victor

From the start of the design we paid much attention to flutter. We were concerned firstly with the problem of estimating flutter derivatives for a swept wing where the mach number went well beyond the critical, and secondly, we had two other problems, the flutter characteristics of a crescent wing and a T tail, both new to Handley Page.

We tackled the problems on a broad front, calculation, wind tunnel test, ground resonance test and finally flight test; mixed up with this there was also a dropped model or two to try and get high M conditions. The calculations owed much to help received from the Flutter Section of the SME Department of the RAE and the use of the RAE analogue flutter computer. The wind tunnel tests were similar to those carried out by the Boeing Aircraft Company, since we had seen their model building technique on a visit to Seattle in 1949. The Boeing models consisted of a light-alloy skeleton to provide the elastic properties, the aerodynamic shape

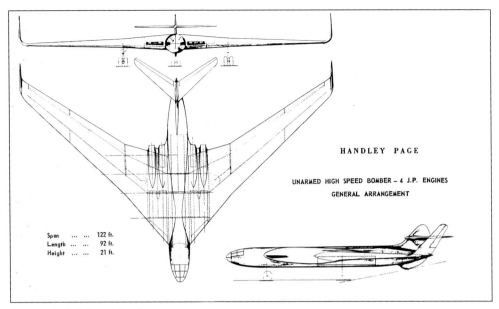

HANDLEY PAGE

UNARMED HIGH SPEED BOMBER – 4 J.P. ENGINES
GENERAL ARRANGEMENT

Span	... ...	122 ft.
Length	... ...	92 ft.
Height	... ...	21 ft.

Unarmed High Speed Bomber

being formed by numerous balsa wood boxes, the gaps between them being sealed by very thin rubber membranes while the mass distribution was brought up to that required by the addition of weights within the contour. Handley Page adopted this technique for the low speed wind tunnel models. As far as the wing was concerned we were entirely successful. On the tail unit, however, despite all that we did, there was a flutter incident with fatal results to the crew. The accident happened during a low altitude high speed run at Cranfield for the purpose of calibrating the static pressure orifice; tail unit flutter occurred and this component broke away.

To begin with this accident was very puzzling because we had assessed (or checked) the flutter speed by three independent means and each time the result showed that the flight programme could be safely undertaken. These three checks were:

1 An assessment of the flutter speed based on low-speed wind tunnel tests.
2 The calculation of the flutter speed using ground resonance tests results.
3 We did rudder jerks up to speeds slightly higher than that attained when flutter occurred.

Unarmed High Speed Bomber in Flight, Model 1.

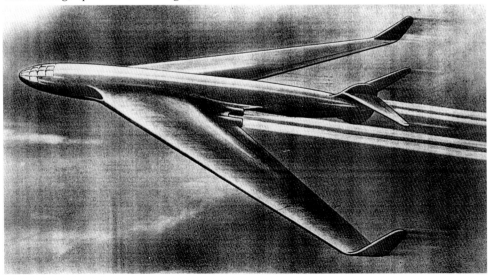

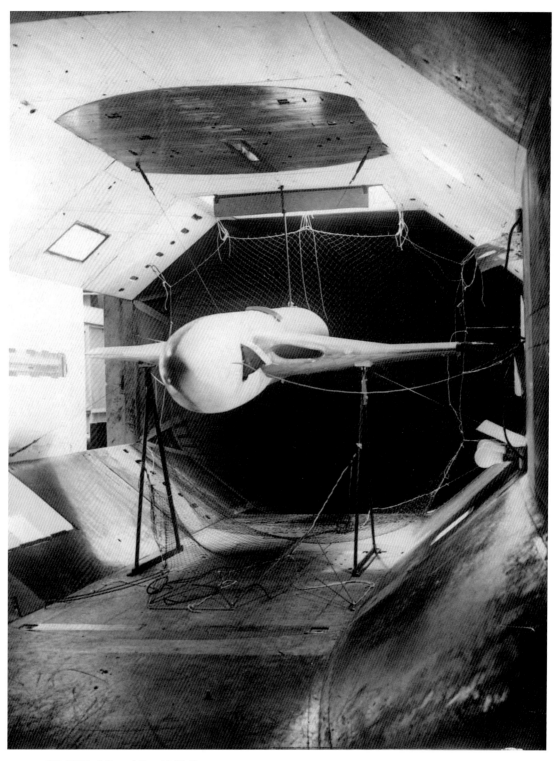

HP 80 Wind Tunnel Test 1947-48.

After some exhaustive tests the investigation showed that increased fin torsional stiffness and increased stiffness of the fin-tail plane joint was the remedy for the flutter trouble; we therefore built a stiffer fin. In fact we built two versions of the stiffer fin, because we decided that the first version had not been sufficiently stiffened.

MINISTRY OF SUPPLY
PRINCIPLE DIRECTORATE OF TECHNICAL DEVELOPMENT
This document is the property of H.M. Government
SPECIFICATION NO B35/46

<u>MEDIUM RANGE BOMBER</u>
This specification is to be regarded for contract purpose as forming part of the Contract Agreement
and being subject to the same conditions
Approved by: H Grinsted Director of Aircraft Research and Development
Date: 24.1.47

<u>I – GENERAL</u>
1.01 This specification is issued to cover the design and construction of a medium range bomber
for worldwide use by the Royal Air Force
1.02 The operational requirements are stated in Appendix B to this specification.
1.03 This specification gives only the particular requirements for the type in amplification of the
current general design requirements stated in:
(i) AP970 with Amendments up to and including AL 38
(ii) Aircraft Design Memoranda, Standardization Design Memoranda, and Standard Instruction Sheets
current to the 1st November 1946
(iii) Specification No DTD. 1208(Issue IV) and amendments 1-5 inclusive thereto.
And these requirements shall be completely fulfilled except where varied by this specification, or
where the prior written consent of P/DTD (A) has been obtained
1.04 It is essential that the design of the aircraft be suitable for economic
production of at least 500 aircraft at a maximum rate of not less than 10 per month.
1.05 Subsequent chapter references in this specification are to AP 970
(as amended by AL 38) in all cases.

<u>II DESIGN REQUIREMENTS</u>
<u>Engines</u>
2.01 Precautions shall be taken to prevent the entry of debris into the air intake.

<u>Engine Failure on Take Off</u>
2.02 In the event of a single engine failure at any stage of the take off the pilot shall either be able to
pull up safely without damage, or be able to continue the take off.
In either event the operation must be completed within 150% of the take off
distance specified in Appendix 'B'. In the event of the take off being continued it
shall not be necessary for the pilot to operate trimmer, flap, and undercarriage
or throttle controls until he has reached a height of 100ft.

<u>Emergency Escape</u>
2.03 The provisions for emergency escape by the crew shall be
in accordance with JAC Paper 339

<u>Protection of Landing Flaps</u>
2.04 The design shall be such as to minimise damage to any part of the aircraft
by water, mud, or stones thrown up by the wheels.

<u>Twin Contact Tyres</u>
2.05 Provision shall be made to allow for the correct operation of the nose
wheel unit with a twin contact tyre of suitable pressure so should shimmy occur, a twin contact tyre can
be fitted without any modification other than a wheel change being necessary.

<u>Cockpit Colour</u>
2.06 The pilots and bomb aimer's stations shall be finished internally in matt black. The only variation
permitted is the use of red for marking emergency controls and exits.

<u>Fire Prevention</u>
2.07 Installation of any combustion heaters or auxiliary power plants shall
be in accordance with JAC Paper 336.

Pressure Cabin

2.08 A pressure cabin shall be installed in accordance with Chapter 718
for which p = 9.0lbs .per square inch.

2.09 With the aircraft on the ground the pressure of the air in the cabin shall be raised to 9lbs.per square inch. With the pressure supply cut off the time taken for the pressure to fall from 9.0 to 4.5 lbs. per square inch shall be noted and shall be not less than one minute.

III EQUIPMENT

General

3.01 Equipment shall be fitted or provided for in accordance with the
Appendix 'A' to this specification.

IV – STRENGTH AND STIFFNESS

Stressing Weight

4.01 Strength calculations for the take off and flight cases (W2 of Chapter 305) shall be based upon the maximum all up weight of the aircraft when carrying the following.

(i) The tare weight items shown in column 10 of the Appendix A and such removable non standard parts as will be necessary for the contractor to supply and fit in order that the military load may be carried.

(ii) The removable military load defined in Appendix 'A' and approximate to the duties of paragraph of the Appendix 'B'.

(iii) The fuel and oil appropriate to the range of paragraph 12 of the Appendix 'B'

4.02 Strength calculations for landing (W1 of Chapter 305) shall be based upon the take off weight less the weight of bombs and half of the total fuel.

Main Flight Cases

4.03 The requirements of Chapter 201 shall be satisfied at the weight W2, with the basic flight envelope of that chapter having the following values: n1 = 2.7

VD = speeds corresponding to Mach numbers up to and including 0.95 but need not exceed 435 knots EAS
VB = 0.8VD or the maximum speed in level flight which ever is the greater.

4.04 The design shall be such that following take-off the above value of n1 will increase to at least 3.0 by the time one quarter of the still air range specified in paragraph 12 has been has been achieved, and will not subsequently fall below this value.

Parking and Picketing

4.05 The design shall be in accordance with JAC Paper 325, except that the factor will be 1.5 and the wind speed 65knots (75mph)

V TESTS

Contractor's Flight Trials

5.01 Prior to the delivery of the first aircraft, it shall be certified to the P/DTD that:

(a) The aircraft has been subjected to a schedule of flight tests agreed at a meeting to be held by AD/RDL2 approximately one month before the first flight. This schedule will in general be based upon Parts 9 and 10 of AP970 current at that time.

(b) The above-mentioned tests have shown the aircraft as safe to be flown by authorised Service Pilots

APPENDIX 'B' TO SPECIFICATION   B35/46

1. The Air Staff require a medium range bomber land plane capable of carrying one 10,000lb bomb to a target 1,500 nautical miles from a base which may be anywhere in the world. The aircraft will be required to attack targets at great distance inside the enemy territory and it must be assumed that it will be plotted by radar and other methods for a large part of its flight. I t must, therefore be capable of avoiding destruction by making the inevitable attack from ground and air launched weapons difficult. To this end it must have:

(a) A high cruising speed – the cruising speed shall be such that attacking fighters will have to fly at a speed at which they will tend to become unmanoeuvrable.

(b) Manoeuvrability at high speed and high altitude – the design must be such that the aircraft can turn rapidly without loss of height or much loss of speed when at maximum cruising height.

(c) A high cruising height – The cruising height must be such that ground launched weapons can only be guided at long range and such that the design of the intercepting enemy aircraft will be difficult.

(d) Capacity for carrying adequate warning devices – these will be needed to detect the approach of ground launched weapons and the proximity of opposing aircraft to be effective the warning device must have long range and may therefore be large. Adequate provision must be made for mounting such a warning system so that it can scan the required field.

(e) <u>Capacity for carrying defensive apparatus</u> – Such as proximity fuses exploders and homing or guided missile jamming devices.

2. The size of the pressure cabin must be as small as possible.

3. Visual and electronic bomb aiming positions are required

4. Maximum performance is the ultimate aim and must not be sacrificed unduly for ease of maintenance

5. It must be possible to operate this aircraft from existing H. B. type airfields and the maximum weight when fully loaded ought, therefore, not to exceed 100,000lbs. The Air Staff is to be informed if the weight will be exceeded

6. The aircraft must be suitable for large-scale production in war.

PERFORMANCE
7. The performance requirements apply to operation in all parts of the world

Speed
8. The aircraft must be capable of cruising at maximum continuous cruising power at heights from 35,000ft to 50,000ft. At a speed of 500 knots.

9. The maximum speed in level flight should be as high as possible but it is not essential that it should exceed the cruising speed.

10. The Flying characteristics must not become dangerous when the speed temporarily rises above the top level speed in the course of combat or other manoeuvres and the Mach No increases to a maximum of 0.90 but a speed restriction is acceptable below 25,000ft.

11. The aircraft will be required to fly under all weather conditions. For this reason it must be capable of comfortable slow speed during the landing approach. The final approach speed should not exceed 120knots and good manoeuvrability must be maintained at this speed.

Range
12. The Maximum operational radius of action with a 10,000lb bomb load must be 1500 miles. To attain this still air range of 3,350 nautical miles at a height of 50,000ft with a 10,000lb bomb carried on the outward and return flight is required.

Climb
13. The aircraft must be capable of reaching 45,000ft with the full load less two and a half hours fuel. The ability to climb above this height is desirable but not essential.

Ceiling
14. The aircraft must cruise at 50,000ft with full load less two and a half hours fuel. The ability to climb above this height is desirable but not essential.

Take Off
15. At sea level under tropical, conditions, the aircraft must clear a 50ft screen within 1500 yards from rest in still air with a cross wind of up to 20 knots at right angles to the take off path. To achieve this rocket take off equipment would be acceptable.
(The development of the RATOG was required to cover this requirement).

Landing
16. The aircraft must be capable under tropical conditions of landing in cross winds of up to 20 knots and coming to rest within 1,400 yards after crossing a 50 ft screen in still air with half the permanent fuel load and no bombs or within 1,700 yards with full fuel/bomb load. When landing with the full fuel/bomb load a slight reduction in the normal safety factors would be acceptable. The Air Staff will accept fuel jettisoning to enable the landing requirements to be met subject to the operation not talking more than 5 minutes. (The use of the brake parachute system was therefore necessary and in addition the fuel jettison system was not installed until the use of under wing tanks on the Mk B2 in RAF service and the conversion to the tanker role for the Mk 1 aircraft when the jettison facility was from the MK 20B pods and the main jettison system terminating in the Mk 17HDU fairing lower extension pipe with the K2 initially using the fuselage jettison facility however it was rendered inoperative and the underwing tanks used along with the Mk 20B pods)
Flight with one or more engines stopped.

17. The aircraft must meet current Air Staff requirements regarding engine failure on take off. It must be capable of maintaining 45,000ft with one engine stopped and 30,000ft with two engines stopped when carrying full load less one hour's fuel. The stopping one engine must not reduce the range by more than 20%.

ARMAMENT

18. The aircraft will rely upon speed, height, and evasive manoeuvre for protection. It will not carry orthodox defensive armament but will be equipped with early warning devices, radar counter measurers to deflect a beam on which a ground or air launched weapon may be launched.

19. A new range of bombs will be carried designed for stable flight frommaximum operational height and speed of this aircraft.

20. The aircraft is required to bomb at is operational ceiling in all weather conditions and therefore the majority of bombing will be with the target hidden by cloud or darkness. It is necessary therefore to carry the new radar bombing equipment under development, which makes use of all radar and D.R navigational data to feed the bombing computer. When the target can be seen, however, a visual bombsight, fed from the same bombing computer, will be used and must be fitted in a position to afford the maximum clear view.

Bombs

21. Capacity is to be provided for a total bomb load of 20,000lb composed of bombs of the following dimensions.

Type	Max Diam.	Overall Length	Distance C.G from nose
10,000lb H.C.	40inch	290inch	80inch
6,000lb H.C.	32inch	225inch	63inch
1,000lb H.C.	16.5inch	110inch	30inch
Special Bomb	60inch	290inch*	80inch*

*First estimate only

22. As an alternative, capacity must be provided for carrying a bomb of the dimensions as shown under 21(Special Bomb) and additional fuel which may be carried in detachable tanks in the bomb cells to meet range requirement stated in paragraph 12 above provided these tanks can be installed or removed in not more than 5 hours.

23. The opening of the bomb doors or other method of release of bombs must not appreciably alter the speed or trim of the aircraft so that it would affect bombing accuracy.

24. It must be possible to release bombs at any speed at which the aircraft is capable of flying. Clearance is required to enable bombs to be released when diving or climbing at an angle of 15degrees or with up to 10 degrees of side slip

Bomb Sights

25. This aircraft will be required to bomb from all heights up to 50,000ft using either visual or electronic bombsights. Provision is to be made for fitting N.B.C. with visual sighting head.

26. The bomb selecting and fusing are to be at the navigation /blind bombing station.

27. Bomb release and jettisoning switches are to be fitted at the pilot's station, the visual bombing position and at the navigation /blind bombing position.

Space is to be made available for bomb guiding equipment.

Bomb Loading

28. Performance must not be prejudiced by designing to use existing bomb handling gear.

Photography

29. Provision must be made for carrying a vertical camera and illuminating apparatus for night photography in order to record the fall of bombs and release points. Photographic recording of the readings of electronic bombsights will be required.

CREW STATIONS

30. The crew will consist of five:
1st Pilot,
2nd Pilot (under training),
2 Navigator/bomb aimer/radar operators,
1 Wireless /Warning and Protective Device Operator

Pressure Cabin

31 The crew are to be accommodated in one pressure cabin. The cabin is to be large enough to allow each member of the crew to move from his seat during flight. The cabin pressure should not be below the equivalent of 8,000ft on the flight to and from the target but may be reduced to the equivalent of 25,000ft in the combat area. Particular importance is attached to keeping the size and hence the weight and vulnerability of the pressure cabin as small as possible. No equipment that can be remotely controlled is to be carried in the cabin. Cabin pressure, humidity and temperature are to automatically control. To reduce fatigue, the maximum crew comfort must be provided.

Pilots Station

32. The pilot must have the best possible view as specified by AP970 and in particular he must have a good view downwards over the nose of not less than 15degrees from the horizontal in level flight. His seat is to be as comfortable as possible. It is too adjusted for height and in a fore and aft direction. The slope of the back is to be adjustable and it is to have folding armrests.

33. The engine instruments are to be visible to the pilot. These are to be kept to the absolute minimum and no instrument is to be provided which is not essential for the correct operation of the aircraft. Instruments required for maintenance check or to indicate something about which the pilot can do nothing in flight are to be excluded. If instruments not required during flight are necessary for pre flight running up and ground test, they are to be provided on a separate and preferably detachable panel outside the pressure cabin. All fuel cocks are to be in reach of the pilot. Engine starting must be from the pilot's seat. Fuel contents and gallons gone meters are to be visible to the first pilot and navigator.

Navigators Stations

34. The two Navigator/bomb aimer/radar operators should be accommodated at a combined station. This station should be as comfortable and quiet as possible and will be required to contain all the navigation instruments, radar navigation controls and indicators, electronic bomb aiming presentation and other radio equipment as detailed in para 62.

Visual Bombing Station

35. A visual bombing station readily accessible from the navigation station is to be provided. The clear field of vision must be 10 degrees aft of vertical to horizontal forward and as wide as lateral, view as possible.

Wireless Operators Station.

36. The Wireless Operators Station will contain all attack warning devices and controls for counter measure devices such as proximity fuse exploders. It must be as comfortable as possible.

PROTECTION
Warning Devices

37. Radar warning devices to detect the launching and approach of ground or air launched weapons or opposing aircraft must be provided to cover at least the whole lower and rear hemispheres.

Crew

38. An appreciation is required of the loss of performance entailed by providing armour against attack by weapons capable of producing fragments equivalent to 0.5 inchA.P. Ammunition and also to provide protection from 0.5 inch gun attack within a 60 degrees including angle from a stern is required. A decision on the requirement for this armour will be made after appreciation for each design submitted has been studied by the Air Staff.

Fuel Tanks and Pipelines

39. (a). Self-sealing is not required but tanks not easily damaged in a crash are to be provided. Neither the tanks nor tank compartments must contain anything capable of acting as a wick for the fuel. Self-sealing pipelines are not required.

(b). Tank purging by inert gas is required for all tanks.

(c) Tanks must be so arranged or compartmented that one whole does not cause the loss of more than 10% of the remaining fuel.

Fire Protection

40. An approved type of fire extinguisher system is required for the engine and tank compartments.

NAVIGATION

41. In order that continuous accurate navigation may be possible over the great distances involved it is essential

that this aircraft should be equipped with:

(a) A long range automatic D.R. System and

(b) A long range fixing system.

42. Since radio systems based on transmission from the ground are liable to jamming, and are unlikely to provide a sufficient degree of accuracy, it is highly desirable that except for homing, the navigation of this aircraft should be independent from the ground.

43. The automatic D.R. system will comprise a type of navigational and bombing computer to which navigational information is supplied by an H2S set of long range and moderate definition, the bombing information being supplied by separate high definition equipment, which may operate on a different frequency. In addition at a later date a system of measuring track and ground speed utilising the Doppler principle may be coupled to the n.b.c.

44. For fixing positions there are two requirements:

(a) H.2.S. To pinpoint and identify over or near land

(b) Astro A completely automatic astro system will be developed during the life of the aircraft and an optically correct glass panel in the roof of the aircraft above the navigator's station will be required.

Short Range Navigation

45. Equipment is required for completely automatic homing, orbiting, approach and landing. The system will also provide a short range fixing aid.

46. An automatic radio compass for use in emergency will also be wanted. This will work in conjunction with the main W/T communication set, which will incorporate automatic coding and teleprinter facilities as soon as they are developed.

OTHER FEATURES
Engine Installation

47. It is preferred that the aircraft has no less than four and no more than six engines.

48. The engines need not be installed as power plants if this will in any way prejudice the performance. Within reason performance must take precedence over ease of access and maintenance.

49. Attention is given to flame damping.

Ground Handling

50. Catapult or trolley launching is not acceptable. Arrester gear for landing is not acceptable.

Icing and Misting

51. A means must be provided to prevent all windows required for flying or for search from becoming obscure by ice, snow rain or internal misting. The system must be effective through out the speed and height range of the aircraft.

52. The aircraft must be capable of flying through all normal icing conditions.

Emergency Exits

53. The complete pressure cabin must be jettison able. Such a cabin must be provided with parachutes to reduce the falling speed to a value at which the occupants will be unhurt when hitting the ground while still strapped in their seats. If such a jettison able unit cannot be provided the seats must be jettisonable.

Ditching and Flotation

54. A good ditching and flotation characteristics are desirable but must not prejudice the performance.

Dual Control

55. The 2nd pilot's seat must be suitable for giving and receiving dual instructions and must be sufficiently comfortable to be occupied for the full endurance of the aircraft. Complete duplication of all instruments is not required but the blind flying panel must be provided for each pilot. A design in which the 2nd pilot must leave his seat to allow access to the nose is acceptable.

Fuel and Oil

56. Controls for fuel cocks and pumps must be as simple as possible.

Under-carriages

57. The undercarriages must be such that the aircraft can use airfields built to the present H. B. Standard.

Controllability

58. The aircraft will be required to land in very bad weather conditions by day and night. It must therefore, be easy to fly with good response to the controls when making the final approach to land. It must also be as manoeuvrable as possible at maximum height and speed as violent manoeuvres will be the only defence against aircraft, and guided or homing weapons. Air brakes are to be fitted.

EQUIPMENT
Flying Equipment
61. (a) Night Flying: – Full night flying equipment is to be provided including U/V cockpit lighting.

(b). Automatic Pilot: – An Automatic pilot is required. This is to be suitable for coupling to the bomb aiming equipment.

(c). Automatic Blind Flying Equipment: – Automatic blind flying equipment is required and will be coupled with the automatic pilot

Navigation
62. The navigational equipment that will be required may be summarised as follows

(a) Non Radio

(i). Remote indicating gyro compass with the necessary repeaters

(ii). Stand by magnetic compass

(iii). Navigation and bombing computer

(b) Radio (including Radar)

(i) Long range navigation system, consisting of H2S with NBC

(ii). Rebecca/BABS or SCS51 in conjunction with autopilot

(iii) High Altitude radio altimeter, preferably incorporated with NBC

(iv). Automatic radio compass for use with main W/T set

(v) Main W/T Equipment

(vi) Multi Channel VHF equipment.

(vii). Intercommunication equipment.

(viii) Radio-teleprinter with automatic coding facilities to operate main W/T equipment.

(ix). Cloud and collision warning system

(x). I.F.F.

Defensive Equipment
63. An early warning system capable of detecting intercepting aircraft attacking from a cone of 45 degrees from the rear.

64. Equipment for detonating fuses will be required.

Window Launching
65. 'Window' or the equivalent counter measure; launching equipment is to be provided outside the pressure cabin.

Oxygen
66. Oxygen is required for the full endurance at 20,000ft. An emergency oxygen system is to be provided in case the cabin is perforated. This must provide sufficient oxygen for all members of the crew for up to four hours at 30,000ft.

Dinghies
67. Each member of the crew is to be provided with a Type'K' dinghy. A type 'H' is to be provided in a blow out storage.

Parachutes
68. Back type parachutes will be worn by all members of the crew

Pyrotechnics
69. A 6-cartridge signal discharger is required.

Air Ministry (D.O.R. (A))

December 1946

DB 57990/3/632 60 1/47

The Handley Page 80 to Specification B35/46, dated May 1947

This article is based on the proposal submitted in May 1947 for an aircraft to the Specification B35/46. This was to be the 'HP 80 Jet Propelled Bomber with 4 Metrovick F9 Units. By Handley Page Ltd. Author's comments are in italics.

The issuing of Specification B35/46 in March to Handley Page and the other selected companies gave the team under Charles Joy with Godfrey Lee as his Research Engineer impedance to produce a brochure and financial documentation for their tender submission that had to be returned by May 1947. It was somewhat of a challenge to achieve the relevant date considering that the specification had not been approved until January 1947 and was I understand issued in March of that year. The company was assisted in this as they had already submitted a design specification for the interest of the Ministry of Supply and the Air Staff in June 1946. This aircraft had an all up weight of 90,000lb and was the product of the preliminary design started in early 1946. The aircraft was still given the Number HP80 this having been allocated back in 1945 by the HP Drawing Office. The change from it just being the HP 80 came in June 1952 with the awarding of the first production contract for 25 aircraft.

The design that was submitted in May 1947 incorporated the crescent wing in virtually the form that we all know, however the wings had fins incorporated in the tips and the tail and fin assembly was of the basic scheme of the production aircraft except that it did not have a rudder and was much shorter than the final design. With a span of 100ft an overall length of 91ft 6in and the overall height of 21ft 6in it was smaller than even the prototype. The aircraft was to be powered by four Metro-Vick F9 jet engines of 7,500 lb static thrust at S.L.9 (*These engines*

H. P. 8 0

G E N E R A L   P A R T I C U L A R S   A N D   L E A D I N G   D I M E N S I O N S

WING AND OVERALL DIMENSIONS

Wing span	100 ft.
Overall length	91 ft. 6 in.
Overall height	21 ft.
Wing area	2,000 sq. ft.
Root chord	30 ft.
Tip chord	10 ft.
Aspect ratio	5.0
Taper ratio	3.0
Thickness/chord ratio tip	0.08
Thickness/chord ratio root	0.14
Sweepback angles on $\frac{1}{4}$ chord	$48\frac{1}{4}^{o}$, $37\frac{1}{2}^{o}$, $26\frac{3}{4}^{o}$.

POWER PLANT

Four Metro-Vick F.9 jet engines giving 7,500 lb. static thrust at S.L.

LANDING GEAR

Undercarriage track	43 ft. 2 in.
Main wheel size	62 x 16.5 – 27
Nose wheel size (twin)	26 x 8 – 12
Main wheel pressure	110 lb./sq. in.
Nose wheel pressure	110 lb./sq. in.

FUSELAGE AND CABIN

Maximum diameter	9 ft. 10 in.
Crew's cabin volume	800 cu. ft.
Total bomb bay length	42 ft.
Height of crew's cabin on centre line	5 ft. 6 in.

TANKAGE

Fuel normal	3,092 galls.
Fuel auxiliary	1,240 galls.
Oil	32 galls.

TAIL UNIT

Area of horizontal tail plane	150 sq. ft.
Area of each tip fin and rudder	85 sq. ft.
Area of central fin	25 sq. ft.

WEIGHTS AND LOADING

Maximum take-off weight	95,000 lb.
Maximum emergency landing	79,000 lb.
Wing loading	47.5 lb./sq. ft.

PERFORMANCE SUMMARY

SPEED

Cruising speed (T.A.S.) . . . .   500 kts.

CLIMB AND CEILING

Mean cruising height with 10,000 lb. bombs . . . . 51,000 ft.
Maximum rate of climb at S.L. at maximum A.U.W.
     at climb thrust . . . .   6,200 ft./min.
Height after 2½ hrs. cruising at 500 kts. . . . . . 50,000 ft.

TAKE-OFF AND LANDING

Take-off run to clear 50 ft. - maximum A.U.W.
    Tropical summer - unassisted . . . .   1,600 yds.
Take-off run to clear 50 ft. - maximum A.U.W.
    Tropical summer - rocket assistance . . . . .   1,500 "
Landing run over 50 ft. - normal landing weight.
    Tropical summer . . . .   1,050 "
Landing run over 50 ft. - emergency landing weight.
    Tropical summer . . . .   1,200 "
Approach speed, normal landing weight (E.A.S.) . .   95 kts.
Approach speed, emergency landing weight (E.A.S.) .   103 "
Maximum take-off or stop distance when one engine
    fails during take-off run - unassisted . . . .   1,700 yds.
Maximum take-off or stop distance when one engine
    fails during take-off run - rocket assisted .   1,650 "
Critical distance for engine failure on take-off
    unassisted (distance from start of run) . . .   800 "
Critical distance for engine failure on take-off
    with rocket assistance (distance from start
    of run) . . . .   700 "

RANGES

Still air range with 10,000 lb. bombs . . . . . .   3,350 naut. mls
Still air range with 15,000 lb. bombs   2,730   "   "
Still air range with 20,000 lb. bombs   2,140   "   "

3-ENGINE PERFORMANCE

Still air range with 10,000 lb. bombs on 3 engines,
    one engine failed half-way, optimum speed .   3,170 naut. mls
Still air range with 10,000 lb. bombs on 3 engines,
    one engine failed immediately after climb,
    optimum speed . . . .   2,930 "
Optimum mean cruising speed with 3 engines (T.A.S.)   420 kts.
Optimum mean cruising height with 3 engines . . . 44,500 ft.
Still air range with 10,000 lb. bombs on 3 engines
    at 500 kts. T.A.S., one engine failed
    immediately after climb . . . .   2,240 naut. mls
Mean height for 500 kts. cruising on 3 engines .   35,500 ft.
Absolute ceiling on 3 engines at maximum thrust
    after 1 hour's normal flying . . . .   44,000 "
Absolute ceiling on 3 engines at cruising
    thrust after 1 hour's normal flying . . . .   41,000 "

2-ENGINE PERFORMANCE

Absolute ceiling on 2 engines at maximum thrust
    after 1 hour's normal flying . . . .   34,500 ft.
Absolute ceiling on 2 engines at cruising thrust
    after 1 hour's normal flying . . . .   30,500 "

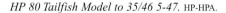

were later taken over by Armstrong Siddeley and developed to became the Sapphire 6 or as known in the Royal Air Force as the Sapphire 100 Series). As an alternative engine the Rolls Royce AJ 65 (Later known as the Avon) was proposed. This engine when developed giving the same thrust and specific fuel consumption as that of the Metro Vick engine was giving the concept of a multi wheeled bogie main undercarriage had not been thought of or even if it had it had not been developed for this submission. So a good old favourite was used a large single main wheel retracting side inboard into the wing. With a size of 62 inches it was too large to retract rearwards into the wing. With twin nose wheels slightly smaller than those used on the prototype and production aircraft the basis of what was to end up as the Mk 1 was beginning to take shape.

The fuel system tankage was rather small compared to that of the Mk1: the total amount

HP 80 Tailfish Model to 35/46 5-47. HP-HPA.

being in the order of 4,330 gallons or as Victor men would know it 34,600lb. (*Hardly enough to supply the needs of a medium bomber that ended up as the Victor Mk1 and 2 versions*)

As to the general shape of the aircraft looking at the drawing of the flight deck one can see the start of an operational Victor layout but only just. The reason behind this layout starts with the first pilot is stagger ahead in order to give a good field of vision and freedom of movement to crew.

The two navigators are seated side by side on the starboard side with a common table and instrumentation. All the indicators would be arranged at eye level with controls immediately below them. The Wireless-Protective Devices Operator sits on the port behind the 1st pilot his instruments and controls arranged to cause as little fatigue as possible on long operations. As to the second pilot his position was behind that of the 1st pilot and is deemed for training and possible operational use. The pilot's windscreens were to be de-iced by embedded heating elements. (*It looks as if the 'Gold Film' window heating system was proposed but failed to get into the Mk 1 versions but was incorporated in the Mk 2 version*)

Each member of the crew has an ejector type seat (*Was this the start of the campaign to provide seats for all the crew it looks as if it got no further*) the exit being through a jettisonable panel in the roof immediately above him.

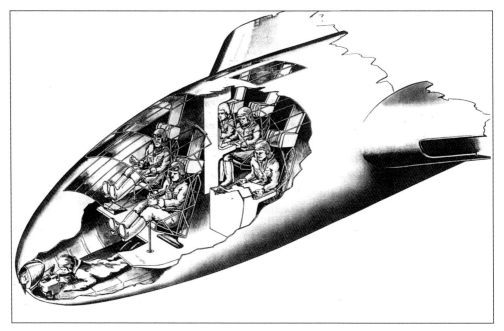

HP 80 Cabin.

The seats would have been fully adjustable and were to be fitted with parachutes and K type dinghies stowed in the head rests. The whole of the crew's cabin can be jettisoned from the rest of the aircraft. The Crew's cabin was to be pressurised to give 8,000ft altitude conditions. (Cruise differential pressure being 9.5psi) The Automatic Control had a manual override facility to achieve 25,000ft cabin altitude over the target (Combat differential pressure being 4psi). Pressurisation was provided by blowers mounted on the outboard engine auxiliary gearboxes. (This system was based on the propeller driven aircraft version).

The air passing through heat exchanger's is either heated, the hot air coming from jet pipe

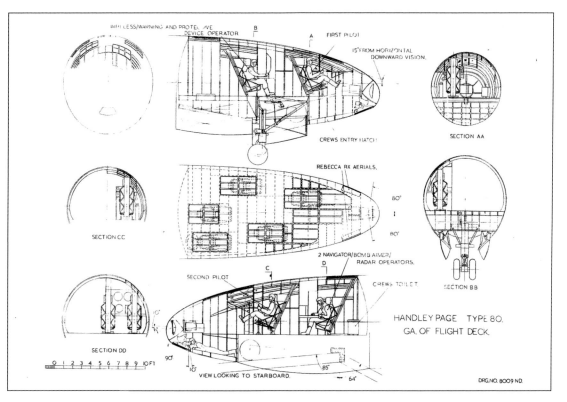

WIRELESS/WARNING AND PROTECTIVE DEVICE OPERATOR

B

A FIRST PILOT

15° FROM HORIZONTAL DOWNWARD VISION.

CREWS ENTRY HATCH

SECTION AA

REBECCA RX AERIALS.

80°

80°

SECTION CC

2 NAVIGATOR/BOMB AIMER/ RADAR OPERATORS.

SECOND PILOT

C

D

CREWS TOILET

SECTION BB

HANDLEY PAGE TYPE 80. GA. OF FLIGHT DECK.

SECTION DD

0 1 2 3 4 5 6 7 8 9 10 FT

90°

10°

VIEW LOOKING TO STARBOARD.

85°

64°

DRG.NO. 8009 ND.

heat exchanger's or cooled by ram air. The humidity being by injecting water under controlled conditions into the blowers. There was to be a facility for air conditioning on the ground from portable equipment. The oxygen system was supplied from nine 750-litre bottles fitted outside the pressure cabin. The system was to ensure a supply for 4 hours at 30,000ft and 2.5hours at 20,000ft. In addition each crewmember had portable emergency oxygen equipment. The crew entry door being on the underside of the cabin forward of the nose undercarriage.

The following equipment was fitted for communications:
1. MF/HF receivers and transmitters, the medium powered in a duplicate installation for general purpose communication, high powered for long-range use. The sets were located in the rear fuselage and remotely controlled by the Wireless-Protective Devices Operator.
2.VHF Equipment. A multichannel set fitted in the rear fuselage and controlled by the pilot and the Wireless Operator.
3.Intercommunication/ Station Boxes are provided at each crew station with radio mixing facilities.
4. Coding and Teleprinting. A coder and teleprinter is mounted behind and accessible from the Wireless Operators seat.

Navigation Equipment fitted
1. A radar installation of H2S Mk IX with a 6 ft scanner and transmitter receiver is housed in the fuselage aft of the nose undercarriage. The indicator and switch units are fitted in the front of the Navigator-Bomb Aimer-Radar Operators, the remainder in the tail of the aircraft.
2. Short Range Homing and Final Approach Guiding are provided by the Rebecca and I.B.A. installations, the latter connected with the flying controls to facilitate automatic landing.
3.An Automatic Radio Compass is fitted as a standby and operates in conjunction with the main GP Radio communication sets. The DF loop is fitted under a flush panel on the top of the fuselage.
4. Radio Altimeters with both high and low ranges are additional navigational aids.

5. An Astro system using an optically flat window above the navigator in the jettisonable panel.
6. A Gyro Magnetic Compass type G4B with remote indication and a small direct reading Magnetic Compass.
7. An Air Mileage Unit fitted in the centre section fuselage.
The H2S, G4B and AMU are arranged to feed into the Navigational and Bombing Computer.

Equipment – Bomb Aiming and Guiding
Bomb aiming was primarily carried out electronically by the use of the NBS and the Mk IX H.2.S equipment at the Navigator Station. Provision is made for the recording of indicator traces automatically.

A visual Bomb Aiming Station with visual sighting head is provided in the extreme nose for the crewmember designated for those duties. When bombing visually the sighting head supplies data to the NB Computer. Bomb selection and fusing controls are situated adjacent to the electronic bomb aiming equipment.

Warning Devices and Defensive Equipment
All indicators and controls are fitted at the Wireless-Protective Devices Operators Station.
1. Cloud and Collision warning-separate scanner and transmitter receiver unit is installed in the extreme nose.
2. Tail Warning – scanner and transmitter receiver unit in extreme tail.
3. Grounds and Proximity Warning.
4. Proximity Fusing.
5. Jamming Devices.
For all of the above three, space is provided for units of the necessary equipment.
6. Window launching chute is situated near the tail and is remotely controlled.

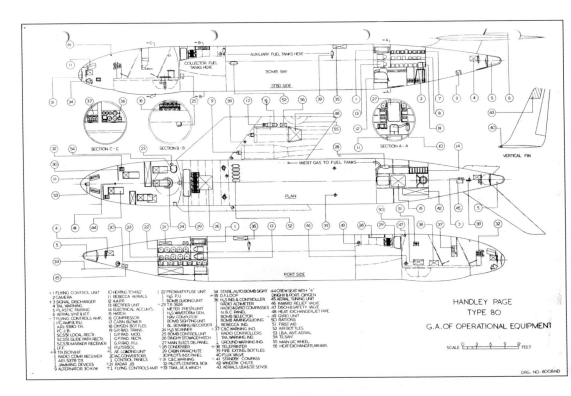

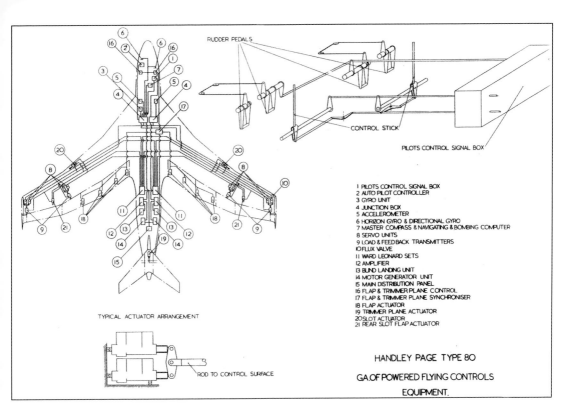

RUDDER PEDALS

CONTROL STICK

PILOTS CONTROL SIGNAL BOX

1 PILOTS CONTROL SIGNAL BOX
2 AUTO PILOT CONTROLLER
3 GYRO UNIT
4 JUNCTION BOX
5 ACCELEROMETER
6 HORIZON GYRO & DIRECTIONAL GYRO
7 MASTER COMPASS & NAVIGATING & BOMBING COMPUTER
8 SERVO UNITS
9 LOAD & FEEDBACK TRANSMITTERS
10 FLUX VALVE
11 WARD LEONARD SETS
12 AMPLIFIER
13 BLIND LANDING UNIT
14 MOTOR GENERATOR UNIT
15 MAIN DISTRIBUTION PANEL
16 FLAP & TRIMMER PLANE CONTROL
17 FLAP & TRIMMER PLANE SYNCHRONISER
18 FLAP ACTUATOR
19 TRIMMER PLANE ACTUATOR
20 SLOT ACTUATOR
21 REAR SLOT FLAP ACTUATOR

TYPICAL ACTUATOR ARRANGEMENT

ROD TO CONTROL SURFACE

HANDLEY PAGE TYPE 80

GA. OF POWERED FLYING CONTROLS
EQUIPMENT.

Miscellaneous

A remotely controlled vertical F.52 camera with a long focus lens was fitted in a heated box in the rear fuselage.

Photoflashes were carried in the bomb bays and released as required.

A six-barrelled signal discharger is fitted in the tail and operated by the pilot.

The H type dinghy is fitted in a hatch within the fuselage aft of the pressure bulkhead.

De-icing

Electrical de-icing is fitted to the leading edges of the wings, fins and trimmer plane.

Flying Controls

The flying controls are power operated without feedback so that mass balance weight and aerodynamic drag is eliminated. The controls comprise:

1. Elevons that control the aircraft in pitch and roll
2. Rudders that control the aircraft in yaw
3. Flaps
4. Tailplane for longitudinal trim
5. Nose flaps coupled with the elevons.

Hydraulic

Electro-hydraulic and electric powered controls were investigated and an all-electrical system incorporated similar to that of the Smiths Mk 9 or Sperry A12 Autopilot except that the servo actuators were fitted close to the moving surface.

Two independent sets are provided one energised by:

a. The Auto Pilot Gyro unit
b. The gyro magnetic compass
c. The auto blind approach and landing unit
d. The Navigational and Bombing Computer
    Or by

e. The pilot controlled follow-up system.

The pilot can operate a duplicate and independent set for standby only.

The nose slats are actuated by duplicate electric motors at a predetermined elevon position.

Electric actuators controlled by a three-position lever operate the flaps.

Fuel System

The fuel system is in two parts:

1. 1. The main system of 3092 gallons capacity with two tanks in the centre section and five in each wing. Four forward and one aft of the spar. Tanks No 2 and 3 are connected by a large diameter pipe.

2. The Auxiliary system of 1240 gallons capacity with four tanks in the rear fuselage above the bomb bay.

All tanks are of the Marflex light-weight crash-proof collapsible bag type. No 1 tank port and starboard are used as collectors and along with the wing tanks on that side form an independent system feeding two engines.

The two systems are connected by a cross feed operated by the pilot. When the auxiliary system is fitted two auxiliary tanks feed each system. Duplicated booster pumps that supply direct to the engine fuel pumps feed the engines. All the tanks are pressurized by the inert gas system to ensure fuel and prevent high altitude 'boilingî.

The fuel can be jettisoned from 2, 3, 5, 6, tanks up to, a total of 2,000 gallons (16,000lbs). Refuelling was carried out under pressure at points on the fuselage side to each system. Additional capacity was allowed for if the operational requirements should change

Fire Extinguisher and Inert Gas System

Fire Extinguisher bottles are fitted for engine and tank protection. High-pressure Methyl Bromide bottles of a 12 lb capacity are mounted easily accessible, adjacent to the areas they

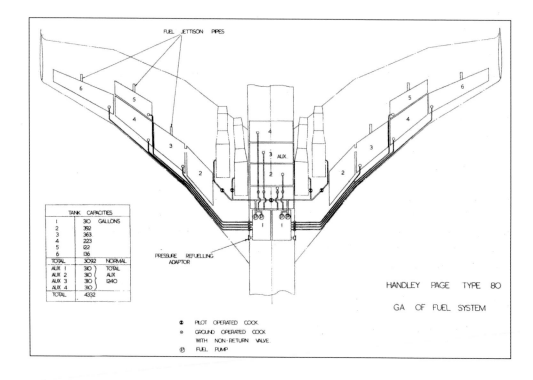

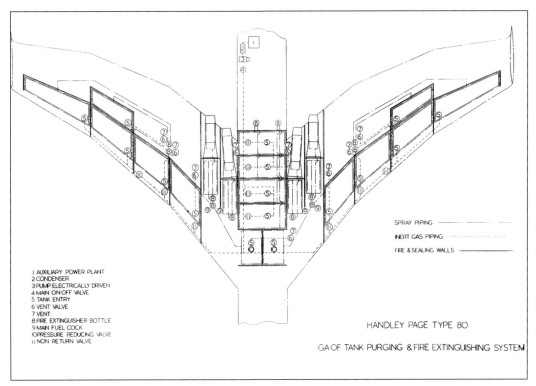

SPRAY PIPING
INERT GAS PIPING
FIRE & SEALING WALLS

1 AUXILIARY POWER PLANT
2 CONDENSER
3 PUMP ELECTRICALLY DRIVEN
4 MAIN ON-OFF VALVE
5 TANK ENTRY
6 VENT VALVE
7 VENT
8 FIRE EXTINGUISHER BOTTLE
9 MAIN FUEL COCK
10 PRESSURE REDUCING VALVE
11 NON RETURN VALVE

HANDLEY PAGE TYPE 80

GA OF TANK PURGING & FIRE EXTINGUISHING SYSTEM

serve. Flame switches and spray pipes are provided for in each engine bay on both sides of the fireproof bulkhead. The fuel tanks are fully covered with fire protection including the auxiliary system.

The inert exhaust gas for the tank pressurization and purging is provided by a feed from the AAPP, through a condenser and then pumped under pressure to the tanks via a non return valve. Special vent valves are fitted to the tanks giving inward and outward pressure relief

Electrical System
A 120volt DC Electrical system with a rectified AC supply similar to that developed for the HP Hermes IV is used on the HP 80.

Power is supplied by four engine-driven alternators of a constant 30kw and one 15kw alternator fitted to the AAPP. The outputs are rectified and paralleled as 120 volt DC with the 24-volt supply obtained from transformers on the DC outputs. Two 30kw alternators are capable of supplying all the systems requirements. The remotely controlled AAPP is arranged to run continuously.

Pneumatic System
This system is used to operate the following services: wheel brakes, undercarriage retraction, nose wheel steering, fuel jettisoning and bomb door operations. Two high-pressure engine driven pumps are fitted to the auxiliary gearboxes on the outboard engines with a 100% standby facility.

Maintenance and Accessibility
All services and equipment can be inspected and maintained through the undercarriage and bomb doors or fuselage hatches. The engines are through large detachable panels over each engine bay. (For the prototypes and production aircraft these were under the engines and varied between 2 and 5 doors depending on the Mark of aircraft.). A major part of the equipment was located aft of the bomb bay in a compartment sized for easy access. (Later known as the rear or back hatch.)

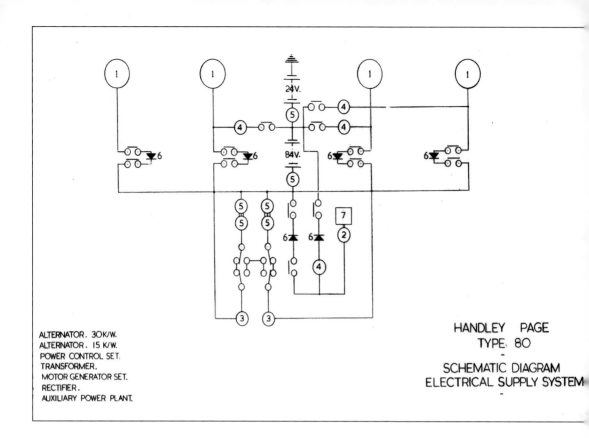

ALTERNATOR. 30K/W.
ALTERNATOR. 15 K/W.
POWER CONTROL SET.
TRANSFORMER.
MOTOR GENERATOR SET.
RECTIFIER.
AUXILIARY POWER PLANT.

HANDLEY   PAGE
TYPE 80
-
SCHEMATIC DIAGRAM
ELECTRICAL SUPPLY SYSTEM
-

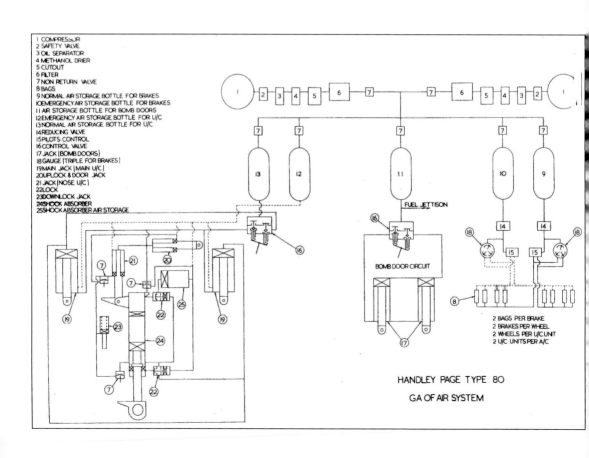

1 COMPRESSOR
2 SAFETY VALVE
3 OIL SEPARATOR
4 METHANOL DRIER
5 CUTOUT
6 FILTER
7 NON RETURN VALVE
8 BAGS
9 NORMAL AIR STORAGE BOTTLE FOR BRAKES
10 EMERGENCY AIR STORAGE BOTTLE FOR BRAKES
11 AIR STORAGE BOTTLE FOR BOMB DOORS
12 EMERGENCY AIR STORAGE BOTTLE FOR U/C
13 NORMAL AIR STORAGE BOTTLE FOR U/C
14 REDUCING VALVE
15 PILOTS CONTROL
16 CONTROL VALVE
17 JACK (BOMB DOORS)
18 GAUGE (TRIPLE FOR BRAKES)
19 MAIN JACK (MAIN U/C)
20 UPLOCK & DOOR JACK
21 JACK (NOSE U/C)
22 LOCK
23 DOWNLOCK JACK
24 SHOCK ABSORBER
25 SHOCK ABSORBER AIR STORAGE

FUEL JETTISON

BOMB DOOR CIRCUIT

2 BAGS PER BRAKE
2 BRAKES PER WHEEL
2 WHEELS PER U/C UNIT
2 U/C UNITS PER A/C

HANDLEY PAGE TYPE 80

GA OF AIR SYSTEM

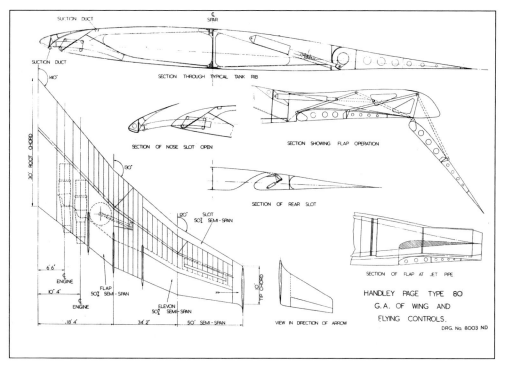

SUCTION DUCT
℄ SPAR

SECTION THROUGH TYPICAL TANK RIB

SUCTION DUCT

SECTION OF NOSE SLOT OPEN

SECTION SHOWING FLAP OPERATION

SECTION OF REAR SLOT

SLOT
50% SEMI-SPAN

SECTION OF FLAP AT JET PIPE

HANDLEY PAGE TYPE 80
G.A. OF WING AND
FLYING CONTROLS.

DRG. No. 8003 ND

ENGINE

FLAP
50% SEM-SPAN

ENGINE

ELEVON
50% SEMI-SPAN

ELEVON
50% SEMI-SPAN

VIEW IN DIRECTION OF ARROW

The Wings

These had a semi-span divided into three parts with the following sweep at quarter chord as follows 48.5 degrees, 37.5 degrees and 26.75 degrees from the centre line of the aircraft. The wingtip fins and rudders are structurally integral with the wings. The relationship between the thickness /chord ratio is designed to give a constant critical Mach number along the span. Leading edge slots are fitted to the outer 50% of the wing with a chord of approximately 15% local wing chord. The elevons that occupy 50 % of the semi-span have plain round leading edges with balance tabs. No mass balance weights are fitted. The wing structure is based on a single spar, a torque box with front and rear webs and closely spaced ribs.

The Fuselage

This is of circular section with a Maximum diameter of 9ft 10in and is divided in to three parts.

The Front Fuselage: Contains the crew compartment up to the pressure bulkhead at frame 92. This section was designed to be jettisoned.

The Centre Section consists of the section aft of frame 92 to the start of the bomb bay.

The Rear Fuselage is from the front of the bomb bay to the end of the fuselage.

The Tailplane This is mounted on a very short fin and is rotatable about a span-wise axis to provide variable incidence.

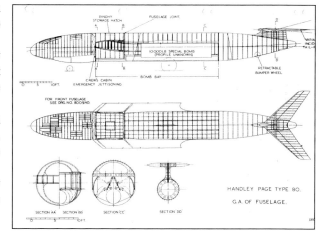

HANDLEY PAGE TYPE 80.
G.A. OF FUSELAGE.

The Engines

These are installed from the top of the wing in separate fireproof bays. Each engine has a 30KVA alternator mounted inside the forward facing air-intake bullet. The aircraft accessories are mounted on gear boxes mounted in the bay adjacent to the outboard engines. The oil tank

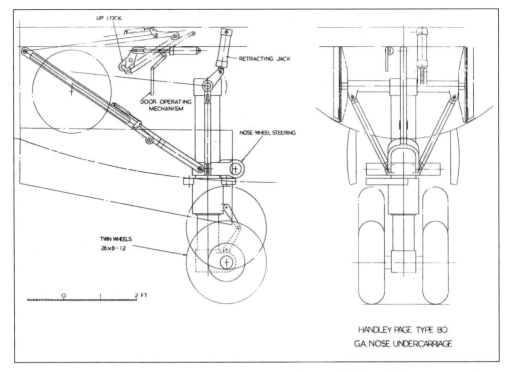

UP LOCK

RETRACTING JACK

DOOR OPERATING
MECHANISM

NOSE WHEEL STEERING

TWIN WHEELS
26×8 - 12

0   1   2 FT

HANDLEY PAGE TYPE 80
G.A. NOSE UNDERCARRIAGE

and the engine auxiliaries are mounted forward of the fireproof bulkhead. The access to these
and the engines is from detachable panels in the upper-wing surface.

The Main and Nose Undercarriage

This had twin nose wheels and single large main-wheels. Tyre pressure being 110lb at
95,000lb.

The nose is located under the cabin floor in the front fuselage and is actuated and steered
by pneumatics.

The Main undercarriage retracted inboard into the wings and again is pneumatically actuated, as are the braking systems.

This design was submitted and resulted in Handley Page being awarded a design and manufacturing contract for two prototypes in November 1947. Over the next few years a considerable amount of redesign and improvement was to be achieved. The Crescent wing was to be retained but the structure was to come under

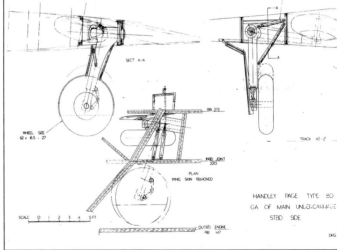

SECT A-A

WHEEL SIZE
62 × 65 - 27

PLAN
WING SKIN REMOVED

HANDLEY PAGE TYPE 80
GA OF MAIN UNDERCARRIAGE
STBD SIDE

SCALE 0 1 2 3 4 5FT

much scrutiny and many design changes as it progressed. There were a number of serious
changes made, and others looked at, until the final design was turned into the manufacturing
process and what we were to see was a vastly different HP80 in late 1952 when Chief Test
Pilot Squadron Leader Headley Hazelden and Chief Flight Test Observer Ian Bennett took
WB771 into the air for the first time at AAEE Boscombe Down on the 24th December 1952
for its first flight of 17 minutes.

AIR STAFF REQUIREMENT NO. O.R./229 (ISSUE 3)
MEDIUM BOMBER

INTRODUCTION

1.　The second issue of O.R./229 for a medium bomber was published in January 1953 and covers the requirements for the Vulcans and Victors now being built to the B.35/46 specification.　This second issue has since twice. been amended and further amendment is now necessary to cover the latest additions such as flight refuelling.　Rather than issue a third amendment list it is more convenient to publish a third issue of the requirement.

REQUIREMENT

2.　The basic requirement is for a medium bomber landplane capable of dropping one 10,000 lb. bomb on a target from a height of not less than 50,000 ft., when a still air range of 3,350 n.m. is needed for the whole sortie.

3.　It is most desirable that the aircraft should be capable of greater ranges than 3,350 n.m. with the same bomb load, but to achieve this, additions to the permanent structure weight needed for the basic requirement must not prejudice the height over the target in the basic case to an extent greater than 400 ft.

4.　For short range targets the maximum bomb load, in combinations described at paras. 33 and 34, is required.　However it is most undesirable that additional permanent structure weight should be built into the aircraft in order to achieve increased bomb load.　Such permanent structure weight as is required for H.E. loads must be included in the maximum penalty allowed in paragraph 3 above.

ROLES OF THE AIRCRAFT

5.　The aircraft is required to fulfil the strategic medium bomber role　by delivering one 10,000 lb. bomb by night and, subject to the tactical situation, by day.

6.　Secondly, should the need arise, the aircraft is required to be able to supplement the tactical bomber force by delivering the maximum weight of H.E. bombs by night, and if practicable by day, on targets at a relatively short distance from base.

7.　Thirdly, the earliest production aircraft should be able to be used in the reconnaissance role by day or by night having been simply converted to carry cameras, photo flashes and such electronic reconnaissance equipment as becomes available.　This equipment may be carried in lieu of bombs.

8.　Fourthly, the aircraft should be able to be used in the flight refuelling tanker role having been simply converted to carry extra fuel tanks in lieu of bombs.

GENERAL DESIGN CONSIDERATIONS

9.　Save where this requirement differs in detail, the aircraft should be constructed to the standard of the second prototype built to the specification B.35/46.

/10.

10.   Since targets will be attacked at a great distance inside enemy territory, it must be assumed that the aircraft will be plotted by radar and other methods for much of its flight.   The aircraft must therefore be provided with a performance ability and equipment to reduce to a minimum the chance of destruction by ground and air weapons which will inevitably be launched by the enemy.   To this end, the aircraft must have:-

    (a)   the highest practicable cruising altitude;

    (b)   good manoeuvrability at high speed and high altitude;

    (c)   a high cruising speed;

    (d)   a capacity for carrying adequate warning devices;

11.   The size of the pressure cabin should be as small as possible.

12.   The aircraft must be capable of operating from airfields having a load classification number of 55.

PERFORMANCE

Operating Height

13.   The highest practicable cruising altitude is required for this aircraft; it should be able to cruise at a minimum height of 50,000 ft. at the target, when flying with a 10,000 lb. bomb after taking off at an A.U.W. consistent with the basic requirement stated at paragraph 2.   After one hour of flight, the aircraft must be capable of maintaining height at 45,000 ft. with one engine stopped and 30,000 ft. with two engines stopped.

Climb

14.   When at an all-up weight consistent with the basic requirement stated at paragraph 2, the aircraft should be capable of reaching 45,000 ft. within one hour after take-off and 50,000 ft, within $2\frac{1}{2}$ hours.

Manoeuvrability and Handling

15.   The highest possible degree of manoeuvrability, particularly at high altitudes, is to be provided.   The flying characteristics must not become dangerous at heights above 25,000 ft, when the speed temporarily rises in the course of combat or other manoeuvres to a maximum of 0.90 Mach.

16.   The aircraft will be required to fly under all weather conditions.   It must therefore be capable of comfortable slow speed flight and under these conditions offer good responses to the controls, especially during approaches to land.

Speed

17.   The aircraft must be capable of cruising at maximum continuous cruising power at heights between 35,000 ft. and 50,000 ft. at a speed of 500 knots.

18.   The maximum speed in level flight should be as high as possible at heights above 25,000 ft., consistent with the preceding performance requirements.

19. A speed restriction as agreed by the Air Staff for the prototypes is acceptable below 25,000 ft. in the interests of saving structural weight.

20.   The final approach speed before landing should not exceed 120 knots.

21.   With a 10,000 lb. bomb the still air range without flight refuelling or external tanks must not be less than 3,350 nautical miles. The stopping of one engine must not reduce the range by more than 20%.

22.   Additional range up to 5,000 nautical miles with the same bomb load is required, provided this does not involve a weight penalty (to the permanent structure needed for the requirement at paragraph 21) exceeding the equivalent to a loss in height over the target of 400 ft. This additional range must be achieved without the use of flight refuelling but external tanks may be used.

23. Provision is to be made for ranges exceeding 5,000 nautical miles without flight refuelling in so far as:-

(a) The reduced strength factors are agreed by the Air Staff after consultation with the M.O.S.

and (b) the permanent structure penalty will not exceed the limits expressed in paragraph 22.

24.   Additionally, to increase flexibility and to still further increase the ranges quoted above all aircraft are required to be capable of accepting fuel in flight. Detailed requirements of this are given in paras. 28 to 31 below.

Take-off

25.   Under A.P.970, Chapter 105, Fig. I, Maximum Temperature, the aircraft must clear a 50 ft. screen in 2,400 yards, from rest in still air or with a cross wind of up to 20 knots at right angles to the take-off path. If necessary, rocket-assisted take-off equipment may be used.

26.   When the aircraft has an all-up weight at take-off commensurate with paras. 21 and 22 and the pilot decides to abandon the take-off before reaching the unstick speed, it must be possible for the aircraft to be stopped within a distance of 3,100 yards measured from the start of the take-off run.

Landing

27.   The aircraft must be capable of landing in cross winds of up to 20 knots. It must be capable of coming to rest within 1,400 yards after crossing a 50 ft. screen in still air at the maximum landing weight under the maximum design temperature conditions as shown in figure I, Chapter 105, A.P.970.   Tail parachute(s) may be used to conform with this requirement. An automatic braking system to provide maximum retardation without skidding should be provided.

FLIGHT REFUELLING

28.   Every aircraft is to be capable of simple conversion to either receive or transfer fuel in flight.

29.   In the Receiver role aircraft are to be capable of accepting at least 500 g.p.m. at any stage of flight.

30.   In the Tanker role aircraft are to be capable of transferring at least 5,000 gallons of fuel at a rate of at least 500.g.p.m. at a radius of at least 1,000 n.m. from base. It must be possible for the fuel for transfer to be used by the tanker if necessary.

31. It must be possible to convert from the basic aircraft to the receiver or tanker role with the minimum of time and labour under Service conditions. It is important that the conversion time does not exceed 5 hours and the Air Staff are to be informed if this requirement cannot be met. The performance

penalty due to the increased weight to the permanent structure needed to cater for flight refuelling must be within the limits stated in paragraph 3 above.

ARMAMENT

Defence Armament

32.   No provision need now be made for rear defensive armament.

Bombs

33.   The following bombs and combination of bombs are the minimum required to be carried by this aircraft as alternative loads:-

 (a) 1 x 10,000 lb. M.C. Mark 1.

 (b) 4 x 10,000 lb. H.C.

 (c) 30 x 1,000 lb. M.C.

 (d) 30 x 1,000 lb. mines.

 (e) 10 x 2,000 lb. mines.

 (f) 2 x 12,000 lb. Tallboy M.C. Mark 1.

 (g) 24 x 100 lb. practice.

 (h) 24 x 25 lb. practice.

34.   It should be noted that the loads at (c), (d) and (e) above will on occasions need to be increased to the maximum load possible subject to the following limitations:-

 (a) Any weight penalty to the permanent structure must be included in the maximum referred to in para. 22.

 (b) Any reduction in strength factors is to be agreed by the Air Staff after consultation with the M.O.S.

 (c) The still air range with this maximum load of bombs should not be less than 1,200 n.m.

Wing bomb nacelles may be used for this maximum bomb load case and for the bomb load specified at sub-para. (b) of para. 33.

Bombing

35.   It must be possible to release bombs at any speed at which the aircraft is flown subject only to the limit mentioned in paragraph 19. Similarly, it must be possible to release bombs from any altitude at which the aircraft is flown subject only to the lower limit set by the danger of the bombs exploding.

36.   The opening of the bomb doors or other methods of releasing the bombs must not appreciably alter the speed or trim of the aircraft or cause snaking or hunting so that the bombing accuracy is affected.

37.   It must be possible for bombs to be released safely when the aircraft is diving or climbing at an angle of 15° or when the aircraft is sustaining up to 10° of side slip.

38.   The temperature of the air in the bomb bay is to be automatically controlled between 0°C. and 18°C., under all operational conditions in flight when the bomb doors are closed.

39.   The system H2S9/NBC/VSA will be fitted to the aircraft for blind or visual bombing for all heights between 7,200 ft. and 50,000 ft.   Blue Study will be fitted for blind bombing at short ranges from heights above 5,000 ft.

Bomb Release and Jettison Controls and Indicators

40.   The following controls and indicators associated with the bombing systems are to be provided at the stations shown:-

(a) First pilot's station:-

(i)   Normal bomb release switch.

(ii) A switch or control for operating the bomb doors.

(iii) Indicators to show when the main fuselage bomb doors and wing cell bomb doors are not in the position selected by the pilot.

(iv) An indicator to show if there is a fire in the bomb bay.

(v)   Emergency automatic jettisoning (safe) switch.   The operation of this switch will cause the bomb doors to be opened automatically, the bombs to be jettisoned safe, and the bomb doors to be closed again automatically.

(b) Second pilot's station:-

(i)   Remote control box for Time of Fall Calculator.

(c) Visual bomb aimer's station:-

(i)   A normal bomb release switch.

(ii) A jettison (live) switch.

(d) Blind bomb aimer's station:-

(i)   A normal bomb release switch.

(ii) A jettison (live) switch.

(iii) A bomb spacing control.

(iv) A panel of bomb selector switches and indicators.

(v)   A Time of Fall Calculator.

(vi) A fuse timing selector.

(vii) An air burst control unit.

(viii) A switch to operate the camera provided for radarscope photography.

(ix) A control for the electro-magnetic nose and tail fusing of bombs.

Photography

41.   Photographic recordings of radarscopes will be required during all bombing runs.

42. The crew will consist of five, viz:-

(a) First pilot.

(b) Second pilot.

(c) Navigator (responsible also for visual bomb aiming and obtaining astro fixes).

(d) Navigator (responsible also for obtaining radar fixes, blind bomb aiming, and photography).

(e) Signaller (responsible also for radio counter measure equipment).

Pressure Cabin

43. The crew are to be accommodated in one pressure cabin. The cabin is to be large enough to allow each member of the crew to move from his seat during flight. Otherwise the size and hence the vulnerability of the pressure cabin should be as small as possible. Equipment which can be remotely controlled should not be carried in the cabin; however, for that equipment which is necessarily installed in the cabin, provision should be made for such in-flight inspection as is practicable without prejudicing the cabin layout. It is to be possible to select cabin differential pressures of 4 P.S.I. or 9 P.S.I. or to select "No pressure". When the cabin pressure differential has been selected at either 4 P.S.I. or 9 P.S.I. the pressure, humidity and temperature are to be automatically controlled. When the cabin is pressurised and "No Pressure" is selected, the time for decompression is not to be less than 6 seconds, but to allow the quickest escape in an emergency this time should not be exceeded appreciably. Provision is to be made for an automatic flood flow of pressurised air in an emergency. This flow is required to maintain at maximum cruising altitude the cabin pressure equivalent to at the most 40,000 ft. if the pressure cabin is punctured to the extent of a hole 1" in diameter for each 12 sq.ft. of the projected area of the cabin. As much cooling of the flood air as practicable should be provided.

44. To reduce fatigue, the maximum crew comfort must be provided. All crew members are to be provided with facilities for using partial pressure (or pressure breathing suits.

Pilot's Station

45. Pilots must have the best possible view and in particular they must have a good view downwards over the nose of not less than 15° from the horizontal when the aircraft is in level flight. Ejector seats are to be provided and are to be adjustable for height. The slope of the back is to be adjustable in the fore and aft direction. Folding arm rests are to be provided and the seats generally made as comfortable as possible.

46. As far as possible, the engine instruments are to be grouped as follows:-

(a) Instruments which will be under observation continuously for the correct operation of the aircraft, are to be grouped so that they can easily be read by the 1st pilot. This group should contain the main fuel contents gauges.

(b) Instruments which only require periodic observation for checking purposes are to be grouped so that they are visible to the second pilot.

(c) Instruments required for maintenance checks and testing purposes only should be grouped outside the pilots' station. This group should expressly include any instrument which indicates a condition about which the pilots can do nothing whilst in flight.

47.   All main fuel cocks are to be within reach of the 1st pilot.

Navigation Stations

48.   The navigators are to be accommodated at a station where they can be seated side by side. This conjoined station is to be as comfortable and as quiet as possible; all the navigational instruments, radar navigation controls and indicators, and electronic bomb aiming equipment are to be suitably displayed at this station.   The equipment is to be illuminated or light screened as appropriate.

Visual Bomb Aiming Station

49.   A visual bomb aiming station readily accessible from the navigation station is to be provided.   The clear field of view from this station must be 10° aft of vertical to horizontal forward and as wide a lateral view as possible.

Signaller's Station

50.   The signaller's station is to be fitted with W/T equipment, attack warning devices and controls for radio and other counter measure devices.   The signaller's station is to be as comfortable as possible.

PROTECTION AND SURVIVAL

Armour Protection

51.   Armour protection for the crew is not required but wherever possible equipment installed in the pressure cabin should be arranged to afford some protection against fragments of ammunition which have been fired at the aircraft from a rearward cone of 60° included angle.

Warning Devices

52.   Warning devices to detect the approach of opposing aircraft or illumination by certain radars will need to be fitted as directed when such equipment becomes available from time to time.

Fuel

53.   Self sealing tanks are not required, but a system of purging the tanks by inert gas is to be provided.   If nitrogen or other stored gas is used for this purging, a sufficient quantity is to be provided for sorties involving the maximum range flown at the maximum operational altitude and one descent at the target down to 25,000 ft.   The tanks are to be so arranged or compartmented that if one is holed there will be a loss of not more than 10% of the remaining fuel.   The fuel system is to provide for the continued functioning of the engines, when the aircraft sustains a vertical acceleration of an equivalent of minus 1 g for a continuous period of 10 seconds.

Fire Protection

54.   Fire extinguisher systems are to be provided for the engine and fuel tank compartments.

Emergency Exits

55.   When jettisoned, the canopy above the pilots' seats must leave the aircraft under all conditions of accelerated flight and fall free without damage to the remaining aircraft structure.   A separate emergency battery must be provided for the escape facilities which are dependent in the first instance on electricity.

56. The crew members other than the pilots are to be provided with an escape exit which protects them, during the process of abandoning the aircraft, from the blast of the air flow.

Ditching and Flotation

57. Good ditching and flotation characteristics are desirable but must not prejudice the performance. A ditching escape hatch is to be provided in the roof to the rear of the pressure cabin. Each crew member is to be provided with a Type K dinghy and a larger crew dinghy is to be provided in a blow out stowage in the upper part of the fuselage close to the pressure cabin.

Parachutes

58. Parachutes appropriate to the ejector seats will be worn by the pilots and back type parachutes will be worn by other members of the crew.

Window

59. At least four window launchers are to be fitted in the basic aircraft; stowage for at least 400 bundles of centimetric Window is to be provided for each launcher.

Oxygen

60. The D.1, demand system for supplying oxygen to the crew members is to be fitted to this aircraft. Sufficient oxygen is to be provided for the five crew members for the maximum endurance of the aircraft on the following basis:-

(a) 10% of the endurance at a cabin pressure equivalent of 8,000 ft.

(b) 40% of the endurance at a cabin pressure equivalent of 25,000 ft.

(c) 50% of the aircraft endurance at a cabin pressure equivalent to the optimum cruising altitude; (sufficient oxygen must also be provided for the use of pressure suits for this duration at this altitude).

For flight refuelled sorties provision is to be made for the carriage of enough additional oxygen to cater for 3 hours extra flight at a cabin pressure equivalent of 25,000 ft.

Air Brakes

61. Air brakes are required; the application of the air brakes must not cause the aircraft to vibrate, snake or hunt. They should be as effective as possible and in any case must be adequate to permit the aircraft to descend from maximum cruising height to 40,000 ft. in 90 seconds or less. The air brakes are not to affect the stalling speed of the aircraft and should not have an adverse effect on its handling qualities at any speed.

OTHER FEATURES

Dual Control

62. The second pilot's seat must be suitable for giving and receiving dual instruction and must be sufficiently comfortable to be occupied for the full endurance of the aircraft. Duplication of all instruments is not essential but a blind flying panel must be provided for each pilot.

Protection against Icing and Misting

63. A means must be provided to prevent all windows required for flying, search or bombing becoming obscured by ice, snow, rain or internal misting. The system must be effective throughout the speed and height range of the aircraft. As a

concession, pending the development of suitable transparencies and other de-icing equipment, it is accepted that windows in the early aircraft will not have full protection against ice and snow. Every effort must be made to meet the full requirement as soon as possible.

64. The aircraft must be capable of flying through all icing conditions.

External Inspection

65. A simple visual inspection device is required so that the crew can see if the aircraft is leaving contrails. Additionally it is desirable that this device can be used to inspect the top and bottom surfaces of the wing. Ideally the signaller should be able to use the device without leaving his seat.

EQUIPMENT

Flying Equipment

66. The following equipment is to be provided:-

(a) Night Flying. Full night flying equipment is to be provided. U.V. and red lighting is to be provided in the pilots' cockpit. Emergency white lighting is to be provided from dry battery cells. A blackout screen is to be provided between the pilots' and the Navigators' compartment.

(b) Automatic Pilot. An automatic pilot Mark 10 is required.

(c) Automatic Approach Equipment. Automatic approach equipment is to be provided by coupling the auto pilot to the I.L.S.

(d) Low Level Radio Altimeter. An approved low level radio altimeter is to be fitted.

(e) Special White Lighting. Special white lighting, now under development, is to be fitted in the pilots' cockpit so that the pilots can see the instrument panel after an atomic explosion.

Navigation

67. The following instruments will be required:-

(a) A G.4B compass with repeaters at the navigation and pilots' stations.

(b) Standby magnetic compass, type E.2.

(c) Air Speed Indicator.

(d) Periscope sextant.

(e) G.P.I. Mark 4 (associated with Green Satin).

(f) Barometric altimeter.

(g) Outside air thermometer.

(h) Fuel flowmeters.

Radio

68. The following radio and radar equipment is to be fitted:-

(a) N.B.S. Mark 1.

(b) Blue Study.

(c) Gee Mark 3.

(d) Green Satin.

(e) I.L.S.

(f) W/T communication equipment STR.18B2.

(g) Intercommunication equipment Λ.1961.

(h) Multi-channel V.H.F. radio communication equipment, TR.1985/1986

(Note: This equipment may be replaced by U.H.F. equipment when available).

(j) I.F.F. Mark 10 and S.I.F.

(k) Red Garter. Early aircraft will be fitted with a modified Orange Putter until Red Garter becomes available.

(l) High altitude radio altimeter Mark 6.

(m) Space structure and power provision for an audio frequency recorder.

(n) Radio Compass ARI.5428.

(o) Low level radio altimeter.

Pyrotechnics

69. A discharger is required for firing window or signal cartridges from the Signaller's station.

In-flight Feeding

70. A power point is to be provided at each main crew station for heating food containers during a sortie.

RECONNAISSANCE

71. Certain specified aircraft including the earliest production aircraft delivered to the Service will be required to fulfil the reconnaissance role mentioned at paragraph 7. The simplest possible modifications should be made to the number of aircraft specified to fulfil this role, compatible with the cameras, photoflashes, and other equipment to be carried.

72. It should be possible for aircraft modified for reconnaissance to revert to the bomber role, or back from the bomber to the reconnaissance role under Service conditions in not more than 3 days. If, therefore, it is necessary to build-in some parts of the modification on the production line as additional weight to the permanent structure, these parts should be kept to the minimum. The majority of the parts associated with the modification should be removable and should take the place of stores in the bomb bay or wing nacelles.

73. These aircraft will be required to do day P.R., night P.R. and survey. It should be possible to change over between roles in not more than 3 hours under Service conditions.

74. The following photographic equipment is to be fitted to these aircraft on reconnaissance sorties:-

(a) Day Role

    (i)   Fan of 8 x F.96 cameras with 48" or 36" lens.

    (ii) Tri camera installation of F.96 cameras with 6" lens or one vertical F.96 camera with 6" lens plus two oblique F.96 cameras with 24" lens.

    (iii) One vertical F.49 camera with 6" lens in a Type 80 Mounting.

(b) Night Role

    (i)   6 x F.89 cameras with 6 photo-electric cells disposed as either:-

       5 with 36" or 24" lens

            or

       3 with 36" lens plus 3 with 24" lens

    (ii) Two F.24 night cameras with 5" lens

    (iii) A minimum of 200 x 8" photo flashes, at least 100 of which must be carried in the bomb bay,

           or

A mixed load of 100 x 8" photo flashes in the bomb bay plus 20 x $16\frac{1}{2}$" photo flashes in wing nacelles.   The carriage of $16\frac{1}{2}$" photo flashes in the bomb bay is no longer required.

(c) Survey Role. The camera installation for the survey role is still under consideration. For the time being survey requirements will be met by the vertical F.49 camera with 6" lens in a Type 8 Mounting which is carried in the day role.

TARGET DATE

75.   The Air Staff require this aircraft in service by 1955.

Air Ministry, D.O.R.(A)
2nd June, 1954.

Crystallising a Concept On Paper and in Metal

With grateful thanks to Mr. R.S.Stafford FRAeS, Chief Designer and
Mr. W.H. MacRostie, Chief Engineer

In the first part Mr. R.H. Stafford describes the way Handley Page Design Department brought the concept of the HP80/Victor into life via the vast amount of work carried out by his department in relating a wooden model into a real aeroplane.

This article by R S Stafford FRAeS, Chief Designer and W H Mac Rostie Chief Engineer was published in the Handley Page Bulletin No. 207 dasted February 1953.

In connection with the design of a large bomber aircraft the name of Handley Page was a tradition because we have always been pioneers in this sphere. It is to be expected that the team which produced countless Hampdens and Halifaxs should think of a new bomber in terms of its experience of World War Two which was just coming to its end and the known and projected developments in bomber inception. It was concluded that, to be effective and to have a reasonable chance of survival, the new bomber would have to cruise at great heights and speed and have range/load capacity far in excess of contemporary bombers. These thoughts led to a few basic requirements; the ability to carry heavy loads long distances high in the stratosphere and at a speed on the brink of the then so called sonic barrier.

In comparison with current achievements, the new bomber had to go twice as far with the same load and operate more than twice as fast and twice as high. Faced with the vast jump in development of such a magnitude, we set up a small team to make an exhaustive study of the problem. Mr. G.H. Lee at that time a Research Engineer was to lead it.

It was soon apparent that, to fly at high subsonic speed, it would be necessary to employ a high degree of wing sweep and, to operate efficiently at great heights, a large wing span would be required.

From a study of the aeronautical, structural and general design problems came the conclusion that the crescent wing offered the best solution. A proposal for a new bomber – based on our studies led to the official specification and finally an order for the HP 80 or the Victor prototype.

To deal with the host of aerodynamic, structural and installation problems a project group was set up under the leadership of Mr. C.F Joy. It comprised a select band of designers, and draughtsmen and technicians who worked in close collaboration with our aerodynamics and stress sections. Its function was to advance the design of the new bomber to a stage where scheming was complete.

An essential was that the external shape should be accurate to fine limits and should remain so when loaded. There were also overriding considerations that the structural stiffness should be adequate to meet the exacting requirements of flight at high subsonic speed.

Some brilliant pioneering work on wing structure led to the development of a low weight structural form that met our needs. Great credit is due to the efforts of Mr. R.H Sandifer, Mr. F. Tyson and Mr. P.H. Wall working in collaboration with our development section and test house. To maintain a high standard of external smoothness, skin panels were to be joined and internal members attached without the use of rivets. When this could not be done, accurate rivet-headed milling was employed.

Front and rear fuselage structures under Mr. B.M. Hubbard and Mr. J.H Vaughan respectively and the tail unit under Mr. R. Little presented difficult design problems. Their solution demanded considerable ingenuity and close collaboration with the shops to evolve satisfactory jigging and fabrication.

On the aerodynamic side a staggering array of new and difficult design problems arose. The need for model data at high subsonic speeds involved the use of a wind tunnel capable of operation at Mach numbers in excess of those obtainable in our tunnel at Radlett. We were not the only constructors in need of such facilities and the time available in the RAE high-speed tunnel was limited.

Flying at high subsonic speeds gave rise to complex problems involving structural elasticity such as flutter and distortions that affect control and stability. They involved much intricate and laborious calculation in the design of the Victor as well as wind tunnel tests. Assessment of flying qualities and the provision of adequate aerodynamic design data with limited facilities called for great ingenuity and application. Under the control of Mr. G.H. Lee our aerodynamic section rose nobly to the task.

A large and comprehensive programme of model tests was handled by Mr. F.R.C Houndsfield in the low-speed wind tunnel at Radlett. In addition flow rigs were set up and tested jointly by the wind tunnel and test house staff.

A great quantity of functional, operational and test equipment – in many instances still under development during the Victor design – had to be accommodated. Mr. S.E. Wells and Mr. P. Chaplin handled all this work. Electrical power requirements have increased in comparison with previous aeroplanes, both military and civil. Mr. P.L Cronbach handled technical and engineering problems in connection with electrical and other equipment.

Retraction of the main undercarriage into the wing and the design of suitable operating mechanism for wing flaps called for much thought. Mr. E.A. Nash handled these problems and the installation of hydraulics and flying controls.

To deal with a multitude of technical problems such as power controls, cooling of equipment, de-icing, cabin air conditioning, etc a section of specialists was set up under Mr. C.D. Holland with Mr. W.R. Shapey as principal assistant.

Our weights control section led by Mr. G. Ratcliffe, dealt with weight expenditure and ensured that it was distributed correctly.

As project engineer Mr. R.L. Hayes made certain that the correct design requirements found correct expression in working drawings. He was responsible for liaison in connection with the HP 88 the scale model for flight-testing the Victor wing on an Attacker fuselage. Many useful data was obtained from this aeroplane that served to confirm the aerodynamic features of the crescent wing.

From the earliest days of design to the consummation of the Victors first flight the guiding hand had been that of Mr. C.F. Joy.

The Chief Engineer Mr. W.H. MacRostie in this second part (written back in late 1952) describes for us the production of the first HP 80 prototype, and the problems they had to solve.

When we were given the job of producing the new Victor bomber, or HP 80, as it was then known, we were up against many problems. Now as I try to write about them, I face another; how to say anything of interest about the work of the Handley Page production team when security restrictions demand no reference is made at this stage of the Victors life to anything, which is not obvious from study of two official photographs.

At once it was evident that in translating into metal the brainchild of our designers, a great amount of research into new methods and materials would be needed.

With operating speeds and altitude so much greater than those of earlier bombers, the aerodynamic requirements became very strict. Wing contours had to be kept within very close limits. Surface smoothness was to be of a much higher standard than ever before.

Conventional methods and materials were not good enough to satisfy the new requirements. A long development programme was set under way.

The design team evolved a new type of structure; our development section under Mr. H. J. Tyte, in collaboration with the test house in the control of Mr. K.C. Pratt, arrived at the ideal form of construction. Not only did this satisfy stringent design needs but also those of production.

Of necessity, new materials have been used in the building the bomber. We have made full use of higher-grade alloys that are stronger and lighter than those in current use. In introducing these a new range of problems was met. Their heat treatment was critical. New plant and techniques were needed to ensure that they fulfilled their promise.

Initial production planning was carried out under my control by Mr. A.W. Braithwaite Assistant Works Superintendent and by Mr. C. Bond and Mr. A. Simpson in our experimental shop.

New methods of construction demanded new methods of jigging . It was here that Mr. W. J. Thorn our chief jig and tool designer came into the picture. The design of jigs for the HP 80 was an immense problem in view of the very close limits and contours required. Success in this very important sphere reflects great credit on all concerned.

To find space for the new jigs was a great difficulty with simultaneous production of Canberras under way in the factories. This problem was solved and gradually more and more sections began work on the HP80. Soon our production facilities were fully engaged on the new bomber under the direction of Mr. D.C. Robinson our works superintendent.

An extensive programme of development work in the machine shop was under the control of Mr. J.C. Wheeler and Mr. J.B. Martin.

It was in the experimental shop under Mr. A.W. Braithwaite that main components, such as fuselage and wings were built. In the main shop, Mr. W.A. Millman was responsible for smaller components.

The swept tail-plane and fin gradually took place under the watchful eye of Mr. J. Inglis.

All three Handley Page factories worked on components of the HP80. At Reading the rudder, ailerons and elevators were built where Mr. E.W. Pixton and Mr. C.S. Lennox took charge of this work. At Park Street Mr. R.A. MacPhail supervised the construction of the huge bomb doors and many items of ground equipment.

While the construction was underway on all sides the progress department, under Mr. H. H. Crooks ensured that materials were delivered on time and nothing was allowed to hold up the work. 'Tin Bashing' on the prototype was under the control of Mr. W. T. Yelland. He was responsible for fuselage skinning panels and cowling. This was no easy job; skinning on modern aircraft is necessarily of a thicker gauge than ever before.

Thousands of details go into a present day aeroplane. Mr. P. Jeffers looked after their production as well as undercarriage and engine doors. The main flaps were the responsibility of Mr. S. Short.

Finally came the day when the fuselage was moved into the main shop. Here Mr. G. Carter's team carried out the installation work. The number of installations in a modern aircraft is formidable and the amount of equipment carried is many times greater than in bombers of World War Two.

Wings and tail plane were temporarily fixed to the main structure at Cricklewood before they were detached and transported to the A&AEE Boscombe Down, where the bomber's final assembly was carried out.

As usual with prototype aircraft, particularly those as revolutionary as the HP 80 there were a number of snags and setbacks. It was the tenacity and skill of my staff, working hard and long that overcame every difficulty in turn.

HP Cricklewood to A&AEE Boscombe Down

Seven column inches greeted the maiden flight of the Handley Page Victor. They said 'World's Greatest Bomber – Crescent Wing HP80 Flies Fastest Farthest and Highest'.

The Spotlight of publicity focused on the designer and pilot of the new bomber. But behind the headlines and the pictures were the years of inspired and painstaking work by a host of men.

Many interesting stories could be told of this development period; little may yet be said. Operation *Geleypandhy*, however is free of the security veto and typifies the thought and care with which difficult assignments have been tackled in building this bomber.

The operation involved the movement in absolute secrecy of the entire aircraft from the Handley Page works 5 miles from the centre of London where it was built to Boscombe Down, the experimental establishment near Salisbury where it was assembled.

Its most difficult phase was the transport of the fuselage over 90 miles of busy roads. Months before, planning under the control of Mr. W.J. Thorn, Handley Page's Chief jig and tool draughtsman. It was decided to carry the load on a London bus axle suitably reinforced, and tow the structure behind a tractor. The combined length of the fuselage portion and tractor in towing trim was nearly as long as the height of London's Duke of York's column.

Much time was spent in planning and surveying the route. Seven trips were made in order to measure the tricky sections. This in itself was no easy task; indeed, the measurements of the carriageway and verge widths of roundabouts along the North Circular Road nearly resulted in several casualties.

From this data, scale drawings of critical points were made. A model of the tractor and fuselage used to discover the best lines of approach to each. It was found impossible to negotiate two T-junctions. With the co-operation of local authorities, bulldozers were called in. In one case, where the Andover road meets the A30 a completely new track was cut through the corner. At the second junction, a triangular section of field of nearly 2000 square feet was flattened to allow us to pass.

An eighth journey was made as a dress rehearsal. Simulating the fuselage section was a large wooden rig mounted on a Queen Mary trailer. All went well and the ninth journey was the real thing.

For security reasons all resemblance between the fuselage and an aeroplane was disguised. A wooden structure was built to mask the shape and this was covered with white sheets. Upon them was printed the impressive pseudonym '*Geleypandhy*' with a fictitious destination, Southampton, beneath. This was all to deceive the casual watche: most thought it was a boat or even a submarine; certainly it did not look like an aeroplane.

On a summer's evening the convoy set out from Cricklewood. In the neighbourhood the label did not fool the spectators; many had worked on the HP80 for months. Steel plates and wooden ramps were used where it had to cross pavements. Traffic was held up as the procession passed. At roundabouts things were very tight, but careful manoeuvre and applied cunning won through. A night stop was made near the beginning of the Great West Road. Here until daybreak slept the fourteen men who were taking the monster to Salisbury Plain.

Dawn came at 4 o'clock and heralded a fine summers morning. The convoy set of at a fair speed along the deserted Great West Road. A police escort through Staines had been arranged for 5am.

The convoy, ahead of schedule, arrived fifteen minutes early. Unchaperoned it pressed on regardless through the town and perforce on the wrong side of the narrow road. The police reaction to this was not recorded. Beyond Staines all went well. Towing became a pleasure and speeds crept above the planned 15mph. No snags were experienced until the Andover road was reached. There a bulldozer had eased the turn. The track was excellent.

The bulldozer had been parked in the cutting. No persuasion would coax it into life and no driver was available. After a great deal of spade work the convoy passed by with careful driving and inches to spare. A triumph of hard work was completed just as the driver appeared and he was not very popular, to say the least.

Onwards went the convoy through Andover with a police escort and many of the residents still in their beds. No stops were made as nobody wanted to tempt fate. So the convoy arrived at Boscombe Down at 10.30, three hours early – a well planned feat. In addition to the fuselage other major parts of the aircraft were included in the convoy carried on Queen Mary trailers. The team of fourteen celebrated their success which had brought the first flight one step nearer. Now the unloading could start and the assembly and all the various functional tests could start.

At Boscombe Down Mr. A.W. Braithwaite assisted me with my Charge Hands being Mr C. Bond and Mr. A.L. Smith. Mr. K Shillcock was handling the installation of the Sapphires. With all the electrical equipment under the control of Mr L. Summerfield. The checking and functional testing of the Hydraulics was under Mr. G. Bolton and its instrumentation under Mr J. Bates the flying controls and instrumentation by Mr. A. King. Work on the airframe was under the control of Mr J. Hutt and Mr. G. Butler, the intakes were the responsibility of Mr J. Pickles. The fuel system and the tanks were installed under Mr. E. Tutchings. All of us had the invaluable help of Mr F. Dare the Handley Page representative at the A&AEE Boscombe Down. The Test Department team did extensive work in testing the bomber before it first flight. The exacting responsibility of inspection was carried out under of Mr. W.A. Robinson and Mr. F.R. Ashworth in conjunction with the AID under Mr. M.C. Brothers. With the aircraft final assembly at Boscombe Down there began the final phase of checking and inspection to ensure that everything functioned in flight. During this phase and that of final assembly the constant attention of experienced design engineers is required. We were well served in this respect by Mr. E.A. Watson who looked after structural and general design matters and Mr S.S. Hall, who had to ensure that the electrical system functioned satisfactorily. Electrical power and actuation was extensively used on the Victor and Mr. Halls contribution was a vital one. Lastly, I must mention the great debt that we owe to all at A&AEE Boscombe Down. The Royal Air Force and the Ministry of Supply personnel could not have been more helpful or encouraging. They made us feel at home and assisted in every way possible.

The unremitting toil of those in Wiltshire following upon the earlier round the clock efforts at Cricklewood, Radlett and Reading were rewarded on Christmas Eve. It was our Chief Test Pilot Squadron Leader Hedley Hazelden accompanied by our Chief Flight Test Engineer Mr. Ian Bennett who set the seal of success on all our endeavours and took the Victor into the air for the first time. It is impossible in a few hundred words to give credit to many people whose work has been vital in addition to those who I have mentioned. The success of the Victor is due to Teamwork. I am proud of our team and always will be. [*This was written in the early 1950s and therefore is rather dated but I think it brings to light the amount of effort that was used to achieve the task so far away from Radlett. Apparently WB771 was partly assembled at the Park Street Experimental site on Radlett Airfield and would have carried out the first flight from there but a Ministry of Supply 'Official' declared the runway too short at 6,000ft for the first flight and so on the 24/5/52 the convoy went to Boscombe Down from 'Radlett' and not Cricklewood.*

The Crescent Wing
by A.H. Fraser-Mitchell ex Chief Aerodynamicist, Handley Page

Flow of Air Over Wings and Wing Design

The trouble with air is you cannot see it, unless you mix it with smoke, say, but then you have a problem because at anything more than very low speeds the smoke gets dissipated and diffuse and then you cannot make out how the air is flowing.

So we start off by looking at the flow of water, for example, the flow of which obeys many of the same laws, though it differs in one respect from air in that it is virtually incompressible, where air is compressible, very much so.

We know that when a river flows through a constricting gorge the speed of the water is in the gorge is much faster than in a wider stream ahead or behind. See Figure 1. This is known as the 'Venturi effect'. We can see that when the distance between the walls of the gorge is small the flow is faster than when the constriction is only slight.

The same thing happens with air, and Figure 2 shows a simple form of Venturi tube. The cross section is usually circular, but does not have to be – it could be rectangular, as shown and give the same effect of the air speeding up in the constriction.

The next principle to grasp is that we can swap speed for pressure – the higher the speed the lower is the pressure on the wall containing the flow, and vice versa. This is expressed mathematically in what is known as 'Bernouilli's Equation' but there is no need to go into that.

Now we go back to our rectangular Venturi seen from the side.

Where the flow speeds up we have a reduction of pressure on the surface. On the outer surface there is no change of pressure from that in the oncoming flow, which we call the 'Freestream' because the surface is lined up with the flow. [There will be some friction on the surfaces but we can ignore this for the moment]

Now let us remove the upper part of our Venturi – Figure 3.

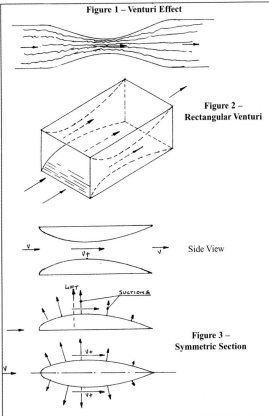

Figure 1 – Venturi Effect

Figure 2 – Rectangular Venturi

Side View

Figure 3 – Symmetric Section

The flow does not change in principle. It is still faster where the bump is, though not as fast as when the upper surface was present. And Bernouilli says there is a drop in pressure there, since the velocity at the bump is higher than the freestream. So now we have the case that the pressure over the upper surface of what is a crude form of cambered aerofoil wing is lower than over the upper surface. So it will lift upwards!

Now we may not want this, and we can get rid of the lift by adding, below the bottom surface, the shape of the upper surface, inverted.

We now have a symmetrical aerofoil and since the reduced pressures on the upper **surface** are matched exactly by the same reduced pressures on the new lower surface there is no lift – provided we don't tilt the whole lot at an angle to the freestream.

Because we have added some cross-sectional area to the aerofoil, the actual velocities and pressures are changed a bit, but not in principle.

Following on from the concept of narrow gorges giving fast flows – see the third paragraph above – a thick aerofoil, which presents a large front to the flow, would clearly have higher speeds round it rather than a thin one, and both would be higher than the freestream speed.

So the thinner the aerofoil the lower the extra speed at its thickest part

High Speed Flow Round Aerofoil Sections in the Air

If we now raise the speed of the freestream until it is an appreciable fraction of the speed of sound, say 70 per cent of it we start to get 'compressibility effects'. This ratio of the speed of a flow to the speed of sound is called the 'Mach Number' and we give it the symbol M for shortness in referring to it. So $M = 1$ means that the flow has just reached the speed of sound in air (or indeed in whatever other gas we are immersed in; helium for example, the speed of sound is higher in air at the same temperature, so our voices sound high-pitched when, like divers, we breathe a mixture of air and helium.)

What happens in air at Mach Numbers higher than this significant M = 1

Due to its compressibility a shock may form, and the loss of energy this represents is shown up as 'Wavedrag'. Another effect is that the sudden change of pressure in the shock wave causes a change to the flow at the surface of the aerofoil, and this also gives rise to drag. These two effects combine to give a sharp increase in the drag of the aerofoil section at speeds a little higher than the speed at which $M = 1$ is reached on some part of the aerofoil surface.

The freestream speed at which this happens is called the 'Critical Mach Number' and is usually called 'Mcrit' for short.

From what we have seen earlier, it is obvious that for a thick aerofoil, where the speed over the thickest part is much higher than that for a very thin aerofoil, the freestream speed at which the flow at the bump just reaches $M = 1$ must be lower.

In other words the Mcrit is lower, and we can put numbers to this – see Figure 4.

We see from there that this is why first generation straight (unswept) wing aircraft had to have thin wings to go fast before compressibility effects set in.

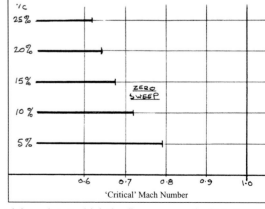

Figure 4 –
Effect of T/C Mcrit. Unswept Wing

The thickness is expressed here as a ratio between the maximum thickness and the 'chord'- the dimension from nose to tail – and given as a symbol t/c or 'Percentage Thickness – Chord ratio'.

We have come to the big breakthrough discovered by Betz [a German Aerodynamicist] a few years before WW2 (and in fact published for all to see though only the Germans took much note of it at the time).

This was that it was the Mach Number at right angles (90deg) to the line of the wing that fixed the point at which the flow over reached M=1. Furthermore the component of the flow parallel to the sweep line of the wing didn't affect the Mach number at all.

As you can see from Figure 5, this meant that the freestream could be much higher than this, provided the wing was swept back (or indeed forward).

So if we have a given thickness of wing section and swing it back, as with the Tornado or F111, it is easy to see that the forward speed at which the shock forms and the drag rises can be raised more and more as the sweep is increased.

Again we can put some numbers to it – but the values depend on how the wing is swept. Rather than rotate the wing on a pivot as above, which causes the span to decrease, the design process treats the wing as if it is 'sheared' back, that is, keeping the same span and 'downwind the t/c ratio as the original straight wing.

Now you will see that although the thickness is unchanged, the chord has decreased when considering the component of flow at right angles to the sweep line. Thus another effect comes in – the section we must consider when finding the drag-rise Mach number of this flow component has a larger t/c than that of the basic wing, since the thickness is the same but the chord has decreased. Hopefully, Figure 6 makes this clear.

Having estimated the Mcrit for the flow at right angles to the wing sweep line, we use this to get the freestream value of Mcrit. Notice that the span wise flow component is not considered at all as indeed Betz pointed out.

This is the design process followed to get the values of Mcrit shown in Figure 7.

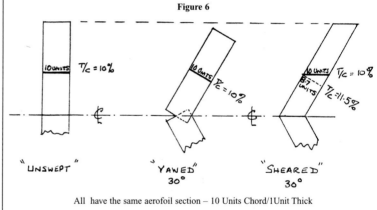

Figure 5 –
How Merit is Affected by Sweep

Figure 6

All have the same aerofoil section – 10 Units Chord/1 Unit Thick

How do we use this information?

Suppose we want to design a wing for an Mcrit of 0.85, which in practice means one can cruise at about M = 0.875 (the design aim of the Victor) with very little drag penalty. We can see from Figure 7 that we may have a wing of 25 per cent t/c but it would need nearly 50 deg sweep. At the other end of the scale with only 5 per cent t/c, we still need about 25 deg sweep.

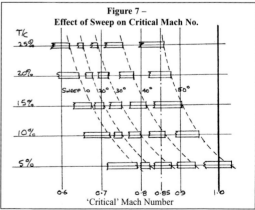

Figure 7 –
Effect of Sweep on Critical Mach No.

So far so good, but then we find that highly swept wings, particularly if they are thick, are very poorly behaved at take-off and landing speeds!

But on the other hand, we want a thick wing at the root in order to resist bending stresses, and, also to be able to house the main undercarriage and/or bury the engines.

However, there is another structural problem – when the swept wing is lifting, it bends

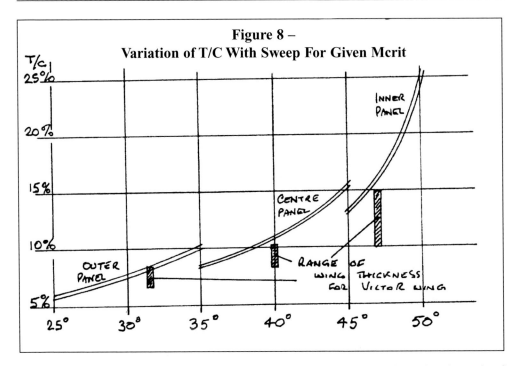

Figure 8 – Variation of T/C With Sweep For Given Mcrit

upwards, this causes the wing to twist along the span, so that the wing-tips reduce in angle of attack, which, at least, is inefficient and at worst results in 'Pitch UP' because the centre of lift is thrown forward.

It can also lead to uncontrollable 'wing dropping' at the lowest speeds needed for flight. The low speed aerodynamic problems get much easier as the sweep comes down, but as we have seen, the wing then has to be very thin, which means it would be very heavy, probably impossibly so. So what the Victor 'Crescent Wing' does is to have a very high sweep and a thick wing inboard, and minimises (though not eliminates) the low speed aerodynamic problems by reducing the sweep, with correspondingly thinner wing sections out towards the tips. One tries to maintain the same Mcrit right across the wing as shown in Figure 8.

Of course the above is a simplified view of a complicated process, but in the Victor two other effects were observed. Firstly the wing cranks effectively cancelled out the bending /twisting effect referred to earlier, and in practice the wing tips do not loose angle of attack as the wing bends. 'Pitch UP ' is therefore minimised.

Second the relative thickness of the wing root and its relation to the diameter of the fuselage (fixed by the required bomb bay and fuel tank volumes) gives an intersection line which is (fortuitously) a very good one for minimising the adverse aerodynamic interference sometimes found at the wing roots of swept wings.

All this came together so well that the 'Father' of the Victor the late Godfrey Lee called it a 'Cohesive Design' the aerodynamic and structural properties dovetailing in extremely well. Even modern designs of wings 50 years later do not show much improvement aerodynamically, especially at high subsonic speeds.

This article was written by C F Jot, Chief Designer and was published in the Handley Page Bulletin No. 213, Summer 1954

SAFETY

in aircraft design

by C. F. Joy, F.R.Ae.S., Chief Designer, Handley Page Ltd.

AEROPLANES, as they have developed, have become more and more complicated.

Mr. C. F. Joy discusses the complexity inherent in today's fast high-flying aircraft and examines the effect which this complexity has on safety.

He shows how designers consider every contingency and do all that is humanly possible to ensure freedom from failure in the air.

C. G. GREY once wrote : "Mail may be lost but never delayed. Passengers may be delayed but never lost."

The first part of this quotation might be questioned, but no one has any doubt about the second. However, not only must passengers be delivered safe and sound, even if late, but their conveyance should bring some profit to the airline operator. Thus it could be argued that the two requirements of paramount importance in transport aircraft design are safety and good earning capacity or low direct operating costs.

Weight Problem

When it is realised that on modern aircraft each pound of additional weight from any cause, including safety precautions, may cost the operator about £60 per year in revenue, the designer's problem in satisfying these two requirements will be appreciated.

On military aircraft, performance (speed, climb, manœuvrability or height over target) makes an important third requirement. In this case, some sacrifice in safety measures may be justified if their weight prejudices a fighting aeroplane's chance of survival.

Safety and earning capacity have each benefited from development; but whereas more simplicity is invariably favourable to the former, improvement in the latter has usually demanded additional complexity.

Vast strides have been made since the first powered flight by the Wright Brothers in 1903. Advances in payload, range and speed since even the first regular airline services were inaugurated

with Handley Page aircraft in 1919 are remarkable for a period of thirty-five years.

On 25th August, 1919, a Handley Page 0/700, developed from the 1914-18 war-time bomber, the 0/400, took off on the first scheduled airline flight from London to Paris with fourteen passengers, and completed the journey in just under four hours. The London-Paris fare was fifteen guineas in 1919.

Our forthcoming H.P. 97 jet liner will take off from London Airport and fly to New York, non-stop, with a load of 100 passengers. Cruising at 600 m.p.h., it will complete the journey in 6½ hours at a direct operating cost of less than one penny per passenger mile.

This noteworthy achievement involves an enormous effort in both design and production. For example, the total design time spent to first flight on the 0/100 involved some 300 man weeks, whereas that required for an aircraft like the H.P. 97 amounts to about 30,000 man weeks.

Spheres of Progress

Speaking generally, this progress has been made on three broad fronts : the result of the quest for safety, higher earning capacity and better operational equipment.

Developments for safety have brought improvement in control and stability, Handley Page slots to give better stalling properties, prevention of spinning, adequate strength and more reliability. These have resulted from experience and a better understanding of the problems involved.

The search for higher earning capacity has led to rather more spectacular changes such as flaps, wheel

B EFORE flight trials begin, every prototype undergoes an
exhaustive series of resonance tests to check flutter and
vibration characteristics.

brakes, cantilever monoplane wings, retractable
undercarriages, pressurisation, powered controls, jet
power plants and swept wings.

The advances in airborne operational equipment
such as radio communication, radio and radar navigation, instruments, ice protection, together with a
whole new range of ground aids, have been directed
towards increasing operational efficiency and regu-
larity of service.

It is interesting to examine the aerodynamic or
structural reasons for some changes in the search
for higher earning capacity, their effect on safety
and the measures taken to ensure adequate safety.
Advances in operational equipment will be discussed
briefly in relation to flight hazards.

Trailing-Edge Flaps

Choice of wing loading is a good example of the
contrary demands made by safety requirements and
low operating costs. A high wing loading results
in a small area and low drag which ensures high
efficiency. But for low speed at take-off and landing
a low wing loading is needed. Many schemes have
been developed and still more proposed for increasing wing lift without increasing area. The one
adopted almost universally is the trailing-edge flap
in a variety of forms.

Since aircraft safety at take-off and landing would
obviously be prejudiced by unsatisfactory functioning of the flaps, alternative or emergency
operating systems are fitted to meet this contingency.

One of the important contributions to increasing
efficiency by reducing wing area has been the introduction of wheel brakes, which permit high but safe
landing speeds. Early aircraft usually had a tail skid
which functioned as a kind of "anchor" on grass
runways. This "ploughing up" of aerodromes was
not popular and was eliminated when tail wheels
became possible with the introduction of main-

wheel brakes. At a later stage, tricycle undercarriages made brakes much more effective since
they enable heavy braking to be used without danger
of the aircraft standing on its nose.

More recently, reversible propellers and tail parachutes have assisted in slowing up an aircraft after
touchdown. We hope reversible jet thrust will soon
be used for braking. Such developments ensure
safer landings since, although speeds are higher, the
braking forces can be more accurately controlled.

Braking must be reliable, since its failure is serious
in almost every case. Here again, apart from
exhaustive rig testing of brakes and operating
mechanism, absolute reliability is usually provided
by duplicating the mechanism.

Cantilever Monoplane Wings

Most early aircraft employed a biplane or even
triplane wing layout having a maze of bracing struts
and wires. This arrangement, which made life easy
for the structural designer, always worried the aerodynamicist because of its high drag, more particularly
as speeds increased.

The development of thick, relatively low-drag
wing sections enabled the structural designer to
make one of the biggest contributions to aircraft
efficiency by introducing the fully cantilever monoplane wing in the twenties.

Since then, insistent demands for lower drag have
reduced the original wing thickness of some 20 per
cent. or more to the 10-12 per cent. in common
use today.

This development in wing design has had an
adverse effect on potential safety but, fortunately,
this has been offset entirely by better knowledge of
air-loading conditions, stress analysis etc., which
will be discussed in more detail later.

Undercarriages have always been considered a
necessary evil; apart from their weight, which on a
long-range transport can amount to as much as
20 per cent. of the payload, the drag of a fixed
undercarriage can make even larger inroads into
earning capacity. Undercarriage drag, which became
an important consideration with cleaner aircraft and
higher speeds, resulted in the early 1930's in the
introduction of retractable undercarriages. On an
aircraft such as the H.P. 97 the weight of retraction

R IGS which simulate the operation of the controls enable these
to be perfected months before a modern aircraft leaves the
ground on its first flight.

costs some 500 lb. in payload, whereas a fixed undercarriage, even if faired, would involve a penalty of more than 5,000 lb., or some 17 per cent. of the payload available for the North Atlantic crossing.

Wheels-up landings are not uncommon, particularly on military aircraft, but they introduce an element of risk which is clearly unacceptable on transport aircraft. Retractable undercarriages, therefore, must never fail to lower. For that reason they are always fitted with a separate emergency-lowering system.

Pressurisation

Fundamentally, the aeroplane appears to suffer a disadvantage compared with surface transport since, in level flight, about half its motive power is expended in overcoming drag due to lift. If the aeroplane always flew near the ground, then this limitation would probably restrict the advantage of air travel to that of speed.

Fortunately, however, flight takes place in a three-dimensional medium, and operating costs when cruising at high altitude can be comparable with many forms of surface transport. Due to reduction in air density, total drag, when cruising at a true air speed of 600 m.p.h. at 50,000 ft., is roughly equal to that at sea level at about 230 m.p.h. From this, it follows that fuel consumption at sea level is nearly three times that at 50,000 ft.

Reduction of engine power restricted high altitude flying in the early days—the less dense air, whilst favourable to the airframe, starved the engine—and it was not until the advent of supercharged piston engines and, at a later date, the gas turbine, that sustained high altitude cruising became practicable. At first oxygen was used by the aeroplane occupants, but it was apparent from the onset that individual oxygen supplies were not feasible for ordinary fare-paying passengers.

Finally, pressurisation was accepted as the only reasonable answer and a whole new range of problems was introduced for the aircraft designer.

Pressurisation requires a reliable supply of air at pressure and a foolproof means of controlling the cabin pressure and varying it with aircraft altitude. In addition, the cabin structure must not fail as a result of the pressure differential (which may be as high as 9 lb./sq. in. at 45,000-50,000 ft.), and it must be sealed against loss of pressure due to leaks.

Of these, the supply and control of air are mechanical problems. Air is usually provided by an engine-driven blower or, in the case of jet-engined aircraft, by tapping the engine compressors. Reliability is assured by having at least two independent sources of supply, each capable of meeting the full requirement.

Considerable care must be taken with pressure-control equipment, since its failure must not lead either to complete loss of pressure or unacceptably high pressures. Here the solution is duplication and careful attention to possible failures in the detail design stages.

Freedom from leaks is important to ensure proper functioning but is not potentially dangerous. A slow leak, even if of such magnitude that normal pressure cannot be maintained, only means that the passengers must suffer some discomfort or that the aircraft must be flown at a lower altitude. But it should be noted that the reduction of a jet transport's altitude may not be possible on a long sea crossing because of the resultant loss in range.

By far the most important requirement is a safe cabin structure since its failure at altitude, as a result of internal pressure, is almost certain to be catastrophic. The reason for this is twofold. The failure of any vessel pressurised with air is explosive and, in consequence, the effect is rarely local while, even if the "blow-out" were only local, sudden "decompression" in the cabin would be fatal to its occupants at altitudes above 40,000-45,000 ft.

Test Fuselage

Aircraft structural designers are keenly aware of these problems and the pressure cabin receives just as much attention as the aeroplane's basic load-carrying structure. Great care is given to the number, size and positioning of all doors and windows; the latter in particular—always a potential source of danger—often consist of an inner and outer sheet of glass or perspex, each capable of withstanding the cabin pressure independently.

A pressure-test fuselage is built for each new aeroplane design; on this must be demonstrated the cabin's ability to withstand at least twice its maximum operating pressure.

Adverse effects of "creep" and repeated loading are also examined by suitable testing since, unlike basic load-carrying structure, the pressure cabin is subjected to its maximum expected load continuously throughout the flight.

In the early days of flying the question of power for operating controls was not important. The effects of control application were the cause of far more speculation than the muscular effort they required.

With increasing aircraft weights and speeds, however, the pilot's strength became a serious limitation and, by the 1920's, numerous ways of assisting him by using energy from the airstream were being investigated. Aerodynamic "balance" in

Continued on page 14

S**TRUCTURAL tests on wings and fuselage confirm strength calculations and ensure that no unnecessary weight is built into an airframe.**   *Photo: Keystone*

Safety in Aircraft Design
Continued from page 11

the form of horns, set-back hinges, servo tabs, etc., became universal and today all aircraft employing manual controls have such aerodynamic assistance.

More recently, the problem of control at high subsonic and transonic speeds has upset all the existing rules governing design of aerodynamic balances. The designer has been tempted to resort to "brute force," that is, power. Although current development may reinstate aerodynamic balance for transonic or even supersonic speeds, power has probably come to stay and for three reasons.

It obviates the necessity for careful aerodynamic design of control surfaces. This invariably results in many hours of flight testing before pilot's control forces are considered satisfactory.

In addition, the absence of aerodynamic balance reduces drag, while carefully-designed power controls enable mass balancing to be eliminated or appreciably reduced. This saving in weight, together with the drag saved by omitting aerodynamic balance, can more than offset the weight of the power-control system on a long-range aircraft.

Power controls inevitably add complexity and therefore adversely affect potential safety. The three most important requirements to ensure safety and satisfactory functioning are a degree of reliability at least as high as that obtained with manual controls, freedom from secondary effects such as servo instability and adequate stiffness to ensure freedom from control surface flutter, particularly when used without mass balancing.

Rig Tests

Compliance with these requirements must be demonstrated by test on a rig representing the complete aircraft control system and having simulated control surfaces with correct inertias and aerodynamic loading.

A single system with complex mechanisms, operated by hydraulics or a combination of hydraulics and electrics, cannot be regarded as infallible. Here again full duplication or an emergency standby system is used. Care must be taken to ensure that any

THIS rig is typical of those used today for proving the pressurisation and air-conditioning systems of new aircraft.

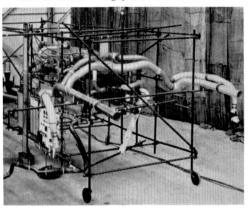

failure of emergency changeover arrangements, or delay in their operation, does not itself create a dangerous situation.

Most aircraft can be broken easily by the pilot if he indulges in violent manœuvres at high speed, since his control forces are arranged to be reasonably light in normal conditions. On manually-controlled aeroplanes, aerodynamic hinge moments provide forces which increase with increasing control surface displacement and are roughly proportional to speed squared. The pilot is therefore warned, by increased control forces, of a dangerous condition due to, say, an abnormally large control surface angle at high speed.

With powered controls having no "feed back," these variations of force with flight conditions must be provided artificially by a feel simulator and, although this involves additional complexity, it results in a major contribution to safety.

Jet Power Plants

Towards the end of the inter-war period, aircraft design appeared to have reached a period of relative stagnation. Aerodynamic "cleaning up" had been developed to a fine art, engine sizes were approaching the limit and further advances other than detail refinements in structures, high lift devices, engine fuel consumption, etc., seemed unlikely.

Then came the jet engine with its enormous power, light weight and small bulk. The whole picture changed; the airframe was literally given a new lease of life. Speeds became limited by the "sound barrier," height seemed to be almost unlimited and the aerodynamicist, in particular, found himself faced with a new set of problems.

Adequate safety was challenged by the possibility of doubling cruising speed and altitude, thus entering the fields of compressibility and atmospheric conditions in the stratosphere about which little was known at that time. Apart from these considerations, which will be discussed later, the jet engine itself presented its own problem in relation to safety.

Since practically all transport aircraft are multi-engined, individual engine reliability is not usually a major factor in safety. In any case, the turbo-jet engine, which is fundamentally simpler than the piston engine, is probably more reliable.

One important contribution to safety, made directly by the jet engine, is its use of kerosene which is far less likely than petrol to ignite spontaneously in the event of, say, a crash landing.

Conceivable troubles, directly attributable to jet engines, and accentuated by the popular buried type of installation, are: The turbo-jet engine, which is in effect a gigantic "blow lamp," may start an airframe fire by burning through the combustion chambers or jet pipe. Some rotating part of the engine, such as the turbine wheel, may burst under high centrifugal loading and scatter fragments which damage airframe structure. Fire is possible also from this cause. Unsuccessful attempts to re-light in the air may result in fuel leakage from the jet pipe into the aircraft structure. A further

A nose fuselage is tested in a water-tank to ensure the strength of a pressurised cabin.

successful attempt may ignite this fuel and cause fire.

Energetic action is taken by both engine and airframe designers not only to prevent these and other troubles but also to minimise their possible effects. Combustion chamber surfaces are air-cooled internally, and turbine wheels are tested at speeds up to 50 per cent. above maximum engine speed, to prove resistance against bursting. Considerable research has gone into selection of the best materials for these and other engine parts, having in mind the working conditions.

Airframe designers install the engine in a fireproof steel "box" which is scavenged by forced ventilation to prevent accumulation of inflammable gases. These boxes are fitted with automatic fire-extinguishing systems which fill them with methyl bromide in the event of fire.

Where possible, even on a "buried" wing installation, engines are located away from the main load-carrying structure. This ensures that, even though fire breaks out or a turbine wheel bursts, the structure is unlikely to be damaged. Jet pipes are made leak-proof and provided with drains so that any surplus fuel left after an unsuccessful re-light is discharged harmlessly overboard. These and other measures are in common use today and there is no evidence to suggest that they are inadequate.

Swept Wings

Sweep-back was first used to provide a tail arm for pitch control (elevons) on a tailless layout, a good example being the Handley Page "Manx" which first flew in 1943. The discovery that sweep delayed the "drag rise" due to shock waves was made by Professor Busemann in 1937 and developed in Germany during the last war. Thus, swept wings and jet engines, two important developments largely interdependent for high speed, arrived most conveniently at about the same time.

Pure-jet engined aircraft cruise most economically at high altitude and at speeds near the "drag rise," that is, the highest Mach number before compressibility drag makes itself felt. In these conditions, compressibility effects other than a sudden rise in drag may develop. These include buffeting, high Mach number stalling, sometimes followed by a wing drop, longitudinal instability and control ineffectiveness. Here, sweep-back has an important advantage in that these effects are usually much less violent than with a straight wing. The behaviour of every aeroplane in these high Mach number conditions is explored thoroughly during prototype test-flying and suitable limiting speeds established for operational use.

One adverse effect of sweep-back on safety, when combined with the high aspect ratios necessary for good range/payload performance, is a tendency towards longitudinal instability near the stall. A successful layout which overcomes this difficulty and, at the same time, combines reasonably high aspect ratio with enough sweep to achieve a high critical Mach number, is the crescent wing used on the Victor.

An important contribution to safety can be made by combining sweep with a suitable tailplane position and size. In this way automatic roundout at touchdown, or self landing, is achieved. This important characteristic of the Victor was described in the last issue of the HANDLEY PAGE BULLETIN.

Structural Design

Aeroplane structures have changed enormously during the last 30 years and there seems little in common between the old "stick and fabric" biplanes and the all-metal stressed-skin monoplanes of today. One link, however, is that they share the structural designer's goal of achieving, to the best of his ability, absolute safety with minimum possible weight. Apart from material changes, big strides have been made in basic understanding of the problem; the designer of today has a much more comprehensive knowledge of flight loadings and their effect on structural safety.

He knows that there are four basic requirements to ensure freedom from failure—that is, primary structural failure and not the secondary effect of, say, fire. These are adequate strength and stiffness and freedom from troubles associated with fatigue and stress corrosion.

The main problems involved in providing adequate strength are the determination of maximum expected loads on the aeroplane and the design of the most efficient structure to support these loads.

The more important design loading results from normal acceleration in manœuvres, gusts, changes in local load-distribution due to application of control surfaces, and undercarriage reactions on landing. Distribution of air loads on wings and tail surfaces are determined by wind-tunnel tests, as are effects of application of the controls. Maximum values for normal acceleration, gust velocity and rate of descent at landing are based on statistical data. Transport aircraft structures are designed to withstand the loads resulting from these maximum values without permanent distortion and have a 50 per cent. reserve of strength before failure.

Test specimens of major components, such as wings and fuselage, are usually loaded to destruction in order to demonstrate a compliance with requirements; this ensures also that no unnecessary strength and, therefore, weight is built into the aircraft.

The statistical data, on which is based this practical approach to the problem of ensuring adequate strength, is being accumulated continuously and covers any sudden development such as the very high altitude cruise made possible by jet engines.

Stiffness

In more recent years, stiffness has become almost as important as strength. Inadequate stiffness or incorrect distribution of stiffness can lead not only to loss of longitudinal stability and to aileron ineffectiveness but also, at very high speeds, to flutter which is all too frequently catastrophic. The importance of stiffness is well recognised by the designer and much work is done, not only on stability and control, but also on the more important job of ensuring freedom from flutter. Mass balancing is combined with the correct distribution of stiffness as a means of raising the flutter speed to at least 25-30 per cent. above the aircraft's maximum design speed which, in turn, is usually some 15-20 per cent. above its maximum operating speed.

The designer has a number of "tools," each of which plays its part in determining flutter speed. These include resonance tests on simple weighted models and the aircraft itself, wind-tunnel tests on scale models having correct representation of stiffness and mass distribution and, more recently, the use of digital and analogue computers.

Fatigue

Some four or five serious accidents since the last war are known to have been caused by fatigue. Previously, very little was heard of this trouble in aircraft structures and the reasons for its more recent prominence are interesting:

Modern materials, particularly high-strength light alloys, have a lower fatigue "life" than their predecessors; that is, the number of reversals of load to failure, at a given percentage of the ultimate stress, is less.

Present-day transport aircraft have a much higher utilisation than was common some years ago. This means that the total "life" expected of, say, a spar boom in a modern aeroplane is some two to four times the average of that experienced before the war.

This reduction of fatigue life inherent in some modern light alloys can have the rather ironical effect of preventing the designer using their high strength properties and therefore reverting to a weaker but less critical material.

Detail design plays an important part in extending the fatigue life of a structure. Examples of this are the avoidance of features such as sudden changes of

section, sharp corners, bad hole-grouping and other forms of "stress raiser."

Critical parts of the structure, such as joints, are subjected to life tests. In some cases a wing or tailplane, or even a whole aeroplane, will be tested by repeated loading until failure occurs.

On some aircraft, danger of fatigue in spar booms is reduced considerably by using distributed flanges. This efficient scheme, in which some 50 per cent. of the wing skin is made to carry a high end-load stress by suitable stabilisation, uses the same material to provide ending strength and torsional stiffness. Spreading the flange material, which is usually fabricated from a number of parts and particularly if in "sandwich" form, tends to localise any cracks due to fatigue. Furthermore, even the tension flange material is seldom stressed as highly as a concentrated boom and therefore its fatigue life is longer.

Stress Corrosion

Modern high-strength light alloys have given prominence also to another phenomenon which the metallurgist has known for some years: stress corrosion.

If a material is subjected to a permanent tensile stress in its outer fibres, then any surface corrosion is liable to start minute cracks which, in time, will extend throughout the area under stress. Unlike fatigue, stress corrosion has no connection with the number of times the structure withstands its design loads. In fact, an aeroplane need never be flown at all but, if conditions are suitable, cracks will appear in its basic structure after a time, which may be three months or three years, depending on the severity of conditions.

Designers have two solutions to this problem: to prevent or minimise surface corrosion by suitable protection; to avoid locked-up stresses. Permanent stresses are caused either by uneven shrinkage during quenching after heat treatment of, say, forged light alloy, or by "assembly stresses." These are stresses imposed on parts of the structure when bolted up during assembly. Quenching stresses can be minimised by careful attention to heat treatment techniques, sequence of machining operations, stretching after solution treatment, etc. Assembly stresses are reduced by use of fine tolerances and careful detail design.

Operational Hazards

Designers can draw on the wealth of experience gathered over the last 50 years and claim, with some justification, that their aeroplanes are almost infallible. But, as with all other forms of transport or, in fact, with life itself, some circumstance or combination of circumstances may lead one day to trouble.

Many of these situations can arise under the general heading of operational hazards and are often beyond control of the airframe designer or those responsible for engines or equipment.

Undoubtedly, an important reason, either directly or indirectly, for many accidents is weather conditions. Weather, usually lack of visibility, is also an important reason for irregularity of airline service. This situation has been improved enormously by various aids, both ground and airborne, such as radio communication, radio and radar navigation and blind approach. Inclusion of this equipment has made a further contribution to complexity in aircraft design.

Other atmospheric hazards are unusually violent gusts or severe icing conditions. Turbulence generally is discussed elsewhere in relation to its effects on strength and pilot's reactions. Icing conditions are usually avoided if possible, but various methods are employed on modern aircraft to enable operations to continue without difficulty.

Fire

Something has already been said about fire in connection with jet engines ; unfortunately, owing to the complexity of modern aircraft, there are many possible reasons for fire. Fundamentally, the difficulty is that aircraft must carry inflammable fluid for engine fuel and, until very recently, for the hydraulic system ; also, the aircraft is a maze of electrical cables. Risk is reduced to an absolute minimum by careful routing of fluid pipes and electrical cables, providing fire extinguisher systems in critical areas such as those around fuel tanks and by scavenging all places where inflammable vapour may otherwise collect.

Fuel tanks themselves are, of course, a potential source of trouble since they always contain an inflammable mixture above the fuel. Methods are now available for overcoming this difficulty by "purging" the airspace with nitrogen or, more recently still, by a system known as "explosion suppression." This makes use of a controlled counter-explosion to kill the flame front and to fill the tank with methyl bromide.

Human Element

After all the care and attention given to design and construction of aircraft and their equipment, there still remains the human element.

Reference has been made earlier to the pilot's ability to break his aeroplane. Although this usually requires considerable effort, blind conditions or violent atmospheric disturbances may temporarily upset his normal reactions.

Despite all modern aids, it is possible for the navigator to make mistakes, a striking example being that of a civil aircraft which in 1952 found itself some 1,300 miles from its scheduled destination.

Modern flight simulators are of immense value for training aircrews to deal correctly with all kinds of emergency. This equipment comprises the complete flight deck of the aircraft concerned including crew stations, controls, instruments, warning lights and indicators. All are made to function correctly and to represent any condition of flight. The simulator is literally "flown" ; any emergency can be represented. Even aerodynamic and other noises are reproduced correctly. Most B.O.A.C. crews train initially on a flight simulator and, from time to time, have refresher courses. In this way emergencies can be experienced and the appropriate action practised much more easily than on the actual aircraft.

Conclusions

Civil aircraft design gives consideration to all possible types of failure and provides means to ensure a standard of safety comparable with other forms of transport.

Extensive research and testing equipment is used, such as wind tunnels, mechanical test-frames, water tanks for fuselage pressure-tests, power-control rigs and air-conditioning rigs. Typical of such establishments are the Handley Page research laboratories at Radlett aerodrome, described in the last issue of this BULLETIN.

Such equipment plays its part in determining requirements and subsequently proving that they have been met. Strength, stiffness and fatigue life of structures are checked, as are the reliability and functioning of systems.

Powered systems, which can seldom be regarded as completely infallible, are duplicated or backed up by suitable emergency arrangements if their failure can lead to a dangerous situation.

Although the demands of safety and good-earning capacity point frequently to differing design solutions, the interest of the latter on civil aircraft is never allowed to prejudice safety.

RIGS of this type are built to test and develop the fuel systems of large modern aircraft.

This article was written by F R C Houndsfield AFRAeS, Chief Wind Tunnel Engineer and was published in the Handley Page Bulletin No. 229 Summer 1958.

A TURBOJET WIND-TUNNEL

BY F. R. C. HOUNSFIELD, A.F.R.Ae.S., Chief Wind-Tunnel Engineer, Handley Page Ltd.

*F*OR several years Handley Page has

operated a turbojet wind-tunnel for tests

up to sonic speeds.

Mr. Hounsfield, the company's chief

wind-tunnel engineer, here describes its

layout and operation and shows how both

high- and low-speed tests play their part in

the design of new aircraft.

As THE greater proportion of model tests in wind tunnels is concerned with the determination of an aircraft's characteristics in steady flight, it is worth while considering the conditions which govern the similarity between tunnel tests and full-scale flight.

In order to achieve dynamic similarity between model and full scale, various requirements must be met. Of these, apart from the obvious one of geometric similarity, the two most important parameters are Reynolds number and Mach number. These are defined as follows:

$$\text{Reynolds number} = \frac{VL}{\gamma} = R$$

$$\text{Mach number} \quad = \frac{V}{a} = M$$

where V = speed of flight or tunnel-wind speed
a = speed of sound in air
L = a characteristic length, e.g. wing chord
γ = kinematic viscosity of air

Both R and M are non-dimensional terms; for model tests to be under conditions of exact similarity their values must be the same for both model and full-scale aircraft.

Consideration of the expression for Reynolds number shows that model tests simulating landing conditions cannot

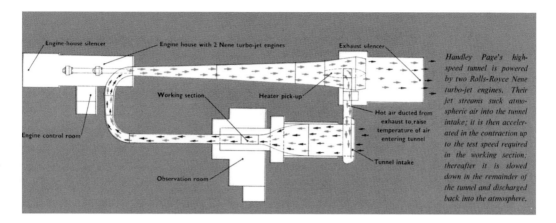

Handley Page's high-speed tunnel is powered by two Rolls-Royce Nene turbo-jet engines. Their jet streams suck atmospheric air into the tunnel intake; it is then accelerated in the contraction up to the test speed required in the working section; thereafter it is slowed down in the remainder of the tunnel and discharged back into the atmosphere.

be made under conditions of exact similarity in an atmospheric tunnel unless the test speed is raised considerably, because the characteristic length on the model, inevitably, is less than the corresponding dimension full scale. While it is possible to minimise this deficiency somewhat by an increase in tunnel speed, this cannot be carried to the required limit because the Mach number of the test would be greater than in full scale. For tests simulating low-speed flight it is therefore important to have as large a model as possible in a relatively low-speed tunnel.

Turning to the consideration of Mach number, it is clear that this is simply the relationship of the aircraft speed to the speed of sound. If again we consider sea-level conditions, where the speed of sound is about 1,100 ft./sec., it is apparent that, to simulate full-scale high-speed flight, a wind tunnel would have to be capable of running up to speeds approaching the actual flight speed.

But the power required to drive a wind tunnel is proportional to the area of the working section and the cube of the wind speed. These two facts alone tend to make any high-speed tunnel much smaller than its low-speed counterpart because of the high capital and running costs. For example, a low-speed tunnel taking models of about 4 ft. 6 in. span would require about 200 h.p. for tests up to 150 m.p.h.; the same tunnel used for tests up to 750 m.p.h. would require about 25,000 h.p.

For a high-speed tunnel the conditions regarding Reynolds number are the same as for a low-speed tunnel; exact dynamic similarity cannot be achieved.

In view of the enormous cost incurred in building a large

A model, set up to show airflow over a Victor, is mounted on its sting in the working section of the tunnel.

tunnel capable of running up to high speed in order to narrow the gap between model and full-scale results, it is usual to consider low- and high-speed testing as separate fields, to have tunnels appropriate to each and to ignore, for example, the effects of Reynolds number at high Mach numbers.

The Handley Page turbo-jet-driven high-speed tunnel illustrates these points. It allows testing at high speeds and, in conjunction with the low-speed tunnel, forms a means of checking the characteristics of a modern aircraft over its whole speed-range in flight.

TUNNEL PROBLEMS

The design of the tunnel was carried out in collaboration with Messrs. Rolls-Royce, Hucknall. This company was primarily responsible for the injector and exhaust side, since its general layout was at the time a new conception in the arrangement of a jet-driven tunnel.

A general arrangement drawing is shown of this U-shaped tunnel. At the second bend are placed the jet pipes of two Rolls-Royce Nene turbo-jet engines. When these are running, their jet streams suck atmospheric air into the tunnel intake.

Following the intake the air is accelerated in the contraction up to the test speed required in the working section. The air is then slowed down in the remainder of the tunnel, and is finally mixed with the exhaust gases from the engines and discharged back to the atmosphere.

Two problems associated with this type of tunnel are those of noise and condensation of moisture in the working section.

Noise was considered at an early stage in the design, as the tunnel is situated close to a residential area. The silencing arrangement, which was designed by Dr. A. J. King of the Metropolitan Vickers research department, consists of an array of acoustic absorbent splitters at the tunnel exhaust and on the engine-house combustion-air inlet.

Noise from the engines can reach the atmosphere, against the airstream, via the diffuser and working section. But this only occurs at low Mach numbers, as the tunnel speed is controlled by a sonic throat where sonic speed is maintained at all working section Mach numbers above 0.6.

When air is accelerated up to test speed in a wind tunnel, it suffers a reduction in temperature. This, increasing with speed, causes condensation of the moisture in the airstream if the humidity is sufficiently high and results in an increase in Mach number. Condensation may also lead to difficulties with instrumentation because of the presence of water droplets.

The open-circuit tunnel has the disadvantage that the air used is drawn from the surrounding atmosphere, whose humidity is dependent on local climatic conditions.

With a closed-circuit tunnel the air can be stored in a pre-dried condition, but the drying by chemical means of a continuous flow of air (about 5 cwt./sec. for the Handley Page tunnel) would require a very large and exceedingly expensive drier.

With jet-driven tunnels a considerable quantity of waste heat is available from the engine jets, and it is normal practice to use some of this to reduce the relative humidity of the air used in the tunnel by raising its temperature. This is done by means of a heater pick-up in the tunnel exhaust which communicates, via transfer ducts, with a series of hollow aerofoils with open trailing edges set in the tunnel intake. When the tunnel is running, a proportion of the exhaust gases mixes with the incoming atmospheric air, and thereby raises its temperature to a point at which condensation does not occur. Valves for controlling the amount of exhaust transferred are set in the transfer ducts.

SPEED CONTROL

Control of the tunnel speed is by means of a sonic throat. Downstream of the working section a portion of the duct has adjustable walls so that the cross-sectional area of the duct at this point may be varied. If the local area is less than that of the working section and the engines are run at sufficient power to produce sonic or slightly supersonic flow through the reduced area, then the mass flow through the working section, and hence Mach number, is fixed.

By varying the area of the throat a precise value of Mach number between 0.6 and 1.0 may be achieved so long as sonic conditions are maintained at the throat. For Mach numbers less than 0.6, variation of engine power is used to control the speed. This is not, however, a region in which tests are carried out normally.

Model tests in high- and low-speed tunnels are fundamentally the same in principle, but, owing to various factors, testing in the former requires slightly different techniques.

For low-speed force measurements, simplified support systems attached to the wings of a model may be used. At high speed this method is unsuitable, owing to the interference between the supports and the model.

One method which avoids support interference is to use a half-span model mounted on the floor so that the floor represents the plane of symmetry. This arrangement has the disadvantage that the fuselage is in the tunnel boundary-layer, and hence the correct flow conditions at the wing root are never exactly represented. However, force tests by this method are adequate for comparing different wing plan forms and modifications to a wing well away from the fuselage.

Although this method has its limitations, it has the advantages that the test Reynolds number will be about 40 per

cent. greater than for a complete model, and, since only half a model has to be made, the time for producing a model for a specific test is reduced.

For half-model force tests an underfloor balance is used. This consists of a frame which is supported by strain dynamometers in such a manner that the three force and three moment components may be measured.

In order to avoid the interference of a strut or wire rig, a complete model is supported by a "sting". This consists of a metal bar attached to the model at its centre of gravity and passing out of the rear end of the fuselage, where it is then held by some "earthed" structure. On this bar resistance strain gauges are attached at various points to measure the forces on the model.

Although force measurements make up the majority of tunnel measurements, the determination of surface pressure distribution forms a not insignificant part of any test programme. This is normally done by burying in the model small-bore nickel tubing and connecting these tubes to a multitube manometer.

When the tunnel is running at the desired conditions, all

Equipment used for testing is seen in the control room. Above are three galvanometers for measuring aerodynamic loads. Below (right) are two multitube manometers used to show pressure variations over test surfaces.

the liquid columns in the manometer may be "frozen" by a clamp on the pressure tubing. The various heights of the columns are read off or photographically recorded while the change to the next incidence or Mach number is being made. From a knowledge of the heights of the liquid columns the pressures on the model may be calculated.

During testing it is often necessary to try to get a better understanding of the flow conditions which give rise to an unexplained force characteristic.

The usual method employed for this purpose is to study the behaviour of cotton tufts attached to the surface of a model. This can be done visually, but records are usually made photographically to save tunnel running time. While this method is purely qualitative in character and must be used with discretion, the fact that the air flow can be "seen" makes its use of particular value in many cases.

MODEL MAKING

The construction of models for tests in the high-speed tunnel is probably the greatest problem of this type of work.

Models must have adequate strength and stiffness when subjected to loadings of about 500 lb./sq. ft. at temperatures in the region of 70°-80° C. The only completely satisfactory materials for them are metals, although these have the disadvantage that manufacturing time is lengthy. To reduce model-making time, various forms of construction have been tried such as metal cores with synthetic-resin coating and compressed timber. Both of these methods are unsatisfactory in one way or another; the resin coating tends to crack and part from the metal core and compressed timber suffers permanent distortion when loaded at elevated temperatures.

For complete models the wings are usually made from aluminium-alloy castings and attached to a steel fuselage which transmits the loads to the model support. For a half-model the wing is also made in aluminium alloy, but since the fuselage does not transmit loads it can be made in mahogany. In the same way such items as nacelles and tip tanks may be of timber.

The models are made by hand to conform to metal

templates based on a master loft-plate. This master is a photographically reduced reproduction of the required shapes drawn on cartridge paper to a scale which may be as much as five to ten times the model size.

TESTING

In order to keep tunnel running time to a minimum it is usual to employ as many observers as there are observations to record. This means that for measurement of lift, drag and pitching moment on a half model, for example, a team of five observers and an engineer would be necessary. Four of the observers would be taking the actual force measurements, while the fifth looks after the tunnel speed control. During a test run the engineer has only to maintain the engines at continuous cruising power, the actual test speed being controlled by the observer on the speed control.

Normally a tunnel run may take about fifteen minutes, either as a run at constant incidence with varying Mach number or over a range of incidence at constant Mach number. In each case measurements are taken at six or seven values of incidence or Mach number.

UTILISATION

Utilisation of a high-speed tunnel cannot, generally, be compared with that of a low-speed tunnel unless there is a considerable stockpile of models awaiting test. This is brought about mainly by the longer time a high-speed model requires for manufacture.

Another factor is that a high-speed model does not normally have all the control surfaces represented, so that the various combinations of model-testing conditions are very much reduced compared with low-speed work.

These two factors militate against a high utilisation over a long time. Over a short period, such as for any given test programme, the utilisation will generally be much higher than for a low-speed tunnel because of the simplicity of the model. Utilisation for detailed test series is usually better than 20 per cent. and has reached 40 per cent. for some work.

That the tunnel uses aircraft-type jet engines for motive power might be considered an embarrassment with regard to utilisation. However, only in a very few instances has testing been held up by engine unserviceability; maintenance work, though, has had to be fairly extensive because of the comparative age of the engines.

The high-speed tunnel forms a very necessary part of Handley Page research facilities and is making a useful contribution to the development of future projects.

A half-span model is attached to the floor of the tunnel for force tests. This method alleviates the disadvantages of support interference affecting full-span models. Tufts show the direction of airflow over the wing surface.

HP 80 Prototypes WB771 and WB775

The company brochure 'High Speed Medium/Heavy Bomber HP 80 Specification No. 35/46 dated February 1951 is used in the coompilation of this article. Author's comments in italics.
Over the next few years a variety of large and in some cases extremely detailed changes were initiated and tested for the developed design. To start with the tail was heightened and the tailplane positioned in mid position. The wing-tip fins and rudders were deleted and a suitable rudder incorporated into the fin. The installation of the engines was developed and this was to end up initially as what we see on the prototypes and the early production aircraft. The nose was looked at in great detail and the location of the radar scanner bay brought right up under the crew compartment. The nose undercarriage was mounted under frame 261. Great changes were made with the introduction of the bogie undercarriages with their multi-tyred wheels retracting forwards and upwards into the wing. This time, along with the flaps, airbrake's, bomb doors and nose wheel steering, they were operated by hydraulic pressure using a 4000psi system with the hydraulic pumps being driven by electric motors and not relying on engine-driven ones. (*This was to make the life of the manufacturing and maintenance staff, whether they were HP or RAF, much easier than is usual in the dreaded petrol driven Hydraulic Test Rigs used by most other aircraft*) The engines were changed to the Armstrong Siddeley Sapphire ASA 3. This was virtually the same engine that Metro Vickers had developed but was taken over by Armstrong Siddeley in May 1948 under direction from the Ministry of Supply when Metropolitan Vickers came out of the Aero Engine business. There were many other changes to come to the forefront and as we describe in detail the HP 80 prototypes we will come across them.

HP 80 Development model HP-HPAI.

The design of the HP 80 in January 1951 was still based on that of the May 1947 brochure, however this was nearly four years on and a considerable number of changes had been made to the aircraft as will become evident as we look at it in some detail.

With its crescent swept-back wing tapering in thickness from root to tip the HP 80 was still basically as it was in the May 1947 brochure, but with important structural and aerodynamic changes evolved during the design to give revised sweep angles of 47.5, 40.5, 32.degrees.

Model tests had confirmed that a 500kt cruising speed at 50,000ft without compressibility drag could be achieved. Development of the aircrafts take-off weight up to 150,000lb was obtainable and along with its operation with a 10,000lb bombs for a range of 5,670 miles or

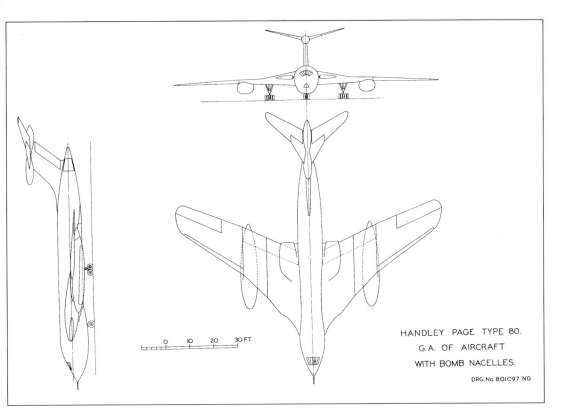

HANDLEY PAGE TYPE 80.
G.A. OF AIRCRAFT
WITH BOMB NACELLES.
DRG. No. 801C97 ND.

with increased load a shorter range.

The high structural and aerodynamically efficiency required to gain this performance in the HP80 is achieved by the wings' sandwich type construction (*developed by HP after exhaustive testing*) which ensures extreme accuracy of contour and aerodynamic smoothness in the loaded condition. Its stiffness eliminates flutter and other undesirable qualities and enables the fuel tanks to be pressurised without undue weight penalty.

Four Armstrong Siddeley Sapphire 3 engines are fitted. Each gives 7,900 lb thrust at sea level. Development of the Sapphire is expected to increase thrust to 9,700lb without increasing specific consumption and without important installation changes. WB775 was to be fitted with the Sapphire SA6 engines in the end.

An all round improvement in performance is achieved particularly in take-off cruising and range. (*Space provision was made for the RR RA8 and Conway and the Bristol Olympus. however more about that in the future*).

The January 1951 brochure outlines the principal features of this version as follows:

Wings: 'Crescent' plan form combines high critical Mach number with good stall characteristics; sandwich construction provides smooth external finish, high strength, and stiffness and enables pressurisation of the fuel tanks.

Fuselage: Very large bomb bay with internal stowage for the maximum of thirty-five 1,000lb bombs (*55,000lb with external loads*); internally retracting bomb doors; no loading ramps or pits required for the largest bombs.

Tankage: Fixed 'overload' internal tanks for 5,200 nautical miles: drop tanks for 5,670 nautical miles and a 10,000lb bomb load.

Undercarriage: Sixteen tyres on main undercarriage to spread the load and enable operation from permanent airfields with the 30-35-strength factor.

Flying Controls: Power operated by fully duplicated and self-contained units at each surface; ideal synthetic feel.

Crew Cabin: Small volume with ample space for crew of five; pressurised and air conditioned; ejector seats for pilots and shielded exit for navigators and signaller; cabin jettisonable.

OPERATIONAL CHARACTERISTICS

Crew's Cabin
The HP 80 crew cabin is heated or cooled as required and pressurised to provide 8,000ft conditions when at 47,000ft, or that equivalent to 25,000ft for combat.

Pilots
The two pilots sit side by side in ejector seats and there is a gangway between them giving access to the prone bomb aimer's position. The windscreen is of flat dry air sandwich glass panels with a direct-vision window on each side. Duplicated flying instruments are fitted on the main instrument panel and the engine controls are on consoles at the side of each pilot. Other instruments, radio controls etc. are on the main panel on the consoles or on a small roof panel between the pilots. (*There was no such thing as panel 'AT' until the production aircraft; the fuel system pump and valve controls were on the pilot's side panel by his left shoulder*).

Duplicated flying controls, fully powered with 'ideal' feel have aileron/elevator hand wheels mounted on push-pull horizontal shafts and so leave the pilot's legs entirely unobstructed. These shafts are telescopic and are connected with the pilots' hatches in such a way that when the hatches are jettisoned the hand wheel's move forward automatically and clear of the pilots knees. Hydraulic brakes are toe operated with a parking lever on the first pilot's console.

Navigators and Signaller
A signaller (*This branch was used in both the commissioned and NCO ranks until the air electronics officer was recruited and trained for the task*) and the first and second navigators (*navigator plotter and navigator radar in production aircraft*) face aft at a bench type table

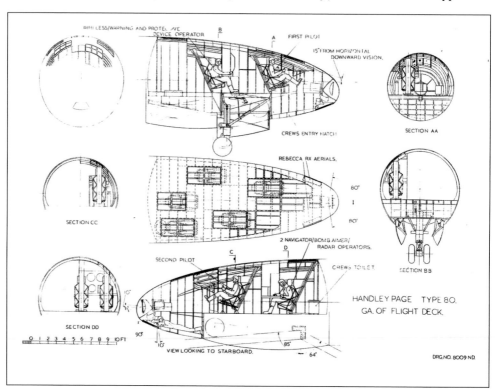

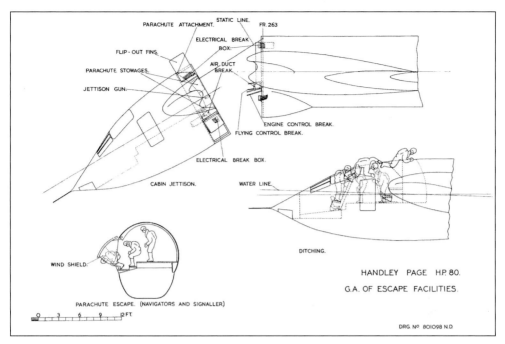

STATIC LINE.

PARACHUTE ATTACHMENT. FR. 263

ELECTRICAL BREAK
BOX.

FLIP - OUT FINS.

AIR DUCT
BREAK.

PARACHUTE STOWAGES.

JETTISON GUN.

ENGINE CONTROL BREAK.
FLYING CONTROL BREAK.

ELECTRICAL BREAK BOX.

CABIN JETTISON.   WATER LINE.

DITCHING.

HANDLEY PAGE H.P. 80.

G.A. OF ESCAPE FACILITIES.

WIND SHIELD.

PARACHUTE ESCAPE. (NAVIGATORS AND SIGNALLER)

DRG. No 801098 N.D.

across the rear of the cabin. Their comfortable seats, fitted with headrests, are arranged so that the first navigator can move easily to the bomb aimer's position.

All H2S, NBC and other equipment that is operated by these crewmembers are on a large vertical panel across the cabin. To obviate parallax it has an inclined upper part.

Visual Bomb Sight

In the aircraft's nose is a visual bombsight that is operated by the first navigator in a prone position. Three large flat glass panels command a wide field of vision in the fore, aft and lateral plane.

Escape Facilities

At low altitude the navigators and the signaller escape through the entry door that is hinged along its upper edge and opening outwards has side screens to enable clearance from the aircraft. Pilots escape in their ejector seats via jettisonable hatches. For escape at high altitude the whole cabin is jettisoned and descends on parachutes. Attached to the wing centre section by four bolts, the cabin is separated by a lever that fires a cartridge gun. This opens the nose stabilising fins, withdraws the attachment bolts and fires the nose from the aircraft in order to ensure a clean separation. As a safety measure the gun is arranged so that normally the cartridge would

Escape trials in wind tunnel. HP-HPA.

discharge into an empty tube. Operation of the lever in the cabin brings the cartridge into the breech first then fires it. This way the cabin is not jettisoned by an inadvertent discharge of the cartridge. In the event of a ditching or crash landing the crew escapes via the pilot's hatches.

Communications

For short range air-to-ground and air-to-air communication the HP 80 has a VHF radio and it has an HF radio for long-range communication. Frequency coverage and standby facilities are

HP 80 WB771 1st pilot. HP-HPA.

HP 80 WB775 front cabin. HP-HPA.

given by twin VHF equipment controlled by the pilots.

The signaller controls the main HF installation mounted in the pressure cabin. Intercommunication between crewmembers is provided.

Navigation

H2SMk 9 and NBC Mk 2 and Green Satin equipment aid long-range dead reckoning navigation. Operating with the air mileage unit and remote indicating (G4B) compass, the H2S-NBC system gives continuous track and radar map information. A direct measurement of true ground speed and drift is given by the Green Satin system.

A periscope sextant and direct reading magnetic compass are installed in case of main system failure. For ferry or similar purpose, structural provision is made for automatic direction finding equipment.

Bomb Aiming and Guiding

A radar bombing system is given by the H2S – NBC installation. Accepting information from the visual sighting head, it comprises the means for highly accurate bombing up to 50,000ft. A radio altimeter duplicating the height finding function of the H2S gives bombing information in the event of full or partial failure of equipment.

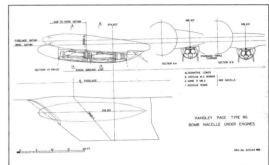

Defence and Warning Devices

A warning is passed visually and aurally to pilots and the signaller of the detection of aircraft or missiles that approach from the rear of the HP80. Electrical and space provision is made for radar jamming and defence equipment to detect missiles as they are launched from the ground and fuse them before they are close to the aircraft.

IFF equipment is installed.

Blind Approach

For blind approach the HP80's instrument landing system uses the D type autopilot that gives automatic approach control.

Thermal De-icing

The wing and tail unit, engines and air intakes have thermal protection against ice formation. Windscreens are heated electrically. (*Not until the Mk B2 was under construction did this come into use*).

Bomb Installation and Loading

The HP 80 has a very large bomb bay unobstructed by either structural members or the mechanism of internally retracting doors (*The bomb bay is stated to be 32 ft 10inches long and has a diameter of 9ft 10inches*). It carries every type of bomb under development and provides a maximum of space to meet future operational requirements. Fuselage height is such that the 10,000lb 'special' bomb can be wheeled into position under the bomb bay. Loading ramps or pits are not required. Provision is made for a small flap at the forward end of the bomb bay if it is required to give a satisfactory bomb flight after release (*These were to end up as the hydraulically operated bomb door gills on the Bomber and SR2 versions only, on the three point Tankers they were manual for servicing use only*).

The HP 80 could carry a wide variety of bombs in the bomb bay and it was proposed to

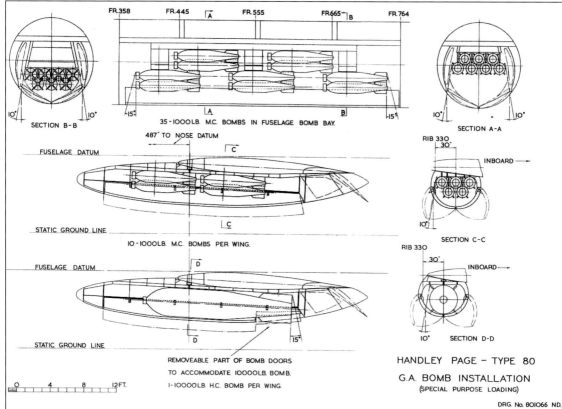

SECTION B-B

FR.358   FR.445   A   FR.555   FR.665   B   FR.764

35-1000LB. M.C. BOMBS IN FUSELAGE BOMB BAY.

SECTION A-A

FUSELAGE DATUM

487" TO NOSE DATUM   C

STATIC GROUND LINE

10-1000LB. M.C. BOMBS PER WING.

RIB 330   30°   INBOARD

SECTION C-C

FUSELAGE DATUM   D

STATIC GROUND LINE

REMOVEABLE PART OF BOMB DOORS
TO ACCOMMODATE 10000LB. BOMB.
1-10000LB. H.C. BOMB PER WING.

RIB 330   30°   INBOARD

SECTION D-D

0   4   8   12FT.

HANDLEY PAGE – TYPE 80
G.A. BOMB INSTALLATION
(SPECIAL PURPOSE LOADING)

DRG. No. 801066 ND.

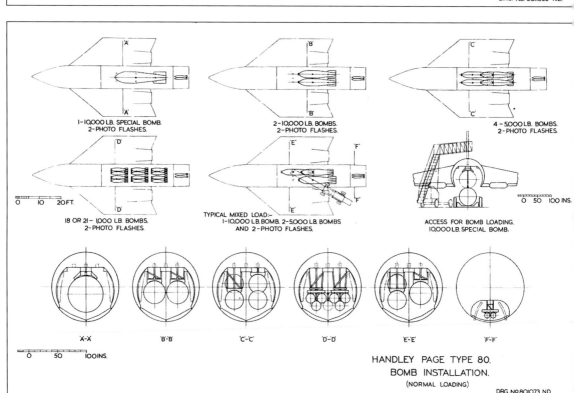

1-10,000 LB. SPECIAL BOMB.
2-PHOTO FLASHES.

2-10,000 LB. BOMBS.
2-PHOTO FLASHES.

4-5,000 LB. BOMBS.
2-PHOTO FLASHES.

0   10   20FT.

18 OR 21-1000 LB. BOMBS.
2-PHOTO FLASHES.

TYPICAL MIXED LOAD:-
1-10,000 LB. BOMB, 2-5,000 LB. BOMBS
AND 2-PHOTO FLASHES.

ACCESS FOR BOMB LOADING.
10,000 LB. SPECIAL BOMB.

0   50   100 INS.

A-A   B-B   C-C   D-D   E-E   F-F

0   50   100 INS.

HANDLEY PAGE TYPE 80.
BOMB INSTALLATION.
(NORMAL LOADING)

DRG. No. 801073 ND.

18

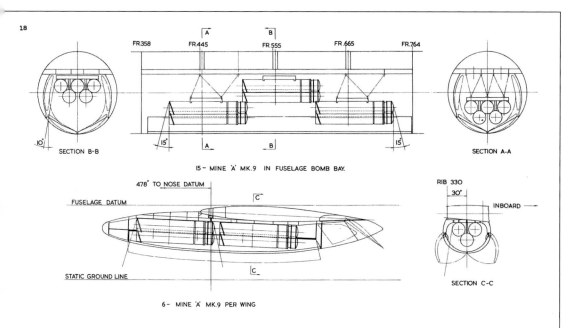

SECTION B-B

SECTION A-A

15 – MINE 'A' MK.9 IN FUSELAGE BOMB BAY.

478° TO NOSE DATUM

FUSELAGE DATUM

RIB 330

INBOARD →

STATIC GROUND LINE

SECTION C-C

6 – MINE 'A' MK.9 PER WING

HANDLEY PAGE   TYPE 80.

G.A. OF MINE INSTALLATION.

0   4   8   12 FT.

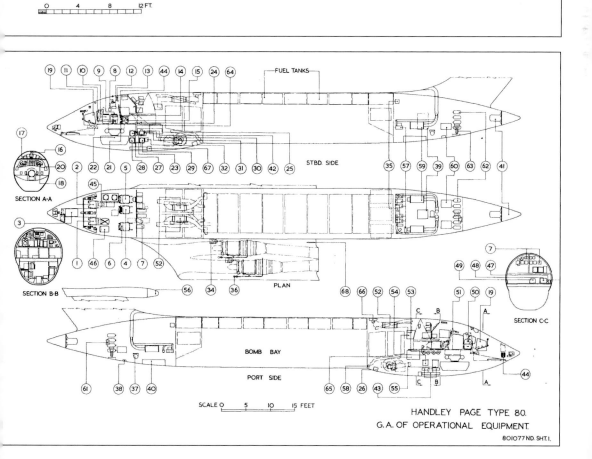

SECTION A-A

SECTION B-B

FUEL TANKS

STBD. SIDE

PLAN

SECTION C-C

BOMB BAY

PORT SIDE

SCALE 0   5   10   15 FEET

HANDLEY PAGE TYPE 80.

G.A. OF OPERATIONAL EQUIPMENT.

801077 ND. SHT.1.

1. 1ST PILOTS STATION:-
    OXYGEN ECONOMISER
    OXYGEN BAYONET SOCKET
    MIC-TEL SOCKET
    V.H.F. CONTROL PANEL
    V.H.F. CONTROL UNIT
    RED GARTER CONTROLLER

2. 2ND PILOTS STATION:-
    OXYGEN ECONOMISER
    OXYGEN BAYONET SOCKET
    MIC-TEL SOCKET
    V.H.F. CONTROL PANEL
    V.H.F. CONTROL UNIT

3. BOMB AIMERS PRONE POSITION:-
    BOMB SIGHT
    BOMB AIMERS PANEL
    BOMB AIMERS RAMP

4. MASTER NAVIGATORS STATION: -
    GYRO-COMPASS MK.4.B
    DEVIATION CARD HOLDER
    CLOCK
    AIR SPEED INDICATOR
    ALTIMETER
    OXYGEN ECONOMISER
    MIC-TEL SOCKET
    AIR MILEAGE UNIT & CONTROL MK.4
    GEE MK.2 INDICATOR
    GREEN SATIN INDICATOR & CONTROLLER
    BLUE BOAR INDICATOR & CONTROLLER

5. 2ND NAVIGATORS STATION:-
    RADIO ALTIMETER
    B.S.U. x 200
    CAMERA CONTROL UNIT
    H.2.S. CONTROL TYPE S.85
    H.2.S. CONTROL TYPE S.95
    H.2.S. INDICATOR TYPE 301
    BOMB FUSING AND CAMERA
                CONTROL PANEL
    BOMB SELECTOR PANEL
    MIC-TEL SOCKET
    OXYGEN ECONOMISER

6. SIGNALLERS STATION:-
    MIC-TEL SOCKET
    MORSE KEY
    OXYGEN ECONOMISER
    GENERATOR CONTROL SWITCHES
    CLOCK
    CONTROL UNITS I.F.F. TYPE 89 & 90
    INTER-COMM. CONTROL
    CONTROL UNIT TYPE A.R.I. 5332

7. RADIO EQUIPMENT :-
    I/C AMPLIFIER TYPE X.576
    I/C JUNCTION BOX TYPE X.578
    H.F. TRANSMITTER TYPE 1570
    H.F. MODULATOR TYPE 107
    H.F. POWER UNIT TYPE 437
    H.F. RECEIVER TYPE R.1571
    H.F. JUNCTION BOX TYPE 146
    GEE MK.3 WAVE FORM GENERATOR
    GEE MK.3 RECEIVER
    RADIO COMPASS RECR. TYPE X.177
    RADIO COMPASS JUNCTION BOX
    V.H.F. T.R. 1934 & 1935
    RUNWAY LOCALISER & MARKER RECR.
    GLIDE PATH RECEIVER

FLIGHT DECK:-
8. PERISCOPE SEXTANT & CASE
9. COMPUTOR TYPE X.230
10. BOMB SIGHTING UNIT TYPE X.200
11. GEE MK.2 RECEIVER

12. AMPLIFIER UNIT TYPE 'A'
13. SIGNAL PISTOL
14. 2ND NAVIGATORS SIDE PANEL
15. BOMB BURSTING CONTROL
16. P.12 COMPASS
17. RED GARTER INDICATOR
18. PILOTS INSTRUMENT PANELS
19. PILOTS SIDE PANELS
20. PILOTS CONSOLE PANELS
21. FIRST AID KIT
22. SCANNER H2S
23. WAVE FORM GENERATOR TYPE A.R.I.1009
24. C.R. FUSING UNIT
25. RESISTANCE UNIT TYPE X.267
26. AIR MILEAGE UNIT MK.4
27. AUTOMATIC CALCULATOR X.1257
28. H.2.S. POWER UNIT
29. H.2.S. WAVE FORM GENERATOR
30. TIME DELAY UNIT
31. PRE SELECTOR UNIT
32. BOMB DISTRIBUTOR CONTROL UNIT
33. AERIAL CAVITY BOX (I.F.F. R.X.)

34. ALTERNATOR
35. ELECTRONIC CONTROLLERS
36. FIRE EXTINGUISHER BOTTLES
37. R.A.T.2.R. UNIT
38. R.A. AERIALS
39. SURVIVAL EQUIPMENT
40. BLUE BOAR AERIAL
41. RED GARTER
42. C.R. FUSING UNIT P.U.
43. GREEN SATIN
44. PORTABLE OXYGEN STOWAGE
45. NAVIGATORS SATCHEL STOWAGE
46. BOMB COMPUTER
47. RADIO AND HEIGHT CONTROL
48. AUTO PILOT AMPLIFIER
49. AUTO PILOT GYRO UNIT S.E.P. TYPE 'D'
50. DINGHY VALISE
51. AXE STOWAGE
52. TRANSFORMER RECTIFIER UNITS
53. OXYGEN BOTTLES
54. POWER UNIT TYPE X.259
55. COMPUTER TYPE X.229
56. GEE AERIAL
57. ROTARY INVERTERS
58. AIRCRAFT DESTRUCTORS
59. TRANSFORMER RECTIFIER UNITS
60. ACCUMULATORS
61. I.F.F. RECEIVER
62. NITROGEN BOTTLES
63. CAMERA STOWAGE
64. AIR BURST DELAY UNIT
65. CABIN PARACHUTES
66. SUPPRESSED LOOP A.D.F.
67. AERIAL CAVITY BOX I.F.F.
68. H.F. AERIAL

HANDLEY PAGE TYPE 80.

G.A. OF OPERATIONAL EQUIPMENT.

use a special container under each wing mounted on the underwing tank hoisting position, with a wide variety of mines in it. (*This was just a proposal and was never proceeded with and all bomb loads were carried internally*).

The loading of internal and the proposed external bombs was to be with the RAE designed bomb loading method which ensures the minimum 'turn round' time and avoids connecting up, crutching or adjustment after bombs are hoisted into the bomb bay.

The variety of loads and their stowage can be seen in the following drawings. It must be remembered that they were all proposals and not all proceeded with.

Powered Flying Controls

The HP 80 has fully powered (*with no feed back*) ailerons, elevators and a rudder. 'Pilot's feel' is given by dynamic pressure. The powered units at the control surfaces are self-contained units and the pilot operates them by a signalling system that is of a normal push-pull type flying control. Auto-pilot servo motors and feel simulators are connected to this system in the centre section and front fuselage. Three-position semi-Fowler main flaps to-gether with contra nose flaps are actuated by duplicated hydraulic motors. Tail-plane nose flaps were proposed to be interconnected with the main flaps and operated electrically. Hydro-pneumatic actuators operate wing nose-flaps automatically. Should the hydraulics fail these flaps are lowered by air stored under pressure. The Dive (*Air Brakes*) at the rear of the fuselage are operated hydraulically.

The Fuel System

This version was a further development from that proposed in the May '47 Brochure. A great deal of redesign was carried out once again and this version was to move greatly towards that as fitted in the production aircraft and form the basis for the remaining versions produced.

Maximum operational flexibility with adequate safe guards in the event of tank damage is given by the HP80 fuel system. This is achieved by the installation of many flexible bag tanks, either singly or in coupled pairs with immersed fuel pumps and refuelling valves.

Provision is made for overload tanks in the fuselage (*not the bomb bay*) and for a 600 gallon drop tank under each wing for use when extra long-range operations are required.

The refuelling valve switching is so arranged that the following tankage can be selected:

a. Short range (2,640 nautical miles) wing
  tanks

b. Normal range (3,630 nautical miles) wing
  + normal fuselage fuel)

c. Long range (5,210 nautical miles) Wing +
  Normal and Overload Fuselage Tanks

d. Extra long range (5,670 nautical miles)
  wing + normal and overload fuselage tanks
  + drop tanks

Intermediate ranges are met by selecting the next highest 'standard' range and neutralising unrequired tanks by the operation of relevant refuelling valve switches in the bomb or main undercarriage bays (*later refered to the 'Not In Use' switches and located in the port side panel, aft of the battery bay Mk1 aircraft*) in the cabin on panel 'AF' on the Mk2 aircraft the refuelling connections and the control panel are on the bomb bay's front bulkhead. (*On the Mk 1aircraft the refuelling connections were on the starboard side in the panel aft of the hydraulic bay and on the Mk2 aircraft in the Port Stub Wing*). (The main control panel is Panel AT in the cabin between the pilots).

As the fuel system is pressurised to a maximum differential of 5psi, the HP 80 can be operated satisfactorily with aviation gasoline. Overload tankage gives the increased capacity required by this fuel. (*Subject to the engines being cleared to run on Aviation Gasoline*).

Engine Installation

The HP 80's four Armstrong Siddeley Sapphire jet engines are mounted two in each wing adjacent to the fuselage sides. Their bays are large enough to accommodate, with only slight modification, other engines up to 10,000lb thrust. The engines are hoisted into the wing from

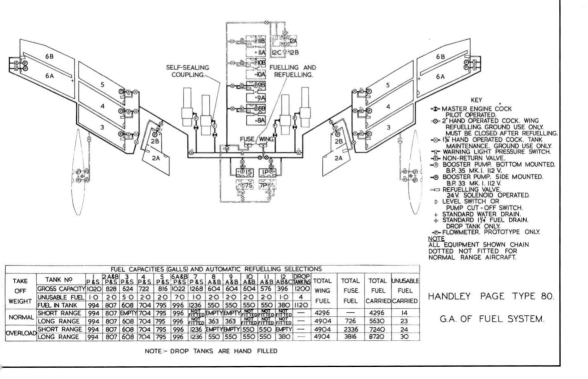

HANDLEY PAGE TYPE 80.

G.A. OF FUEL SYSTEM.

	TANK Nº	1	2 A&B	3	4	5	6 A&B	7	8	9	10	11	12	DROP TANK P&S	TOTAL WING FUEL	TOTAL FUSE. FUEL	TOTAL FUEL CARRIED	UNUSABLE FUEL CARRIED
		P&S	P&S	P&S	P&S	P&S	P&S	P&S	A&B	A&B	A&B	A&B	AB&C					
TAKE OFF WEIGHT	GROSS CAPACITY	1020	828	624	722	816	1022	1268	604	604	604	576	396	1200				
	UNUSABLE FUEL	1·0	2·0	5·0	2·0	2·0	7·0	1·0	2·0	2·0	2·0	2·0	1·0	4				
	FUEL IN TANK	994	807	608	704	795	996	1236	550	550	550	550	380	1120				
NORMAL	SHORT RANGE	994	807	EMPTY	704	795	996	NOT FITTED	EMPTY	EMPTY	NOT FITTED	NOT FITTED	NOT FITTED	—	4296	—	4296	14
	LONG RANGE	994	807	608	704	795	996	363	363	NOT FITTED	NOT FITTED	NOT FITTED	—		4904	726	5630	23
OVERLOAD	SHORT RANGE	994	807	608	704	795	996	1236	EMPTY	EMPTY	550	550	EMPTY	—	4904	2336	7240	24
	LONG RANGE	994	807	608	704	795	996	1236	550	550	550	550	380	—	4904	3816	8720	30

FUEL CAPACITIES (GALLS) AND AUTOMATIC REFUELLING SELECTIONS

NOTE :- DROP TANKS ARE HAND FILLED

underneath through two easily removable access doors. The single intake in each wing passes through the main wing torque box and splits just forward of its rear web. Easily made connections are provided between the fixed intakes and the front face of the engines. The jet pipes are connected in a similar manner (*both the connection of the intakes and the jet pipes was not as simple as stated and required some special expertise especially on the Mk1 production aircraft*). The use of auxiliary gearboxes was no longer needed as the alternator was the only engine driven component.

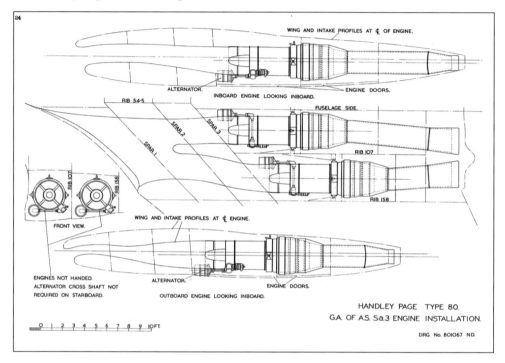

Cabin Pressurisation

The pressurisation, heating and cooling of the cabin are controlled automatically using bleed air from the main engines via heat exchanger's and a variety of control valves. The cabin is pressurised to 8 PSI to provide 8,000ft conditions when flying up to 47,000ft and a pressure of 4 PSI equivalent to 25,000ft can be selected for combat conditions. Oxygen is available to all crewmembers through pressure breathing apparatus supplied from four 2,250-litre bottles beneath the cabin floor.

Ice Protection

Thermal ice protection is provided throughout the HP80. Hot air bled from the engine compressors and mixed via a jet pump is served at the correct temperature to the wing and the tail unit leading edged. The nose flaps are heated in the same way as the normal fixed surfaces. The intake lips and intake walls of the engine are heated from the wing jet-pumps. There are a considerable number of intakes that have electrical heater mats on their extremities to provide the ice protection as required.

Fire Protection

All the engines and their bays are covered by a comprehensive system so that if the need arises they can be shut down. There is a fire protection system covering the inner wings of the rear hatch compartment, the battery bay, the bomb bay front bulkhead.

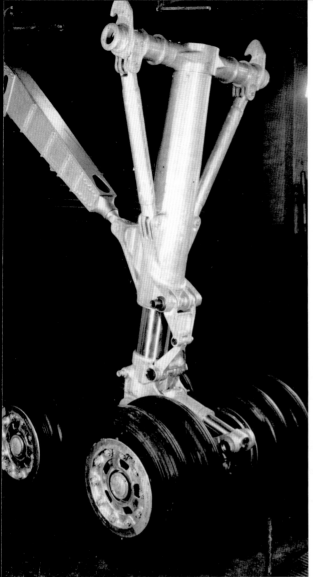

Undercarriage. HP-HPA.

Nose Undercarriage.
HP-HPA.

Undercarriage Retracted. HP-HPA.

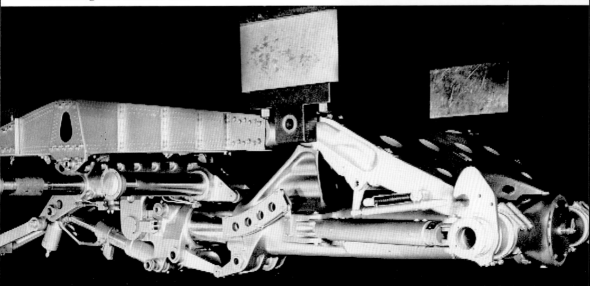

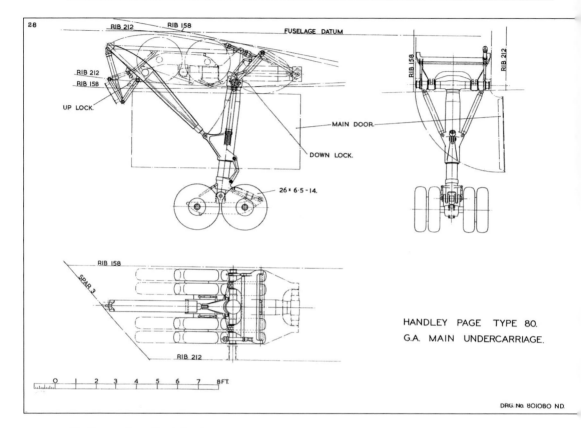

HANDLEY PAGE TYPE 80.
G.A. MAIN UNDERCARRIAGE.

DRG. No. 801080 ND.

Undercarriage Installation

The main undercarriages are of the four wheeled eight-tyred type and retract forward and over into the bay using a 4,000psi hydraulic system. The nose undercarriage being twin wheeled and steerable and fully castoring retracts rearwards into its bay.

The undercarriages can be operated by both the normal and emergency hydraulic systems.

The Hydraulic System

This system is unique to the HP 80 in that the hydraulic pumps are driven by electric motors that supply the required pressure to operate the following systems under carriage retraction: nose wheel steering, wheel brakes, bomb doors, main and nose flaps and the airbrakes at the rear of the aircraft. The motors and therefore the pumps are only running when a service is selected, thus providing long life. The main feature of this method of hydraulic pressure production is that there is no need for a hydraulic supply rig to provide the pressure and therefore the aircraft is self-contained. The operation of all services is by the use of solenoid-operated selectors and their associated hydraulic jacks backed up by sequence vales and protection units.

Electrical System

To support the various auxiliary services including the flying controls, the system uses four engine-drive 73KVA alternators that provide the following power supplies: AC 200 volts frequency variable for heating loads, DC 112 volts for main loads and DC at 28 volts for light loads and radio services, transformer rectifier units obtain the DC supplies, invertors that take their main power from the 112volt DC system provide power supplies for radar, instruments and special stores. (see diagram page 36)

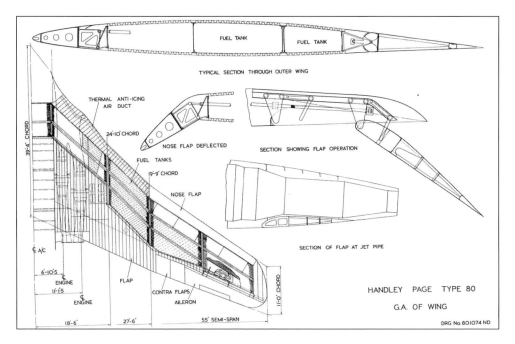

TYPICAL SECTION THROUGH OUTER WING

THERMAL ANTI-ICING
AIR DUCT

24-10' CHORD

NOSE FLAP DEFLECTED

SECTION SHOWING FLAP OPERATION

FUEL TANKS

19'-9' CHORD

NOSE FLAP

SECTION OF FLAP AT JET PIPE

¢ A/C

6-10·5
ENGINE
11-1·5
ENGINE

FLAP

CONTRA FLAPS
AILERON

HANDLEY   PAGE   TYPE 80

G.A. OF WING

18'-6'   27'-6'   55' SEMI-SPAN

DRG No. 801074 ND

Structural Characteristics

The HP 80 Structure is characterised by a smooth external finish – Flush Rivets or spot welding are used throughout.

Wings

The wing structure has the lightest possible weight in combination with a smooth surface free from waves or buckles when in the loaded condition, high torsional and flexural stiffness and fuel tank pressurisation to 5lb/sqin differential.

Although in many ways dictating the structural layout, the HP 80's crescent plan-form has not been allowed to involve a weight penalty. Exemplifying this is the arrangement of ribs. A heavy rib being necessary at each kink: the inner-kink also picks up the main undercarriage and the outer-kink rib also functions as a transport 'pipe' joint and fuel tank bulkhead. This 'pipe' joint, and a similar one at the fuselage side, divide the whole wing into four sections for transport purposes. The part between the fuselage sides and the centre section is integral with the rear fuselage.

Basically the wing is of sandwich construction with multi-shear webs dividing it into a series of span-wise cells for the stowage of fuel. The sandwich has an inner and outer skin of approximately 14swg high-grade light alloy with a span-wise corrugated core of the same material in approximately 16 SWG. The outer skin is spot welded to the core and has a smooth finish; the inner skin is attached by 'blind' riveting. This assembly, a very stiff sandwich, carries practically all the normal wing bending-loads, no spar booms being necessary except for a short distance each side of the inner kink and on the rear web at the fuselage side. Sandwich construction, used also for the spar webs that have tanks on both sides, gives a smooth surface for the bags. Other webs are of single sheet with vertical stiffeners. Leading edges have double skins, the inner with chord-wise machined groves for thermal de-icing. Double skins are used also on the 'droop' type nose-flaps that extend from the outer kink to the tip. Single skin construction with closely spaced chord-wise stiffeners, is used aft of the rear spar-web. There are large quick release doors beneath the engines and the aileron power control units.

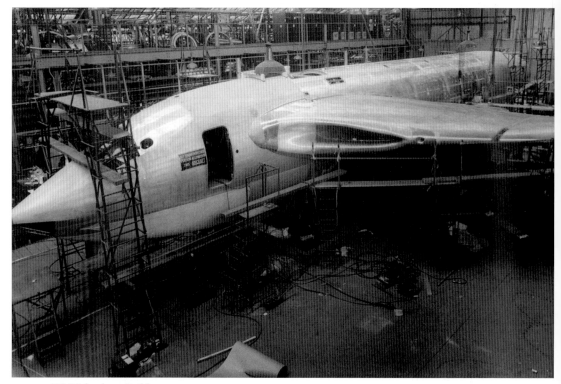

HP 80 fuselage Build. HP-HPA

Front Fuselage

The front fuselage, of light alloy skin stiffened by longitudinal stringers and frames, comprises the crew's pressurised cabin above floor level and below floor level is an unpressurised part with the H2S scanner in a removable radome.

At the rear of the cabin, which is terminated in a domed pressure bulkhead, the fuselage surface is composed of flip-out fins for stability when the nose is jettisoned. Detachment from the main rear fuselage is by four special bolts at the bulkhead coincident with the front wing-spar.

Rear Fuselage

The rear fuselage includes the wing centre-section and extends back to the main fin pick-up bulkhead.

Immediately aft of the rear spar web bulkhead is the 7ft 3in high and 32 ft long bomb bay. To prevent buffeting when the doors are open there is a 7ft 6in long rear extension with a sloping roof. It will hold two flash bombs. Above the bomb floor is a compartment for bag tanks. It is skinned on the inside of the stringers to give a smooth housing and this sandwich structure facilitates tank pressurisation.

Structurally, the rear fuselage comprises longitudinal stringers attached to hoop frames and a single skin. Heavy lingering at the bottom edge of the bomb bay are stabilised over the greater part of their length by the lower surface of the wing. Three heavy double frames at bomb hoisting points carry all bomb loads.

Tail Cone

This part of the fuselage is detachable at the main fin pick-up bulkhead and carries the air brakes and the rear scanner.

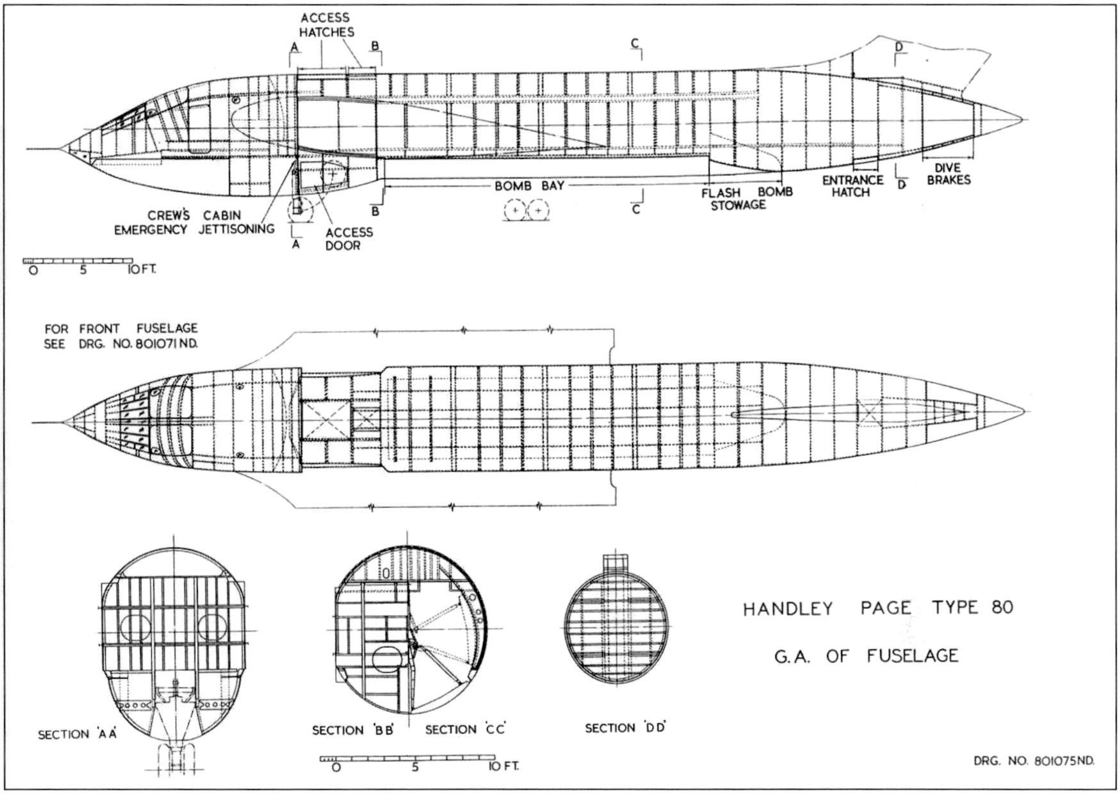

HANDLEY PAGE TYPE 80

G.A. OF FUSELAGE

SECTION 'AA'   SECTION 'BB'   SECTION 'CC'   SECTION 'DD'

DRG. NO. 80I075ND.

Tail Assembly

The fin, tail-plane and elevator are single spar structures with closely spaced ribs and single skins. Leading edges have local double skinning with machined grooves for thermal de-icing. A large panel in the side of the fin gives access to the rudder power-control unit. That for the elevator is mounted on the aircraft's centre line and is removed via a panel on the tailplane's upper surface.

The Aerodynamic Design

The overall requirements that are met by the HP80's aerodynamic design are:
(a) Good range bomb-load characteristics at 45,000ft to 50,000ft at 500kts TAS (M = 0.875)
(b) Good stability and control characteristics throughout the speed range from stalling to the service limiting conditions (365kts. EAS M = 0.90).
(c) Good take-off and landing performance.

By carefully distributed sweepback, a high critical (drag rise) Mach number, not less than 0.875 is achieved with a wing thickness giving reasonable structure-weight and good stowage space.

In the centre wing, where structure weight and stowage spaces are of primary importance, the quarter chord sweep is 47.5degrees permitting the use of 16 per cent wing thickness. Sweep is successively reduced in two steeps, being 40.5 degrre for the intermediate wing and 32degrees for the outer wing, thus avoiding tip stalling and loss of longitudinal stability inherent in the retention of high sweep at the tips. Constant critical Mach number is maintained by reduction of the t/c ratio from root to tip.

The wing sections are chosen for high critical Mach number and favourable pressure gradient under cruising conditions.

A series of tests made in the high-speed tunnel at RAE Farnborough confirm that the target Mcrit of 0.875 will be achieved.

To obviate tip stalling at low speed consequent on the use of high-taper-ratio nose flaps, extending at a predetermined wing lift coefficient, are fitted in the outer wings. These droop at all angles of attack when the main flaps are extended.

Rearward moving slotted main flaps, proved by tests to be more effective than simple split or slotted flaps, provide good take-off and landing performance.

Short span contra flaps, fitted between the outboard end of the main flap and inboard end of the aileron and operated during landing, provide increased drag, low stalling speed and improved stability in the stall.

Flying controls, entirely power operated, ensure good control, adequate power and steady operation despite variations of hinge movement to be expected at high Mach number.

Power controls permit the use of a tailplane with elevator large enough to be used for practical purpose as an all-moving surface. For a given size of horizontal tail surface an unusually powerful elevator control results.

Together with simple unbalanced controls with a small trailing edge angle (*less than 11 degrees*), reliable 'positive' response to control movements at high Mach number is ensured.

To increase the useful range of tailplane incidence for down load at large angles of incidence, nose flaps are incorporated in the elevator. This additional trimming power is only needed when the main lift flaps are deflected. Selection of main flaps down extends the elevator nose flaps, which remain retracted in flight.

Dive (*Air*) Brakes fitted at the rear of the fuselage in preference to wing-mounted design are considered less likely to cause trouble at high Mach numbers.

Engine air intakes, located adjacent to the fuselage side, have a duct to carry away fuselage boundary layer which would otherwise be drawn into the engines with consequent loss of efficiency. Wind tunnel tests show the ram recovery efficiency to be high and that the arrangement of intakes and nacelles does not reduce the aircrafts critical Mach number.

The fuselage shape, of the requisite high critical Mach number, results from extensive pressure plotting.

Engine Performance

Engine characteristics and performance were based on data from Armstrong Siddeley publication AEDO/S3 Iss 3 dated August 1950, but with nominal static sea level thrust increased to 7,900 lb and with the cruising specific fuel consumption reduced by 2.5 per cent in accordance with further data supplied by the engine makers.

The following corrections are also made:

(1) Allowance for air intake ram efficiency of 93.5 per cent based on model tests

(2) Due to the added length of the jet pipes there is a 1.6 per cent loss of thrust.

(3) A loss of thrust varying from 0.3 per cent at sea level to 1.3 per cent at 50,000ft is due to bleeding air from the compressors to feed the air-conditioning system;

(4) Also approximately 30lb loss of thrust (*per aircraft*) is due to engine driven accessories

(*Alternators and engine fuel system pump*).

With these allowances, the characteristics of the engine are:

Maximum Thrust at Sea Level Static	7,960lb
Cruising Thrust 50,000ft 500kts	1,087lb
Fuel flow 50,000ft and 500kts	1,238lb/hr
Specific Consumption 50,000ft 500kts	1.14lb/hr. thrust/hr.

Weight and Centre of Gravity Data

The HP 80's basic equipped summary is derived from the detailed analysis given in M.O.S.Form 2492 issue 9 dated December 1950.

H.P. 80

Range — bomb load.

TYPICAL SERVICE LOAD ITEMS.
Two main items of additional typical service load, not included in the basic equipped weight are.

(A) External, streamlined wing-bomb containers:
weight of a pair of these is approximately 2,000lb

(B) Fuel Drop-Tank of 600 gallons capacity each a pair weighs approximately 1,000lb. Carriage of these external loads appreciably increases the wing relief loads at high all up weights.

Design All Up Weight
Governed by the range requirements of the spec B35/46 issue 2 Para 4.01 the design all up weight is as follows:

Basic equipped weight	60,000lb
Bomb load	10,000lb
Fuel for required range	45,000lb
Design all up weight	115,000lb

Landing Weight
For the design weight the normal landing weight is 82,500lb and made up as follows: -

Design all up weight		115,000lb
Less bombs	10,000lb)	
Less half-fuel	22,500lb)	32,500lb
Landing weight		82,500lb

This is based on Case 1, the most severe of Spec B35/46 Para 4.02.

HANDLEY PAGE

H.P. 80

GENERAL PARTICULARS AND LEADING DIMENSIONS

WING AND OVERALL DIMENSIONS

Wing span	110 ft.
Overall length	114 ft. 6 in.
Overall height	28 ft.
Wing area	2,400 sq.ft.
Root chord (stn. 60" from ₵ aircraft)	35 ft. 2.9 in.
Tip chord	11 ft.
Aspect ratio	5.04

Thickness chord ratio
- (at root (Stn. 60") . . 16%
- (1st kink (Stn. 212") . 10%
- (2nd kink (Stn. 330") . 8%
- (Tip (Stn. 660") . . 6%

Sweepback angles on ¼ chord . . . . . 47½°, 40½°, 32°

FUSELAGE AND CABIN

Maximum diameter	10 ft.
Crew's gross cabin volume	694 cu. ft.
Overall length of jettisonable cabin	27 ft. 4 in.
Total bomb bay length	32 ft. 11 in.

TAIL UNIT

Fin and rudder area	146 sq. ft.
Tailplane and elevator area	263.6 sq. ft.
Fin and rudder sweepback angle on ¼ chord	43°
Tail plane and elevator sweepback angle on ¼ chord	40°
Tailplane and elevator dihedral	15°

POWER PLANT

Four Armstrong-Siddeley Sapphire Series 3 jet engines giving 7,900 lb. static thrust at sea level.

LANDING GEAR

Undercarriage track	30 ft. 2 in.
Main wheel size	26 x 6.5 - 14
Nose wheel size	29 x 8.0 - 15
Main wheel pressure) normal take-	(125 lb./sq.in.
Nose wheel pressure) off weight	(130 lb./sq.in.

TANKAGE

Normal tanks	5630 Imp.gals.
Overload tanks (internal)	3090 Imp.gals.
Drop tanks	1120 Imp.gals.
Total capacity	9540 Imp.gals.
Oil	9 Imp.gals.

WEIGHTS AND LOADING

Normal take-off weight	115,000 lb.
Overload take-off weight	150,000 lb.
Landing weight	82,500 lb.
Wing loading (normal take-off weight)	48 lb./sq.ft.

H.P. 80

COMPARATIVE RANGE PERFORMANCE WITH ALTERNATIVE ENGINES

Under I.C.A.N. Conditions

	SAPPHIRE 3		SAPPHIRE 4		CONWAY	
	Range Naut.Miles	Mean height feet	Range Naut.Miles	Mean height feet	Range Naut.Miles	Mean height feet
NORMAL STILL AIR RANGE Take-off at Design A.U.W. 115,000 lb. without drop tanks						
With 10,000 lb. bombs (bombs brought back)	3,470	46,600	3,520	52,900	3,870	51,600
With 10,000 lb. bombs (dropped half way)	3,630	47,600	3,710	54,000	4,060	52,800
With 21,000 lb. bombs (dropped half way)	2,640	47,600	2,650	54,000	2,840	52,800
With 35,000 lb. bombs (dropped half way)	1,380	47,600	1,300	54,000	1,280	52,800
OVERLOAD STILL AIR RANGE Take-off at overload A.U.W. 140,000 lb. without drop tanks						
With 10,000 lb. bombs (bombs brought back)	5,000	44,500	5,130	50,500	5,760	49,300
With 10,000 lb. bombs (dropped half way)	5,210	45,400	5,350	51,500	6,140	50,200
With 21,000 lb. bombs (dropped half way)	4,320	45,400	4,420	51,500	5,040	50,200
With 35,000 lb. bombs (dropped half way)	3,180	45,400	3,230	51,500	3,620	50,200
Take-off at max. overload A.U.W. 150,000 lb. with drop tanks						
With 10,000 lb. bombs (bombs brought back)	5,460	43,800	5,630	49,800	6,420	48,800
With 10,000 lb. bombs (dropped half way)	5,670	44,600	5,890	50,800	6,660	49,600
With 21,000 lb. bombs (dropped half way)	4,810	44,600	4,990	50,800	5,600	49,600
With 35,000 lb. bombs (dropped half way)	3,720	44,600	3,840	50,800	4,240	49,600
Take-off at max. overload A.U.W. 150,000 lb. with wing bomb nacelles						
With 55,000 lb. bombs (dropped half way)	1,920	42,500	1,920	48,500	2,080	47,200

TANKAGE

(a) Short range (2,640 nautical miles) - Wing tanks.
(b) Normal range (3,630 nautical miles) - Wing + normal fuselage tanks.
(c) Long range (5,210 nautical miles) - Wing + normal and overload fuselage tanks.
(d) Extra long range (5,670 nautical miles) - Wing + normal and overload fuselage tanks + drop tanks.

HANDLEY PAGE

H.P. 80

PERFORMANCE SUMMARY WITH SAPPHIRE 3 ENGINES

SPEED

Cruising Speed (TAS)   500 kts

CLIMB AND HEIGHT

Commencing at Design A.U.W. 115,000 lb.

Maximum rate of climb at S.L. climbing thrust	4500 fpm
Height at ½ hour after take-off	43,400 ft.
Height at 2½ hours after take-off	45,500 ft.
Mean cruising height with 10,000 lb. bombs	46,600 ft.

TAKE-OFF AND LANDING

At sea level, tropical summer (41°C)

Take-off distance to 50 ft.	)	1400 yds
Critical distance	) at	1750 yds
Emergency landing distance from	) design	
50 ft. with dive brakes open	) A.U.W.	1670 yds
Emergency landing approach speed E.A.S.	) 115000 lb.	129 kts.
Critical speed for engine failure	)	
on take-off E.A.S.	)	97.5 kts.
Take-off distance to 50 ft. at maximum overload A.U.W. 150000 lb.		2550 yds
Landing distance from 50 ft. with dive brakes closed	) at normal) landing) weight	1220 yds
Landing approach speed E.A.S.	) 82500 lb.	109.5 kts.

NORMAL STILL AIR RANGE

Commencing at Design A.U.W. 115,000 lb.

With 10,000 lb. bombs (brought back)	3470 naut.miles
With 10,000 lb. bombs (dropped half-way)	3630 naut.miles
With 21,000 lb. bombs (" " ")	2640 naut.miles
With 35,000 lb. bombs (" " ")	1380 naut.miles

OVERLOAD STILL AIR RANGE

Commencing at Overload A.U.W. 140,000 lb.

With 10,000 lb. bombs (brought back)	5000 naut.miles
With 10,000 lb. bombs (dropped half-way)	5210 naut.miles
With 21,000 lb. bombs (" " ")	4320 naut.miles
With 35,000 lb. bombs (" " ")	3180 naut.miles

Commencing at Overload A.U.W. 150,000 lb.

With 55,000 lb. bombs (dropped half-way)	1920 naut.miles

THREE AND TWO-ENGINE PERFORMANCE

Commencing at Design A.U.W. 115,000 lb.

Absolute ceiling after one hour's flying	
On three engines - climbing thrust	40,000 ft.
cruising thrust	38,500 ft.
On two engines - climbing thrust	29,250 ft.
cruising thrust	27,250 ft.
Still air range, one engine failed at end of climb, with 10,000 lb.bombs (brought back)	
At 500 knots T.A.S.	2630 naut.miles
At optimum speed (435 knots T.A.S.)	3240 naut.miles

With the exception of take-off and landing, performance is given for I.C.A.N. conditions.

HANDLEY PAGE

H.P. 80

BOMB LOADS AND FACTORS

For longer ranges or bigger bomb loads, the H.P. 80 takes-off at weights up to 150,000 lb. Internal tankage is sufficient for a range of 5,210 nautical miles with a 10,000 lb. load of bombs at 140,000 lb. take-off weight. Longer ranges or very large bomb loads are met by the use of drop-tanks or bomb nacelles under the wings.

Strength factors in the following table are estimated.

Improvements are expected when actual strength figures are obtained from the current programme of component strength tests.

As the normal landing weight is substantially unaffected by overloading, this case is not included in the table. For emergency-landing at 150,000 lb., the maximum permissible vertical velocity will be reduced by 10-13%.

Take-off weight		lb.	115,000			140,000			150,000			
Bomb load	Fuselage	lb.	10,000	21,000	35,000	10,000	21,000	35,000	10,000	21,000	35,000	35,000
	Wings (bomb nacelles)	lb.	-	-	-	-	-	-	-	-	-	20,000
Drop tank (including fuel) weight per side		lb.	-	-	-	-	-	-	5,000	5,000	5,000	-
Permissible manoeuvring	Fuselage		2.7	2.7	2.7	2.4	2.2	2.2	2.4	2.2	2.2	2.2
acceleration (g)	Wings		2.9	2.9	2.9	2.1	2.1	2.1	2.1	2.1	2.1	2.4
Reserve factor with specified up-gust Wings.			>1.0	>1.0	>1.0	0.9	0.9	0.9	0.9	0.9	0.9	1.0

N.B. The specification requirement for permissible manoeuvring normal acceleration at design A.U.W. (115,000 lb.) is 2.7g. The overload factors on the tail unit are greater than 2.4.

Normal loading in bomb-bay standard carriers

1	-	10,000 lb. Special
2	-	10,000 lb. H.C.
4	-	5,000 lb. H.C.
21	-	1,000 lb. L.C., M.C., or "Cluster"

Special loading

35	-	1,000 lb. M.C. (in bomb-bay, special carrier beam).
15	-	2,000 lb. Mine "A" Mk.9 (in bomb-bay, special adaptors).
(4	-	10,000 lb. H.C. (2 in bomb-bay standard carriers).
x(27	-	2,000 lb. Mine "A" Mk.9.
(55	-	1,000 lb. M.C.

x In these arrangements, a special container is fitted under each wing on the drop-tank mountings. This container is designed to carry one - 10,000 lb. H.C. bomb, six "A" Mk.9 mines or ten 1,000 lb. M.C. bombs.

C.G. Range

Representing 8.8 per cent of the geometric mean chord, the CG range is 1342 to 1552 aft of the manufacturers datum.

There was an addendum to the February 1951 brochure issued in June 1951 to introduce the 'Special Purpose Bomb Installation'.

The carriage of still greater bomb loads over short ranges has been investigated and the following are proposed.

Additional bomb nacelles have been added, one being under each pair of engines on the port and starboard wings. Each of these nacelles carries the following alternative bomb loads:

6-1,000lb MC
1-5,000lb HC
4-Mine A Mk IX

Therefore the HP 80 is able to carry the following alternative loads:
6-1,000lb MC
4-10,000lb HC plus 2-5,000lb HC
35-2,000lb mine A Mk IX
This bomb loading is achieved at a take off weight of 150,000lb

Range: With Armstrong Siddeley Sapphire 3 units 830 miles maximum.

Cruising Height With Armstrong Siddeley Sapphire 3 units 41,000ft

In addition to the foregoing data the attached graphs give a good idea of the original HP80 performance data.

The first prototype was purely a flying shell with the intention of proving the aerodynamics of the aircraft and the basic handling of this design. It was fitted with limited services and did not have operable bomb doors; neither did it have a brake parachute system. No operational equipment was fitted and that communications and navigational equipment was to a very basic level. The two prototypes were to have changes made to their colour schemes just prior to them displaying at the 1953 and 1955 SBAC shows to reflect their outstanding design features.

Full details of the colour schemes, engine details, avionic equipment and refuelling equipment for all the versions of the HP80/Victor are to be found in the relevant appendix.

Victor production spot welding unit. HP-HPA.

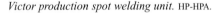

The Construction Phase

Although the ITP had been issued way back in 1947 and the official contract letter sent in early 1949 there was a great deal of work to do on the design of this aircraft as we can see from looking at the design as submitted for approval way back in early 1947. There were incorporated a vast number of changes after 1947 that meant that Handley Page were to end up with a total different aircraft. All this took a great deal of time and a considerable amount of effort from the various departments involved in the design process. Many hours were taken to build and test in the wind tunnel the test models, and the results had to be calculated by hand. Remember that in the late 1940's there were no easily available computers or calculators as we know them – the calculations were done by slide rule or by basic maths using 'Log Tables'. The Stress Department had considerable input and had to approve the majority of the items as they were designed. The Weights Department was always trying to keep the weight down so that the aircraft, when loaded, would meet the design requirements. The Costing and Estimating department soon became involved as the manufacturer was always under pressure to keep costs down.

Within days of the IPT being issued an Advisory Design Conference was set up and various meetings took place on a vast number of subjects in order that the customer's wishes were taken into consideration and also to discuss and resolve problems as they came to light during the design phase. In November 1948 the mock-up of the crew stations was examined by the Ministry of Supply at HP Cricklewood and after that these meetings were conducted on a regular basis for many years and well after the Victor was in service.

It was not until the summer of 1951 that the DOR (Director of Operational Requirements) confirmed an interest in Photographic Reconnaissance Development for the HP 80(Victor) and this was to add to the design changes that were ongoing.

With the design approved and authorisation received to start the process of cutting metal,

Panel construction. HP-HPA.

Tailplane. HP-HPA.

the Experimental Shop at HP Cricklewood began the change from the manufacture of the various mock-ups to the manufacture of the various major components that were in due course to be transported to AAEE Boscombe Down for final assembly and testing prior to the first flight.

While all the design work and mock-ups had been going on. There had been considerable work on the development of the sandwich skin for the wings. There had been thoughts of using Redux bonding but these were rejected after various tests had been carried out. The use of a corrugated section between the inner and outer skins was developed into a smooth outer skin, without the use of rivets, by spot welding of the aluminium alloys together. The inner skin was to be riveted to the corrugated section because the use of the smooth finish produced by welding was not required. It took some time to get the current of the welding equipment to produce a successful weld but once it had been set up and the process passed all the tests required by the Test Department it was possible to go into limited large-scale production of the prototypes.

The rear fuselage in an assembly jig

In this major assembly jig the Victo
rear fuselage is skinned.

The fuselage was constructed in the familiar method of using frames at the critical sections joined by stringers and then skinned over in the conventional manner. The frames are the main strength sections of this type of construction and in certain areas they are complex. The critical ones in the construction of the Victor are: the cabin, the fuel tanks housed in the front of the fuselage, the frames at the front and at the rear of the bomb bay including half frames that divide up the top section of the bomb bay and provide the strength for a number of fuel tanks that are positioned up there. (*There are a number of differences in this area when comparing the prototypes with the production aircraft.*) Heavy longerons at the bottom edges of the bomb bay are stabilised over the greater part of their length by the lower surface of the wing. Heavy double frames at the various bomb-hoisting points carry all bomb loads. After the bomb bay there is the rear end of the rear fuel tanks and the frames associated with the tapering section of the rear fuselage. The design of the front fuselage comprises a pressurised cabin for the crew and an unpressurised section below floor level with the H2S scanner and other services in a removable radome.

As the crew cabin was pressurised this called for more frames and in some locations extra strength frames to provide the rear face of the cabin with sufficient strength although, this was, in fact, domed. It was at this point that the four special bolts that hold it to the rear fuselage were fitted. As this is the only area to be pressurised the construction of the remaining fuselage is more conventional. The rear fuselage includes the wing centre section and extends back to the main fin pick-up bulkhead. The tail cone part of the fuselage is detachable at the main fin pick-up bulkhead and carries the airbrakes and the tail radar scanner.

The numbering of the frames and associated sub-frames is in inches starting from frame 0 which is the first frame and is located at the inboard side of the bomb aimers windows. One of the most familiar frame numbers is frame 398, which is at the front face of the bomb bay.

The tail unit comprises the fin; tailplane and elevators are single spar structures with closely spaced ribs and single skins. Leading edges have local double skinning with machined grooves for thermal de-icing. A large panel in the side of the fin gives access to the rudder powered flying control unit. That for the elevator is mounted on the aircraft's centre line and is removed via a panel on the tailplane upper surface.

The port inner wing section
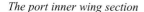

The construction of WB771 and WB775 was carried out in total at the Cricklewood factory in the experimental shop, well away from the main production area devoted at that time to the production of the Canberra for the RAF. It was envisaged that final assembly would have been at the Park Street Experimental and Test Facility but even though the assembly was started it was all dismantled and moved to A&AEE Boscombe Down due to a strange decision that a 6,000ft runway was too short by somebody in the Air Ministry or the Ministry of Supply. All the major assemblies were produced at this location eventually for all Victor production and transported by road to HP Radlett Colney Street Works for assembly and fitting out prior to their first flight.

The construction of the two prototypes was under the control of Chief Engineer Mr Mc-Rostie assisted by Mr A W Braithwaite and Charge Hands from all the relevant HP Radlett and HP Cricklewood sections as required.

The story of the transportation of WB771 to A&AEE Boscombe Down is related by Mr McRostie and it was a traumatic journey for all those concerned but it was not one journey. There were quite a few journeys to bring all the major sections of the aircraft, along with all the associated team who were to carry out the assembly and to complete the various systems and test them to such an extent that they were completely functioning as they had been designed to do. In some cases this was a tortuous task and led too much discussion of what had happened, or not happened, and why it did not happen.

The hydraulic system took quite a time to function properly and it was while work on this system was in progress that a disastrous incident happened in the rear equipment bay. On the Prototypes this bay had a considerable amount of electrical equipment in it along with the hydraulic services for the air brakes passing through it. As the aircraft was in what is called a Power On state the equipment in the rear equipment bay was all live with 112vDC and 28VDC. This made the bay a rather lethal place to be, especially as the hydraulic system was still under test and the tracing of faults with it in progress. A hydraulic high-pressure leak occurred at 4000psi, most probably from the piping supplying the airbrakes. The hydraulic fluid atomised as it sprayed out and ignited on coming into contact with the various electrical contactors and motors of the rotating equipment. This caused a severe fire and with the hydraulic fluid being sprayed on to the fire it became intense and engulfed the electrician working in that area at the time. In addition, the fire caused severe damage to the lower part of the fin and this had to be replaced by that from WB775. The fire was eventually extinguished but the death of the electrician, Eddie Eyles, was tragic. There was also found to be need to adjust the C of G position and this was the cause of the 42 inch insertion that was to become the 'Plenum Chamber' on all production Victors along with all the various HV electrical equipment from the rear hatch forward.

Eventually all the problems were sorted out and the aircraft was ready for the initial ground runs and the other systems functional checks to the required specifications and for approval not only by the Handley Page Inspection Staff under the control of Mr W.A. Robinson and Mr F.R. Ashworth but by the AID Inspectors from the Air Ministry under the control of Mr M.C. Brothers who would issue the relevant documentation for each individual test flight before the first taxi trials were able to be under taken in mid-December 1952.

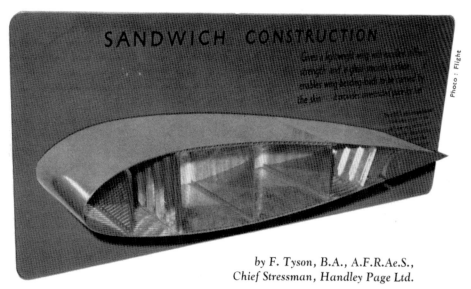

Photo : Flight

by F. Tyson, B.A., A.F.R.Ae.S.,
Chief Stressman, Handley Page Ltd.

B^Y using sandwich construction for its new aircraft, Handley Page is leading the way in the development of this new form of aircraft fabrication which combines high structural and aerodynamic efficiency.

Structurally, it results in a lightweight wing with excellent stiffness and strength whereby bending loads are carried by the skin; it enables fuel tanks to be pressurised without weight penalty; it gives unrestricted space and a smooth inner-surface for bag tanks.

Aerodynamically, it gives a glass-smooth surface and accurate contour which are maintained under load and reduce drag by increasing the area of laminar airflow.

Mr. Tyson describes the development of sandwich construction for the wing of a large, fast, high-flying aircraft. His article is based on a paper which he read recently before the Royal Aeronautical Society.

A SANDWICH is a structural element which consists of two face-plates of comparatively thin but strong sheet separated and stabilised by a core of very light, and therefore weak, material. The whole assembly has considerable bending and shear strength with stiffness in all directions.

The principal factors which governed the design of the wing structure for a large, high-speed, high-altitude aircraft were the need for: smooth external finish and an accurate profile of the skin surfaces; high internal pressures in the wing fuel tanks; great torsional stiffness.

These requirements led to the choice of a wing design with sandwich skins, multi spars and very few ribs. The smooth and accurate wing surface was not merely a manufacturing standard but one that was to be maintained in level flight at cruising speed. Furthermore, it was a necessity after the wing had been loaded to its proof load in any stressing case. The standard required was a waviness not exceeding 0.004 in. to 1 in. and a wing profile accurate to 0.025 in. It was considered difficult to achieve this standard with conventional stringer

construction, but a sandwich offered good chances of success.

The next consideration was high fuel-tank pressures. To prevent fuel boiling at high altitude requires pressurised tanks. With aviation gasoline loaded at 50° C., a pressure of 7 lb. per sq. in. is needed at 50,000 ft. To this must be added the pressure due to fuel inertia which, owing to the high speed and manoeuvrability of the aircraft, is about 7 lb. per sq. in. With a factor of safety of 1.5, the ultimate design pressure was slightly greater than 20 lb. per sq. in.

It is impractical to design conventional stringer-and-rib wings to stand this high pressure because of the increased structure weight involved. Apart from strength considerations, there is the aspect of wing deflection and the need to prevent the wing surface from assuming a quilted shape under internal pressure.

It was found that with a wing having sandwich skins, multi spars and very few ribs, high tank pressures were catered for satisfactorily.

A typical arrangement of spars and ribs for a

stringer wing and that for a sandwich wing are shown in the diagram below.

In the stringer-wing case, tank pressures are carried by the stringers as beams supported at the ribs. This produces bending stresses in the stringers which add to the stresses due to wing bending.

In the sandwich wing, tank pressures are taken by the sandwich panel acting as a beam supported by the spars. This is because the sandwich, unlike the stringer panel, has approximately equal bending stiffnesses in both directions and the spars are put much closer together than the ribs.

Thus the bending moment in the sandwich due to tank pressures produces tension and compression stresses in the face-plates which are at right angles to the stresses due to the main wing bending-moment. These stresses do not add directly together as in the case of a stringer wing. Thus, when a sandwich wing of this sort has been designed to take the main wing bending-moment, it also can take considerable tank pressures without any appreciable increase in structure weight.

Shear Stiffness

Limiting wing-surface deflection under tank pressure is chiefly a matter of providing adequate shear stiffness in the core to keep the shear deflections of the sandwich small. Consideration of wing torsional stiffness led to skins sufficiently thick to keep the bending deflections small.

When the sandwich has been designed to meet other conditions, the deflections under tank pressure are very small—and no weight penalty is involved in meeting the condition of a smooth wing under tank pressure.

A further advantage for the sandwich wing in this particular case is that the skins can be made to work in compression up to a stress approaching

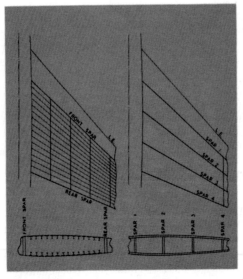

SPAR and rib arrangements show the different wing layouts required by stringer (left) and sandwich construction.

proof with a 1 in. thick sandwich on spars 30 in. to 36 in. pitch.

A stringer wing can, of course, be designed to work up to the same stress. But the stringers would have to be considerably deeper than 1 in. or the ribs would have to be very closely spaced. Either of these alternatives encroaches on the space available inside the wing (already small enough in a high-speed aircraft) and complicates and restricts the design of the wing fuel tanks.

Another advantage of the sandwich is a smooth internal surface for thin bag fuel-tanks.

Two Types

Development was concentrated on two types of sandwich. The first had a honeycomb core of aluminium alloy attached to aluminium-alloy face-plates by an adhesive; the second had a core of corrugated aluminium-alloy sheet attached to aluminium-alloy face-plates by spot-welds and rivets.

An example of corrugated sandwich construction is shown opposite.

The choice of core was a difficult problem. Thicknesses of the skin sheet are fixed by consideration of wing torsional stiffness. Over much of the wing it is necessary to stabilise these sheets to work to a compression stress approaching their proof stress. The pitch of spars and thickness of sandwich depend, of course, on the properties of the core. These were chosen to suit the best core characteristics which were thought likely of achievement.

Properties required in the core are those needed to develop a high compressive stress in the face-plates. In this respect, the suitability of the core is finally proved by compression tests. The shear strength necessary is that required to carry the tank pressure, as the core of the sandwich is the web of the beam carrying tank pressures.

The density is a most important consideration because of the large total volume of the core. It was hoped that a figure of 4.5 lb. per cu. ft. could be obtained consistent with the other properties required. In considering core densities, it is interesting to remember that the density of aluminium is 175 lb. per cu. ft.

Stringent Needs

The core and its attachments must also meet a number of requirements which cannot be expressed in figures. The strength and stiffness values must be maintained over a temperature range −70° C. to +70° C. in all conditions of humidity. They must be resistant to damage by all aircraft fluids and to attack by insects and fungi.

The core, preferably, must be of a material which can be produced and inspected to aircraft standards and specification. In addition, the manufacture of the core and its assembly to the face-plates must be capable of control and inspection to similar standards.

Many cores have been proposed for use with metal face-plates. Most fall into one or other of a number of groups.

First come wood cores. Characteristically, balsa has low shear strength and stiffness figures compared with the end-grain direct stresses and stiffness. Its strength properties are reasonable, but the density is high. Balsa trees do not grow to an aircraft specification, and density varies from 6 to 12 lb. per cu. ft. with strength roughly proportional to density. The wood must be chosen within a certain range of density with consequent rejection of much of the raw material. Even so, strength figures must be based on minimum density, while weights depend on average density.

Expanded rubber is a possible core, but its strengths and stiffnesses are low and density not impressive.

Some foamed or otherwise expanded materials have been proposed as cores. Calcium alginate is one of the best of these, but its properties are less than those sought. All these cores can be produced in a variety of densities with strength figures varying accordingly. Their attraction is that they provide a continuous surface for the attachment of core to face-plates. But all these materials are water absorbent and lose strength both at moderately high temperature and in humid conditions.

Light Core

Another way of making a light core is to provide a structure which connects the two face-plates with empty spaces between structural members. These are kept sufficiently close to provide a continuous support for the face-plates. The structure must provide shear strength and stiffness as well as end-load strength and stiffness in the direction normal to the face-plates.

A core of this type, in the form of a honeycomb of paper impregnated with resin, was produced during the war. Its properties are superior to the expanded cores. It can be produced in a range of densities, the strength and stiffness varying with the density. But this honeycomb does not have the strength-to-weight ratio we aimed at and the control of paper manufacture is not in accordance with aircraft standards. If used in primary structure, an additional factor of safety (with consequent increase of weight) would be required to cover variation of quality.

Another type of core, the impregnated fabric honeycomb, has been made and has involved cotton, linen and glass-cloth. Each suffers from one inherent disadvantage : if it is made stiff and strong for taking forces normal to the face-plates by putting the fibres normal and parallel to them, then it is weak and flexible in shear ; if it is made stiff and strong in shear by arranging the fibres at 45° to the face-plates, then it is weak and flexible under loads normal to the face-plates.

Metal Honeycomb

The best solution is a honeycomb core of metal foil. This, made from 0.003 in. hard aluminium foil with an ultimate tensile strength of 42,000 lb. per sq. in., gives very good strength qualities in conjunction with satisfactory density.

However, in our tests the shear strength, though better than with other honeycombs, was less than required. When tested in shear, tension-field waves in the core led to its collapse.

The shear strength can be increased by raising the waving stress either by a reduction of cell size or by an increase of foil thickness. Either method increases the density of the core. A better way is to put a flute down each cell wall. This was our solution.

A further increase in strength is obtained by using an aluminium alloy instead of aluminium. Most of these need a protective treatment against corrosion in the form of paint or its equivalent. As the foil is so thin (0.003 in.), a normal paint spread of $1\frac{1}{2}$ oz. per square yard increases weight by nearly 50 per cent. The strongest alloys needing no protection for internal use are the magnesium aluminium alloys ; one of these, M.G.5, was chosen.

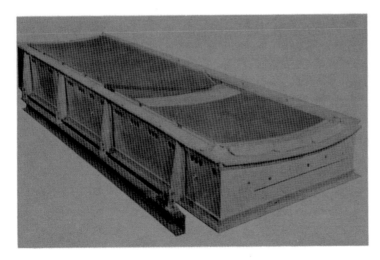

A METAL-HONEYCOMB core is ideal for the production of curved sandwich panels.

The Victor

This article by Sqn Ldr H G Hazelden DFC and Bar, Chief Test Pilot was published in the Handley Page Bulletin No. 207 dated February 1954.

It was shortly after I joined the Company in 1947 when Mr Stafford our chief designer told me very casually one day about a new bomber project and the revolutionary performance in speed, range and height to be achieved.

'Sounds a bit advanced', I reflected, 'but I reckon if that's what you want to do I'll have plenty of time to find out how to fly it while you find out how to make it'.

That, for me, was the beginning of a project, which made its biggest step on Christmas Eve 1952 when I took the HP 80 into the air for the first time. On that day in 1947, when Mr. Stafford told me all about it, the HP 80 was an embryo design study. The dimensions were a surprise, for it was not easy to see how an aeroplane with the performance and load carrying capacity which he envisaged could be only a little larger than the Hastings transport with which I was mainly occupied.

The aeroplane, I remember, was to be powered by four Metrovick F4 engines which, I believe, were supposed to give about 7,000lb of static thrust each. The undercarriage would have to be a bogie with four, possibly eight, wheels in order to make it retract into the small depth of wing.

Crescent wing

The pros and cons of all the different plan forms were explained to me: how thin straight wings do the trick aerodynamically but are difficult to build strong enough and are unsuitable for engines, undercarriage and fuel tanks (of which many obviously would be required) to be housed in them; how, if the necessary depth were obtained by the use of straight swept wings, aerodynamic characteristics at low speed were possibly bad; how deltas without tailplanes have a restricted C.G. range.

It seemed to me that whatever course was adopted something was going to be a bit chancy. Since the bomber had to have its engines, fuel and undercarriage stowed, it looked like being a sweptback wing job and I would have to master the aerodynamic drawbacks.

Then Mr. C. F. Joy our deputy chief designer told me of the compromise when he said 'We think that we can overcome most of the difficulties'. Our wing was to have three different angles of sweep: sharply swept back at the root (where a good depth is needed for strength and for housing engines, undercarriage tanks etc) moderately swept back in the centre (where less depth still allows fuel tanks to be stowed) and finally at the wing tip the angle of sweep was to be only slight since here, from the stowage standpoint, it was possible to use a much thinner section which met the aerodynamic needs.

Leap into the unknown

When I left Mr. Stafford and Mr. Joy that day I confess that I felt a little overawed at the tremendous step forward which was being proposed. I wondered whether perhaps we were taking too big a bite that might lead to some painful indigestion. However as I thought more about it, I became as enthusiastic as everyone else.

In due course the Ministry of Supply gave the order to proceed with the design and, in a very short time, I found myself being called upon to give advice on matters concerning flying qualities. I was asked about such items as the required movement range of flying controls, desirable forces to be provided artificially for different manoeuvres and a host of other points.

A mock-up of the nose and crew cabin was built and frequently I sat in this to consider the best position for controls, instruments etc. Almost every idea for the position of anything in the cockpit was discussed in the mock up and, with few exceptions; the first idea was modified as a result. Our design people were very patient about my criticisms. We realised that the combined efforts of a team and not those of individuals would produce the best answers.

Another manifestation of advanced design was the strange framework of girders which grew up at our Radlett aerodrome. Where, of course, the bulk of my time was spent. Although not directly concerned with this structure, I found it was a mock-up of the fuel system with tanks in the relative positions that they would occupy on the aeroplane. This rig could be moved to simulate different flying positions and tests were carried out to ensure that the correct fuel supply would reach the engines whatever the aircraft attitude.

There were, by this time, developments regarding the engines that we had selected. Metrovick's F4 had been taken over by Armstrong Siddeley at Coventry and developed into the well-known Sapphire. In order to gain experience with the Sapphire arrangements were made to fit two engines to the outboard positions of a Hastings (Second Prototype TE583) for use as a flying test-bed. I did some flying on this aircraft and later on a Sapphire-engined Canberra, WD933, and found it was a very fine engine. I remember on one Hastings flight I stopped one of the Sapphires and the two Hercules inboard engines and flew comfortably on the other Sapphire at 175knots with no more than normal cruising power. It was a fore-taste of the power to be given to the HP 80.

HP 80 (Victor) Project

My impressions of the whole HP 80 project from its conception to the first flight, are those of one who looks on from the outside, but who has frequent visits to investigate points of special interest. Everyone else had so much more to do than I. My efforts to learn more must have annoyed some, for they must have wanted to get on with their own jobs rather than talk to me. However, I think that sometimes my inquisitive mind helped because in explaining things to me they made it clearer to the other man's mind as well.

When I first saw the shop in which theories and drawings were being transformed into the components of the aeroplane itself, I realised the magnitude of the project that had been undertaken. Jigs of strange shapes were fixed to the concrete floor. To my eyes, unskilled in such matters, they seemed to be in complete and utter confusion. Where space was limited pits had been carved in the shop floor. Sections of wings in their respective jigs were unrecognisable as such.

Intense activity

Despite the patient explanation of Mr. W.H. MacRostie, our chief engineer, I found it difficult to visualise how each separate part was to dovetail into the others. The intense activity and purpose of all engaged in that shop gave me the impression of mystery and a feeling of wonder that I had been watching an anthill. Because of the noise, endless questions remain unasked and unanswered. I came away confident that somebody knew the answers and, as the amateur actor is apt to say, that everything will be all right on the day.

A big moment in the HP 80 life came one Saturday in June 1952. Its fuselage, covered in a huge canvas cover as a boat hull destined for some foreign port, was mounted on a reinforced bogie and towed along the roads to Boscombe Down where final assembly was to take place. All vehicles used in this operation had the Handley Page name carefully concealed in an effort to preserve the secrecy in which the project had been wrapped since its inception. I saw this huge shape moving along with special motorcycle police to control the traffic at crossings. How impossible that such an apparent monstrosity could ever fly!

HP80 fuselage loaded and on the road at Radlett. HP-HPA

HP80 WB771 in the Hangar at A&AEE. HP-HPA

HP80 WB771 being towed out of the A&AEE Hangar. HP-HPA

Boscombe Down

In a few weeks after this I visited Boscombe Down. For the first time I could see what the HP80 was going to look like. Much remained to be done but the wings and fin were in position. Climbing onto one of the huge erection platforms, I saw the whole structure from above. At last the HP80 began to look like an aeroplane.

Days slipped by. The SBAC Show loomed up; I began to wonder whether our hopes of demonstrating the aircraft there could be realised. Indeed there was too much to do and our new bomber did not appear. But in the tired faces of the men who were building her was reflected the great effort that had been made. They had worked such long hours through night and day for so many weeks.

In spite of the keen disappointment, there was no let-up afterwards and the work continued to forge ahead. Unfortunately, another setback occurred and like the end of the HP88 it had tragic results. A small fire broke out at the rear end of the fuselage during tests on the hydraulic system.

It took some weeks to repair the damage (this included replacing the fin which was damaged at the base) and it was not until the middle of December that I decided to move to Boscombe Down in readiness for the first flight.

Personal feelings

'What do you feel about it?' was a question frequently put to me. Rarely did I answer it truthfully. The HP 80 was all but completed. I thought of all the work which had gone into the new aeroplane from so many people over so long a period – about five years. Two men had died in the process of giving it birth. Now, at the end of the line, it was to be put into my hands. I must discover whether or not all that tremendous effort had been successful. I hoped I would measure up to the task and to the trust placed in me.

It was about a week before Christmas 1952 that I first moved the aircraft under its own power when I taxied from the hangar to the base for a compass swing. (This included speeds up to about 20mph and a check of the various systems required for the fast taxi runs). It handled delightfully on the ground and although there was a gale blowing at the time I felt none of the adverse effects. Two days later, (20/12/52 at 14.30hrs) when it was pouring with rain, I took it out onto the runway in order to do some fast taxi runs. Rain seemed to have as little disturbing effect as had high wind earlier. I did four runs. (The trials actually took 1hr 45mins) I was happy with the aeroplane and the next time out I was sure it would fly.

Bad weather continued to take a hand and it was Christmas Eve before conditions allowed a maiden flight to be contemplated. The aircraft was on the apron and, in company with Mr. Ian Bennet, my flight observer, I climbed aboard. This was it, the thing we had waited for! Cockpit checks were completed, engines started and I taxied to the runway.

Conditions were perfect with a slight breeze straight down the runway, bright sunshine through a few woolly cumulus clouds and visibility up to twenty miles in crisp December air.

First flight

I locked my radio on to transmit so that all we said could be heard on the ground. In a matter of seconds now we would know if the HP 80 could fly. I opened the engines to fairly low power and released the brakes. The aircraft rolled up the runway rapidly gaining speed. I pulled the control column back and the nose-wheel left the ground. So far so good. I held the aircraft like that for a few seconds: the rumbling ceased and I knew we were off. (After a take-off run of only 1,500ft)

I kept close to the runway, still gaining speed, for a few more vital seconds, and then I knew it was all right. An imperceptible movement of the control column and the ground

HP80 WB771 Fast taxi at A&AEE. HP-HPA

HP80 WB771 prior to first flight. HP-HPA

started to fall away as we climbed.

Smoothly, effortlessly the aircraft had slid into its natural element. By so doing it had become an aeroplane instead of just the expression in metal of so many drawings and hieroglyphics on paper. Whatever happened know we knew it could fly.

After a few minutes in the air my thoughts turned to landing. I had got the aircraft up there; now could I get it back again? I tried reducing speed to see how it would behave at a suitable speed for the approach. Once more it was all right and, coming in on a long straight approach, I headed for the runway. Lower and lower we came until the beginning of the runway was only a few feet below the wheels. I throttled right back, and in a few seconds the wheels started rumbling and we were down. The HP80 had come back to earth as smoothly as it had left. We had had a comfortable flight with no anxieties.

Thus ended the most important stage so far of a great project. My own part has been a small one; my main work was ahead. The success and pride of achievement belong to all who have worked on the aircraft. They are not only in our company, but also in every one of the concerns great or small, which have supplied individual components.

I like to think that the final success is a monument to my friends Duggie Broomfield and Eddie Eyles who died in making it possible.

HP80 WB771 take-off run on first flight, 24.12.52. HP-HPA

Testing the Prototype

This article by Ian K Bennett BSc, AFRAeS, Chief Flight Test Observer was written only a few days before his death in the crash of WB771 in July 1954 and published in the Handley Page Bulletin No. 214 Autumn 1954

Nowadays a new aircraft is in the design and construction stages for three, four, or even five years before the time is reached when all is ready for the prototype's first flight. Then, resting on the tarmac, is a new creation; a complex machine which awaits its loss of contact with the earth for the first time. It is the culmination of several years of work by many people in research, design and construction. It has its maiden flight: a gentle take-off, a few gentle circuits and an oh-so-gentle landing.

Then in next to no time it is claimed a new wonder airliner, or a bomber able to fly higher, faster and farther than ever before, or a fighter able to crash invulnerably and at will through the sound barrier. So often the public believes that in a very short time such airliners will be flying all over the world with their passengers or, if warplanes, will be in full squadron service.

Many months must pass before this becomes a reality; they are months of intensive test flying and development that cover every conceivable aspect of aeronautical engineering.

To do this work, an aircraft constructing company has its flight-test fraternity: an integrated team of test pilots, flight-test observers, aerodynamicists and engineers. A highly developed team spirit is essential and it is most desirable to keep the same group of experienced individuals together during the development of a new aircraft.

HP80 WB771 take-off on first flight, 24.12.52. HP-HPA

Why so thorough
People ask why the flight-testing of a prototype takes so long and why is it so thorough. It is because a prototype is not only a new flying machine but also because it is equipped with many components, such as engines, electrical equipment, and hydraulic systems etc., which are virtually prototypes themselves. Thus we are dealing with much new and complex machinery assembled into a lightweight structure that has to be proven as airworthy.

When, for example, an aircraft has been designed to take fare-paying passengers around the world, obviously every conceivable test must be made to prove that their passage through the air may be made in reasonable safety. Again a modern bomber represents a great expenditure of technical resources. It must be capable of carrying out its operational duties as efficiently as possible and, at the same time, afford the small flight crew as little worry as possible. One bomber of the 'V' class is possibly a great factor in the defence of this country at the present time than a whole fleet of warships. Therefore, flight tests by its constructor and by representatives of the Ministry of Supply must be very exacting.

Handley Page has always been associated with large aeroplanes, the flight-testing of which is more complex than that of small ones. However there is one advantage in that more space is available in the large prototype for the flight-test equipment.

Principal tests
It is appropriate here to list the main items to be tested on, say, a large four-engined jet aircraft.

Initial flying
Early test flying is usually done at light weights and mid centre of gravity positions and includes: initial handling, take-offs and landings and general circuit flying; initial functioning of flying controls, engines and fuel system, hydraulics and electrical systems; general handling at low speeds and low altitudes.

General performance and handling
After the aircraft has been found generally airworthy, a more systematic programme of tests is started. Beginning at moderate weights and mid centre of gravity positions, it extends up to the maximum design weight and through the centre of gravity range. This includes: measurement of air speed systems error; assessment of flight at high Mach number at various altitudes; assessment of behaviour near the stall; stability and control about three axes; flight flutter (Sustained oscillation usually on wing, fin or tail caused by interaction of aerodynamic forces, elastic reactions and inertia which rapidly break the structure) tests and measurement of certain vibrations and stress; behaviour with one or more engines inoperative; assessment of climb and level speed performance; assessment of take-off and landing performance and engine thrust.

System and functional testing
This can be done concurrently with performance and handling tests and includes: checks on functioning of engines, hydraulics, electrical system, pressurisation and flying control units; measurement of air intake efficiencies and engine thrust.

Miscellaneous
Testing of operational equipment and other items usually coming towards the end of a programme includes: checks on cabin comfort, noise level and air-conditioning; checks on cooling of electric motors and other auxiliaries; checks on cooling of engine bays, jet pipe shrouds, etc; auto pilot trials; radio and radar trials; trials under expected conditions of operation.

This list is very incomplete but it is sufficient to show how much has to be covered. It must be remembered that, with a new prototype, each step forward may result in the need for adjustment or modifications.

Obviously, all sections of the constructor's design organisation require information as soon as possible. This, and the fact that there are always periods when test flights are few and far between (due to bad weather, aircraft inspection periods, ground work on modifications or time taken up by demonstrations to would-be customers), mean that on each test flight the opportunity must be taken to gain every possible scrap of information. This is done by fitting a great quantity of test instrumentation and by arranging a test programme that makes full use of all flying time available.

Instrumentation
In pre-war days most test flying consisted of qualitative assessment by test pilots and, although this is still of supreme importance, there is a growing tendency for more comprehensive and more accurate quantities measurements.

The testing of a large prototype aircraft requires the fitment of about three hundred instruments. Most of them have to be arranged on specially designed panels that are illuminated so they can be photographed by remotely controlled cine cameras; the remainder need to be situated in the cabin so that they can be seen and recorded by the flight crew.

In addition, there is an increasing need to fit equipment to measure high frequency oscillations and stresses and strains in various parts of the structure. This is done by using acceleration pick-ups and strain gauges and by amplifying their signals to make them suitable for trace presentation in special boxes or by oscillographs.

With modern prototypes it is essential to plan the test instrumentation so that it can be fitted during initial construction of the aircraft. This is because the difficulty of running pipes and cables at later stages and also because of space considerations.

An example of this scope of instrumentation is the test to check level-speed performance at a given Mach number. To do this, accurate recordings at frequent intervals must be taken of height, speed, Mach number, gallons of fuel used, air temperature engine rpm, jet pipe temperatures and jet pipe total heads (for thrust calculation). In addition during these levels, records are required to show all the control surfaces angles and also to indicate there is no side slip or bank or change of direction. Thus in this one test on a four engined aircraft we need to record the indications shown on some thirty instruments.

Flight Observers duties
The duties of flight observers are many. They act as flight-test engineers when necessary; they keep logs of test flights and note pilot's comments; they make sure that the agreed test programmes are being adhered to; they operate the cameras; they record all-important visually read instruments.

It is a sobering thought, to the flight test section in particular, that on a typical test sortie over 40,000 quantities are recorded on film and paper and in addition, there are long lengths of sensitised paper covered with trace recordings.

Many man hours (and woman hours) are spent in sorting out the quantities required and in correcting and transposing these quantities from the records. We find that for every flying hour undertaken by each flight-test observer there are some twenty hours of work on the ground. They involve analysis of results, writing of technical reports and checks on instrumentation and cameras.

Before flight-testing even begins, a schedule of tests must be compiled together with some order of priority. As every opportunity must be taken to make use of all available flying time, a detailed programme must be worked out before each flight.

Let us consider what can be undertaken on a typical test flight whose primary object is to obtain information on the handling qualities of an aircraft at say 47,000ft at a Mach number of 0.93. To check this feature entails a nine-mile climb into the stratosphere and there is much

The HP 80 WB771 at A&AEE. HP-HPA

that can be checked on the way up, on the way down and even on the ground.

For example, there is a strong cross-wind blowing on the airfield and so we plan to photograph, at say two frames per second, all the instruments that will show the aircraft's behaviour during take-off at full power with this cross wind blowing.

There are several cloud layers at low altitudes and thus there is an opportunity to measure the aircraft's behaviour in turbulent air.

At 10,000ft, conditions will allow a performance climb to be started. So we plan to climb at maximum climbing power and agree the speed to be used.

Plans are made to record control angles, air temperature, fuel used, speed, time, height, and engine conditions every 1,000ft up to 47,000ft.

Various checks

An outstanding test may be the measurement of the cooling air to the flying control units and the recording of operating temperatures and electric current within these units. It is arranged, therefore to take records of the quantities during the climb and subsequent high-altitude flying.

The climb also affords the opportunity to record engine behaviour, the temperatures in and around the engine and the fuel pressure to them. It also gives the pressurisation system another check.

On reaching 47,000ft conditions have to be stabilised in level flight. The power is set to a pre-determined value and the speed allowed to build up and stabilise at this constant altitude, in order that a check can be made on level-speed performance, engine thrust and aircraft drag.

The conditions will be set for the main object of the flight; to check control characteristics at high Mach numbers. Here film records of all the relevant quantities must back-up the pilot's assessment at frequent intervals.

By this time it is estimated that the aircraft is 'running out of land' and so a turn through 180 degrees is made. Here is a chance to record the behaviour in a 45 degrees banked turn at high speed and high altitude.

A test left over from a previous flight is to record the aircraft's response to a sudden rudder bar 'kick' when flying at an indicated speed of say 240knots at 45,000ft; this is fitted in.

Next comes the descent to base. It is a long way down and here is a chance to measure the rate of descent with engines throttled back and with dive brakes extended.

We presume the cross wind will still be blowing and so the landing will be worth recording.

After each such test flight, all cameras are quickly removed and we bite our nails until we are assured that every thing on film is readable.

Need of prototypes

Most of the analysis work is laborious. It would help very much to have instruments capable of giving direct and accurate indication of true air speed, true ambient air temperature, of true engine thrust, the lift coefficient of the aircraft, the aircrafts weight and its centre of gravity position at any time during flight.

At times progress seems to be very slow and in fact if in a year one achieves 100 hours of really useful test flying in a prototype, one is doing well.

Undoubtedly, progress would be much faster if two or more prototypes were available from the start. On one prototype all characteristics could be investigated quickly; on the other any desirable developments or modifications could be proceeded with.

If there is a shortage of prototypes, full operational use of production aircraft is liable to delay due to underdevelopment of certain features.

In addition it must be remembered that a modern long-range aircraft has to be suitable for operation in any part of the world and tests have to be made at some time in the tropics and under arctic conditions.

In any reference to test flying, mention must be made of the pioneer work carried out by the Aircraft and Armament Experimental Establishment at Boscombe Down. There a watching brief is undertaken on the progress of every new type of aircraft. Its experts are always available to give advice. Eventually they do check tests on each new type in order to clear it for service use. Hence the old saying, 'What goes up-Boscombe Down'.

Mention must also be made of the valuable work of the Empire Test Pilots' School that produces pilots of great experience. We, as flight test observers, must have great faith in the man at the controls. We are confirmed in our faith in him when a pilot has been to EPPS.

(*This article by Ian K Bennett BSc ARAeS was written before his tragic death along with A. Cook and B. Heithersay, all who were flight test observers and Test Pilot R Ecclestone in the crash of Victor WB771 on the 14 July 1954 at Cranfield*)

Testing and Development Flying of the Victor Prototypes WB771 & 775

The variety of test carried out on a prototype of a new aircraft have already been described. To illustrate the complexity of this type of testing I have decided to describe the progress of the two HP80 prototypes, WB771 and WB775.

Chief test pilot Sqn/Ldr H.G. Hazel Hazelden had spent many hours since the end of 1950 preparing himself to fly the new aircraft. He had, of course, been closely associated with the design and production departments so that he was familiar with every detail of it. A Hastings prototype had been fitted with two Sapphires in place of the outboard Hercules piston engines and he flew this machine for many hours to familiarise himself with the engine; for high-speed experience he flew a Canberra B.2 with Sapphires.

Just before Christmas on the on 20 December he taxied WB771 from the Boscombe Down hangar to the compass base in a gale with just himself and Ian Bennett on board, he was pleased with the way it handled. Two days later on 22 December he and Ian Bennet commenced taxiing trials with fast runs along the runway up to the calculated take-off speed. This activity took 1 hour and 45 minutes and gave the crew a good insight into the ground handling and proved that the aircraft would fly without a problem. Heavy rain prevented a short flight. The weather had cleared on Christmas Eve and the wind blew directly along the runway so, with his flight test observer Ian Bennett, later to lose his life in this machine, he took off for a 17 minute flight making a trial approach and overshoot before a landing which confirmed Godfrey Lee's prediction that the aeroplane would have the ability to land itself as it entered its ground cushion which would initiate the flare out. All that was needed was an accurate alignment with the runway centre-line.

Over the next eight weeks 771 was to undertake fourteen flights from the A&AEE and all were to carry out investigations into the handling of the aircraft. On 9 February 1953, on the seventh flight, the undercarriage was raised for the first time. It had been a design requirement that the brakes must be applied to stop the wheels rotating before retraction commenced since gyroscopic forces might cause the gear to foul the interior of the undercarriage bay with serious results. To ensure that this condition was met a small flap was attached to the parking brake lever so that it covered the undercarriage 'UP' selector button until the lever was moved to the brake 'ON' position. The small flap then covered the undercarriage 'DOWN' selector button until the lever was moved to the brakes 'OFF' position as required for landing – it seemed a reasonable solution to the problem, requiring no complex hydraulic sequencing.

However, apart from handling reports the design department called for retraction and lowering times so, for this purpose, several 'up' and 'down' cycles were made. When, on this flight, the undercarriage was about to be raised, the parking brake was applied but before the 'UP' button was pressed a red warning light came on to indicate high temperature in the hydraulic system. The undercarriage was then retracted. Hazel checked the cockpit indicators for landing – three greens on the undercarriage – dive brakes and half flaps at take-off position – there was no need for further use of the hydraulic system so he proceeded to land, it seemed to be a very smooth one until the toe brakes were recognised as inoperative. Hazel realised that the parking brake was still 'ON', he instantly moved it to 'OFF' but it was too late – all sixteen tyres on the main legs burst and the wheels, too, were damaged beyond repair. As Hazel said, 'A mistake – yes – but a lesson had been learned so modifications ensured that it was not repeated'.

Further handling flights were carried out with the undercarriage up before finally leaving the A&AEE WB771 carried out two Pressure Correction Error flights on the 20 and 21 February. It was on the 22nd that the second Handley Page Test Pilot Mr Dalton Goulding was to fly 771 and carried out a short conversion flight lasting 48 minutes. On 25 February, WB771 returned to HP Radlett flown by Sqn/Ldr Hazelden and Ian Bennett in a flight lasting forty minutes,

It had flown 8hrs and 42 minutes whilst at the A&AEE including its return flight to HP. Now back at HP Radlett with its main runway extended to 7,000ft it was time for the test programme to develop further. On 28 February this started with preliminary stall investigation. The aircraft was then grounded for just over two months for modification and the completion of some additional services to be fitted, including a camera to view the operation of the undercarriage. [This was repeated later whilst in service with the RAF]

Flying started again on 5 May 1953 with a number of handling flights including hatch jettison trials. In May a further undercarriage problem arose when, on landing, the port bogie bounced and stayed in the vertical position. Hazelden made a very smooth 'tip-toe' landing with no damage to the aircraft. On a later flight as Hazel brought it in to land, he selected flaps down and immediately a roll began to develop; thinking that he had a flap actuation malfunction he landed without them. To his astonishment he found that the whole of the flap assembly on one side had disappeared. Appropriate modifications to the fixings were made.

A very intensive test programme checked out the function of the Mach trimmer fitted to compensate for centre of pressure changes due to compressibility effects. It was found necessary to fit a yaw damper to control the tendency, common to swept-wing aircraft, to develop a Dutch roll instability at high altitudes. In a Dutch roll the aeroplane yaws and swings in the rolling plane giving an unpleasant wallowing motion.

As the summer came along it was time for the demonstration flights to senior RAF Officers. The pilots were intrigued by the Victor's ability to land with no flare-out action by them. The later fin height reduction was welcome as it eliminated the capability that was seen by them, and by RAF pilots, as an invitation to exercise less care on the approach. The unusual effect was due to the high tailplane being out of the downwash created by the flaps when in the landing attitude. As soon as the machine arrived at the point where the ground cushion effect became apparent and the throttles were closed, the Victor levelled out and touched down. There then followed rehearsals for the Queens Review of the RAF Flypast on the 15th July at RAF Odiham.

In early September a number of demonstration flights were made from RAE Farnborough before returning on the 14th for a change in paint scheme before the demonstration flights on the 17th 18th, 19th and 21st to the SBAC Airshow at Farnborough, these all being flown from Radlett.

After a break of about a month handling flights were restarted again on the 15 October. Hazel had flown to 50,000ft (15,240m) without experiencing buffet and had reached M0.80 at 47,000ft (14,330m) with power in hand. His assistant, Ken Dalton-Golding, achieved M0.88 at 47,000ft (14,478m) at which height he extended the dive brakes that were in the form of 'petals' at the tail cone. Deceleration was smooth. He was critical of damping in the yaw plane at altitude with the aircraft continuing to 'snake' slightly after the rudder was centralised. These flights continued up to the 31 December with an odd demonstration flight thrown in. The New Year started in mid January with the continuation of the handling flights. It appeared that drag rise due to compressibility had not yet materialised, a good augury for the high-speed end of the range. Hazel reached M0.91 at 47,500ft and reported a slight nose down trim change. In February 1954 he flew at M0.925 at 45,000ft again reporting the slight nose down trim change between M0.90 and 0.91. Steep turns were made at M0.88 and these were buffet free. By the end of the year problems with the braking parachute system had been overcome. [This is a slight aircraft location error; the Braking chute was apparently not fitted to WB771] Unfortunately another flap problem emerged when one of the inboard flaps broke away. The pilots were

HP 80 WB771 at RAE Farnborough. No sign of the Brake Chute doors. HP-HPA

unaware of the loss until after they had landed. By the end of February 1954 the prototype had logged 60 hours and was ready for a major checkout and various modifications to improve aileron effectiveness and some minor changes to extend the flight envelope.

Back in service in June 1954 Hazelden prepared for a series of airspeed indicator calibration trials. This work required steady runs at a height of about 150ft past a special ground-based camera, at different speeds from just above the stall to maximum permissible. The low-level circuits necessary for this test caused considerable annoyance in populated areas such as that surrounding the Radlett airfield so the trials were planned to take place at the airfield of the College of Aeronautics at Cranfield, Beds, in fairly open country. The trials were planned for 14 July and the ground crew, with camera, set off for Cranfield by road with instructions to telephone Radlett when everything was ready. Hazelden would then take-off in the Victor to carry out the test runs and return to base without landing at Cranfield. Since all the flying would be at very low level the endurance of the aircraft would be restricted to little more than two hours. The all clear call came from Cranfield and, almost immediately came another call, this one was from Handley Page's Woodley, Berks, plant asking Hazel to come to Woodley immediately to fly a HPR.2 Marathon, a small four-engined airliner, on an acceptance flight for a Japanese customer. This had been planned for the afternoon to follow the Victor trials at Cranfield, but the customer had to alter his plans so the flight had to take place before lunch. Hazel's deputy, Ken Dalton-Golding had been killed tragically when the

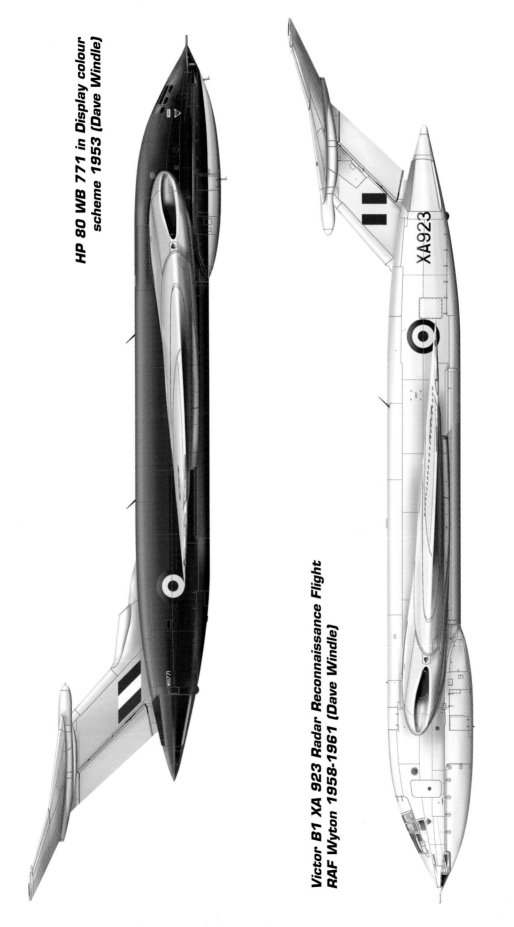

HP 80 WB 771 in Display colour scheme 1953 (Dave Windle)

Victor B1 XA 923 Radar Reconnaissance Flight RAF Wyton 1958-1961 (Dave Windle)

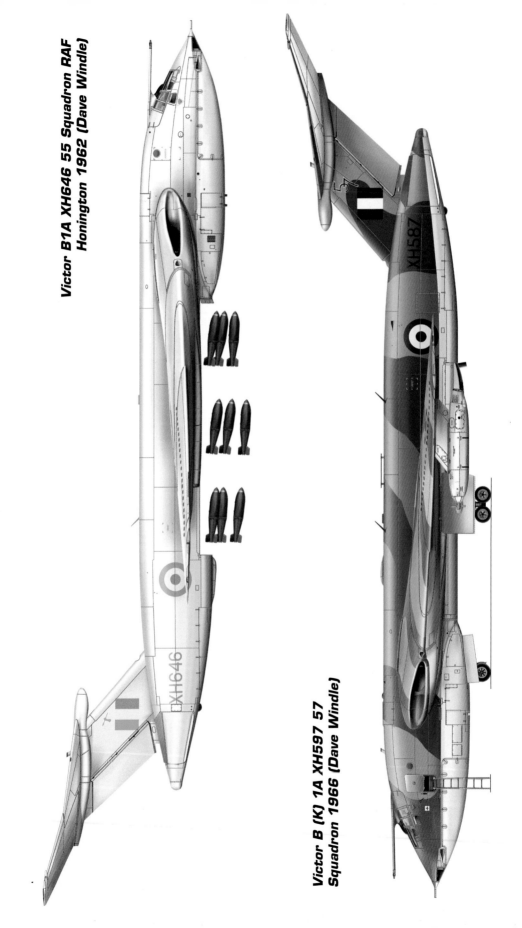

Victor B1A XH646 55 Squadron RAF Honington 1962 (Dave Windle)

Victor B (K) 1A XH597 57 Squadron 1966 (Dave Windle)

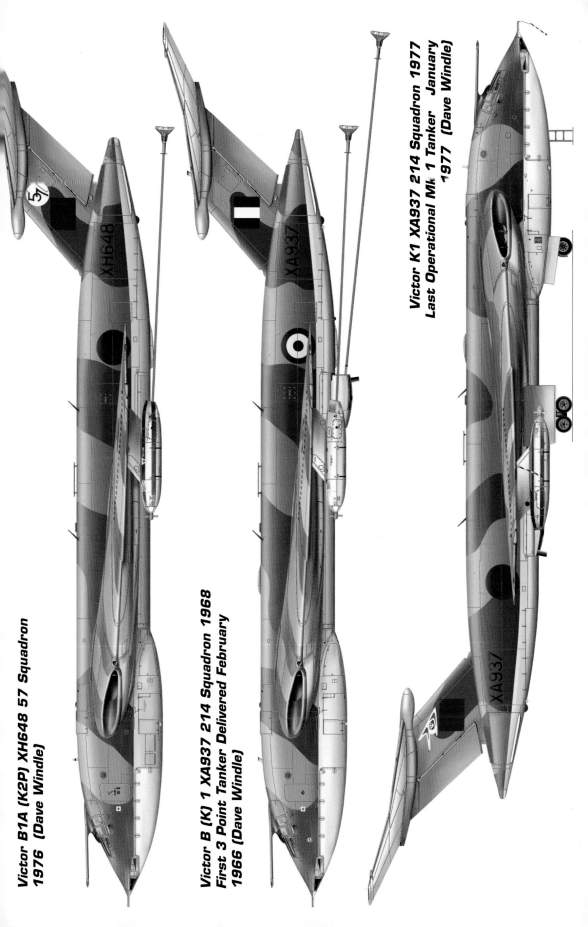

Victor B1A (K2P) XH648 57 Squadron 1976 (Dave Windle)

Victor B (K) 1 XA937 214 Squadron 1968 First 3 Point Tanker Delivered February 1966 (Dave Windle)

Victor K1 XA937 214 Squadron 1977 Last Operational Mk 1 Tanker January 1977 (Dave Windle)

Victor B1 XA 918 on Test and Development flying from HP Radlett 1957 (HP-HPA)

HP 80 1st Prototype in the special colour scheme for the SBAC Show at RAE Farnborough September 1953 (RAF Museum.)

Victor B1 on a Low Level Cross Country Flight showing its unique wing design. (Authors Collection)

Victor B1 XA918 landing at the SBAC Show at RAE Farnborough 1957 (Authors Collection)

Victor B1 XA937 10 Squadron landing at RAAF Butterworth Malaysia 1963 (Authors Collection)

Victor B (K) 1 XA928 57 Squadron 8/66
refuelling Lightning F6 XR761 5 Squadron
[Authors Collection]

Victor K1 XA930 55 Squadron undertaking Air-to-Air Refuelling Trials with Phantom F4M XT852 in the USA (Douglas Photo)

Victor K1 XA939 214 Squadron Old Colours Scheme 1966 (Authors Collection)

Victor K1 XA939 214 Squadron Revised Markings and post Cart Spring Repair 1974 (Authors Collection)

Victor B1 XA 927 10 Squadron Pre Anti Flash Markings 1958 (Authors Collection)

Victor K1 XA937 214 Squadron at RAF Laarbruch January 1975 attending 15 Squadron 60th Anniversary Display (Authors Photo)

Victor B1 XA930 Landing at A&AEE Boscombe down whilst under taking Probe Trials 2/58 (Authors Collection)

Victor K1A XH588 55 Squadron undertaking refuelling trials with CAF F5 150 1971 (Authors Collection)

Captain and Co-Pilots Position of Victor B1A (K2P) XH648 at IWM Duxford 1984 (Heather Brooks Photo)

Victor XH589 15 Squadron Pre Anti Flash Markings 1959 (Authors Collection)

Victor B (K) 1A XH618 Production TI aircraft at A&AEE undertaking trials with Belfast XR371 (via Alan Fisher)

**Victor K1A XH618
57 Squadron 1973
(Authors Collection)**

**Victor K1A XH650
214 Squadron 1975
(Authors Collection)**

**Victor K1A XH618 57 Squadron refuelling Buccaneer S2A XV348 1974
(Authors Collection**

Victor B1A XH587 15 Squadron in the USA on joint ECM Trials 1963 (Authors Collection)

Victor B1A XH591 RAF Honington Wing at RAF Luqa Malta 1965 (Authors Collection)

controls of his Canberra jammed on his approach to Radlett over the railway embankment,

On the 24 June Taffy Ecclestonee had his first familiarisation flight and then on 27th a further four flights were undertaken. Taffy Ecclestone's first solo was on 28 June and over the next two weeks he was to gain further experience. On the 14 July he could see that Hazelden could not be in two places at the same time and therefore he immediately asked if he could do the Victor job. After some thought Hazelden agreed and gave Taffy a thorough briefing on the trials, going into detail on the circuit and its landmarks. He was quite confident in Ecclestone's competence to carry out the trials and so set off by road for Woodley.

At 1226hrs on that day Mr Ecclestone and his flight-test observers Ian Bennett, A. Cook and Brian Heithersay took off to carry out Pressure Error Correction Flights at Cranfield. However, after a few runs and at 13.10hours the tail plane parted company with the fin and the aircraft crashed killing all the crew. (Tailplane flutter leading to the separation of the tail plane from the top of the fin during high-speed low-level flypast for position error calibration was the cause)

The Marathon flight was carried out and afterwards the Japanese was taken to a local restaurant to be entertained to lunch. As the party arrived Hazelden was asked by the manager to telephone Radlett most urgently. He was shocked to receive the news that the Victor had crashed. Taffy, with his observer, Ian Bennett, Bruce Heithersay and Albert Cook were flying above the runway at high speed, after several such runs ground observers saw the leading edge of the tailplane rise fractionally from the fin and suddenly detach, the Victor immediately nosing down and disintegrating as it hit the runway at high speed. This tragic accident to a prototype that had shown such great promise and killed a highly skilled and dedicated crew was a fearful shock to all who had an interest in it and a 24 hour-a-day test programme was

Park Street Test House. HP-HPA

Victors at Handley Page Test Facility, Park Street. HP-HPA

instituted to resolve the problem that had caused it. Two weeks later it was announced that the metal around the three tailplane fixing bolts showed fatigue cracks that had allowed the bolts to loosen and shear one after the other. Modifications to the fin included an alteration to its construction, the fixing of the tailplane by four bolts to reduce the stress concentration and the reduction of the fin and rudder height to decrease even further the stress levels at the fin to tailplane joint.

The aircraft had carried out a total, of 90 flights and flown 86 hours 10 minutes.

The test flying carried out by WB775 was much more comprehensive and went on over a number of years. The most significant piece of testing was the Flutter programme and the following is a detailed account of what was undertaken.

Flutter

'Jock' Still joined Handley Page as a test pilot with some trepidation, he was aware of the deaths of Duggie Broomfield, Ken Dalton-Golding and Taffy Ecclestone and wondered if the Victor programme was a fairly dodgy one, however, he had total faith in Hazelden as an extremely competent test pilot with long experience in 'B' Squadron at Boscombe Down. He also had equal regard for John Allam so agreed to join the company. He was allotted the flutter programme that had already commenced with the second prototype, WB775, which had been equipped with eccentric excitation devices in the rear fuselage; these were weights that were rotated by electric motors to give differing vibration frequencies at different motor rpm.

Right from the original design studies for the Victor, flutter had been recognised as one of the most crucial and difficult areas. There was concentration upon the swept wing at a Mach number well beyond the critical number and, from that point, the particular problems associated with a crescent wing; the T-tail was a new concept for the company so it, too, required special consideration. The study was approached on a broad front: calculations, wind tunnel tests,

HP 80 WB775-1. HP-HPA.

ground resonance testing and, finally, flight tests. Some dropped model tests were also carried out.

The work on the wing had been entirely successful but, as has been recounted earlier, the calculations on the tail were not wholly successful for three reasons: the joint between the fin and tailplane was less stiff than on the wind tunnel test model, the dihedral on the tailplane was large to give additional lateral area at little structural cost when the fin twisted in a roll the forces exerted by the dihedral were much larger than had been anticipated. Excitation of the weights was inertial during flight and, as the critical frequency was low at around 2-10 cps, the amplitude applied at the important frequencies was also low. To avoid turbulent air affecting the recorded readings the sorties were carried out in calm air early in the morning. To identify the flutter speed the tailplane of WB775 was deliberately weakened so that when the instrumentation indicated proximity to the disintegration speed, strengthening of the tailplane would take the maximum flight speed into the 'safety zone'. When the exciters had been used to initiate the vibration they were immediately braked so that the rate of decay could be recorded, the illustrations show the principles involved. If the decay does not occur satisfactorily, as soon as the exciters

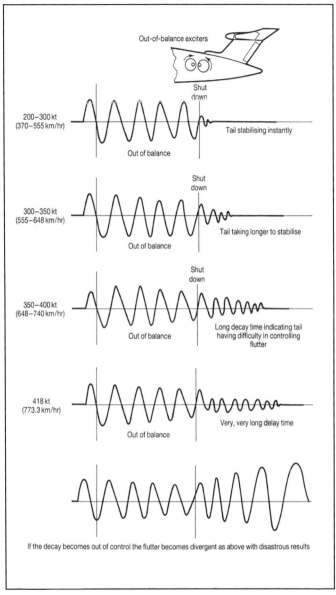

are braked the flutter can become divergent and end in structural failure. Jock approached all these flights with a high degree of prudence but, on one of the last ones, at around 415kts the exciters were started at 20,000ft, somewhere over Lincolnshire the problems arose. In Jock's own words: '*There was a BANG and the aircraft started to buck and weave, pretty well out of control; many emergency "dolls-eye" indicators started flashing on the instrument panel and an enormous degree of vibration developed. I warned Jock Ogilvy, my observer; to stand by to eject and then pulled the machine into a fairly steep climb, at the same time I closed the throttles of all four engines. As speed dropped the vibration diminished but did not vanish entirely, although, by the time I had reached 25-30,000ft speed had fallen to about 250kt. The aircraft appeared to be controllable so I turned south giving quick résumés on the RT to Radlett control, at the same time I called out "Mayday" on the radio. As I flew south, by deduction from the evidence on the dolls-eyes of the emergency panel, I concluded that*

HP80 WB771take off at SBAC Farnborough 1953. HP-HPA

HP80 WB771 fly-by at SBAC Farnborough 1953. HP-HPA

HP80 WB771 landing at SBAC Farnborough 1953. HP-HPA

something had happened to the starboard wing. I was also losing fuel rapidly from the tanks in that wing. Quick calculations indicated that fuel might suffice to reach Radlett. However, some of the gauges were entirely blank and I did not know if the tanks were empty or the gauges unserviceable. A bonus was a radio message from Peter Bugge, a de Havilland test pilot flying a Comet out of Hatfield in the vicinity of the Victor and he offered assistance. I gratefully acknowledged and asked him to fly alongside to investigate the condition of the starboard wing. Within two minutes he was formatting with me and reported that I had lost a large part of the wing and fuel was pouring out of the hole.

By this time Radlett control had everything on emergency standby – ambulance, fire wagons and British Rail whose London to the North line passed alongside the airfield and had to be crossed to land! I decided upon a "straight-in" approach, but as speed reduced I experienced more and more difficulty in holding up the right wing until all the trim facility was used up. As I lowered the flaps on the final approach, we experienced even greater vibration – this was caused by the aircraft shedding even more of the damaged wing plus some of the landing flaps. At l50kt I found that I could only just hold the wing up, although the control column was fully over so I decided to land at this speed even though the normal was 125-130kt so, at the higher speed I managed to place the wheels firmly on the runway and deployed the tail-braking parachute.

I was very thankful when I felt the "slow-down" jolt as the 'chute opened and, with full foot brakes on, we came to a halt 200 yards from the end of the runway. It transpired that I had lost a substantial section of the wing area at the trailing edge between the aileron and the landing flap – but, as each piece tore away with the vibration, it also took additional pieces with it. The RAF did a great job in recovering virtually all the wing debris spread over miles of countryside between Lincoln and Huntingdon with another large amount on the run-in to Radlett when the flaps were lowered. Thankfully, all the bits, about 200 in all, fell in open country.

The design office was able to establish that the cause of this near-disaster was the trailing-edge box of the wing that was not supposed to be taking any strain during flutter tests. This area was suitably strengthened and we went on to clear its maximum flutter "envelope".'

This extraordinary occurrence showed the Victor to be an aeroplane of remarkable aerodynamic and structural quality in that it could continue to fly after such a major aberration and was capable of being landed safely back at base by a pilot of great courage and dedication. The incident led to Handley Page being recognised at the time as the leader in flutter investigation and they advised many other aircraft builders at home and overseas. Boeing was experiencing some wing flutter with the '707' due to uneven consumption of fuel in the wing tanks. Jock Still had a number of discussions and flights with their test pilots including Boeing's chief test pilot the renowned Tex Johnston who, at the Seattle Power Boat Races in 1954, was due to carry out a flypast in the prototype Dash 80, as it was known. Not content with just a sedate pass over the crowd of 200,000 people he carried out two rolls at altitude and then came down to a very low level and repeated the manoeuvre – with a full test crew on board! John Allam and Spud Murphy demonstrated barrel rolls and half loops at the 1958 SBAC Show.

In concluding the account of the flutter programme it is appropriate to quote Godfrey Lee who, in an Aerospace article on Victor development, commented 'In my opinion these flight tests were outstandingly and courageously done and I consider that the crew, Jock Still, the pilot, with Frank Haye and Jock Ogilvy, the observers, deserve great credit for this work'. John Allam, Geoff Wass and other pilots were also involved in this part of the programme.

I do not intend to elaborate on all the aircraft used for test and development flying. Therefore I have compiled the following compilation of the aircrafts' history. The date precedes the activity on all the test and development aircraft and you will find further listing as you proceed through the book.

WB 771. Manufacture started in 1949 at HP Cricklewood in the Experimental Shop. Ready to move 24/5. Components moved to A&AEE Boscombe Down 6/52 for final assembly and system testing. The Compass Swing and Taxi trials were carried out on 20/12 1430-1615 1.45hrs: Sdn/Ldr H G Hazelden Chief Test Pilot and Mr. I K Bennet Chief Flight Test EngineerFirst Flight 24/12 1215-1235. 20 mins (17min) at A&AEE Sdn/ Ldr H G Hazelden and Mr I K Bennet.
1953: 3/1:30/1:4/2(two): 5/2:9/2:13/2:18/2:19/2:20/2:21/2:22/2(two) 24/2:Handling Flights: First U/C retract 9/2 1546-1606 20 mins: 20/2: 21/2 PEs at A&AEE Boscombe Down. First Flight for Mr. Dalton-Goulding 22/2: First Flight with Mr. Dalton Goulding I/C 22/2 48 min with Mr. I.K Bennett: Returned to HP Radlett 24/2:1249-1329 40mins Sdn/Ldr HG Hazelden Mr. I.K Bennett: Total Flying 8.36hrs: Preliminary Stall Investigation Mr. Dalton Goulding; 28/2:2/5:12/5:16/5:23/5:7/6(two): 14/6:17/6: Handling Flights: 17/6: (photography): 17/6 (Mr Dalton Goulding, Mr. W Steele & Sdn/Ldr Baldwin): 22/6 (Sdn/Ldr Hazelden Mr. R Williams Sdn Ldr Baldwin) (PEs): 25/6: (Mr. Dalton- Goulding & Mr. R Williams) 26/5(two) Mr Dalton Goulding Mr. R Williams, (2nd Flight) Sdn/Ldr Hazelden Mr. Steele (2 Handling Flight at 45,000ft): 28/6 Handling Flight Mr Dalton Goulding Mr R Williams: 30/6 Mr Dalton Goulding, Mr. R. Williams Handling Flight Photo and Stalls: 10/7(two) Fly Past Rehearsal and Air to Air Photography: RAF Review at RAF Odiham 15/7 1530-1626 (Sdn/Ldr H G Hazelden & Mr. R Williams) (24.05hrs): 17/7(two) (Stalls) 19/7:20/7:21/7 (Demonstration Flight ACM Vernon Brown) 18/8 Demonstration Flight: 21/8 (two) (42000ft): 2/9(Air test): 3/9 (Demonstration Flight): 5/9 to SBAC Show (Sdn /Ldr Hazelden, Sdn/Ldr Baldwin & Mr W. Steele):7/9:8/9: 9/9/ (Sdn/Ldr Hazelden, Mr. Dalton Goulding Mr. W Steele) 10/9:11/9:12/9:13/9: (Mr. R. Williams) Returned HP Radlett 14/9 (Sdn/Ldr Hazelden, Mr Dalton Goulding, Sdn/Ldr Baldwin, Mr. W Steele) painted Matt Black/Red Cheat Line/Silver Grey for the 1953 SBAC Show 17/9: 18/9(2): 19/9: 21/9: (Demonstration Flight): 15/10: 16/10:30/10:2/11:3/11:4/11(2)12/11:13/11: Handling Flights:14/11 (Demonstration Flight): 16/11:28/12:31/12: Handling Flight: Camera to View U/C 5/53: Hatch Jettison Trials 5/53
1954:16/1:19/1 21/1:26/1:2/2(three): 3/2(two): 4/2:5/2:14/6:(two) 16/6:18/6:24/6(three)

Handling Flights 27/6(four)(Mr.R Ecclestone 1st Flight): 28/6(two) (Mr R Ecclestone I/C first flight): 29/6(two): 30/6: 1/7(two): 2/7: 8/7:9/7(two) 13/7:Handling Flights:
WO Cranfield 14/7: 1226- 1310hrs last flight time 44 mins.
Pilot Mr R Ecclestone. Mr. I K Bennet, Mr. A Cook and Mr B. Heithersay: All killed:
The Pilot had carried out eight flights.
Tail plane parted company with fin. (Tailplane flutter leading to separation of tail from top of fin during low-level high-speed flypasts for position error calibration).
Total flying time 86 hrs 10 min 90 test flights.

HP 80 WB775 Take Off HP Radlett. HP-HPA

1954: WB775

First Flight 11/9 0939-1035. 56 min (Sdn/Ldr Hazelden) (305 HP Test Flights (366Hrs) 11/9:12/9:(SBAC Demonstration): 12/9:(Handling Flight): 18/9(RAF Demonstration Flight:) 28/9(J W Allam First Flight): 29/9:1/10: 2/10: 7/10:9/10:13/10(First Flight J W Allam I/C)(two): 25/10(two): 26/10: 22/11: 27/11:30/11: 3/12(two): 9/12: (Handling Flights): 9/12: (Demonstration Flight): 10/12(Stalls): 11/12-1/2/55 Modifications:

HP 80 WB775 with HP Flight Crew and Sir Fredrick Handley Page. HP-HPA

HP 80 WB775 landing at Farnborough 1955 using four Brake Chutes. HP-HPA.

1955: Handling Flights unless indicated

1/2(Main Bomb Bay opened) 3/2:6/2:15/2(Demonstration Flight): 1/3(First Yaw Damper): 2/3(Flash Bomb Bay Opened): 3/3/: 4/3/: 10/3/: 14/3/(3)(Familiarisation Flights for A&AEE) 15/3(2)(A&AEE): 17/3(A&AEE) Sdn/Ldr Tomlinson & Flt/Lt Moreau): 18/3:20/3:21/3: (Handling Flight A&AEE Crew) 28/329/3:30/3:31/3:1/4 (Handling Flight): 1/4: (Demonstration Flight): 4/4 (Demonstration Flight): 6/4:23/5: (Handling Flight): 24/5 (HP Radlett to A&AEE Boscombe Down: 24/5 to 26/5 (eleven flights covering Handling and Night flying) (Sdn/Ldr Hazelden & J W Allam): 26/5 A&AEE Boscombe Down to HP Radlett: 6/6:10/6: (Handling Flights) 14/6: 5/7 (Demonstration Flights 3) 13/6: 15/6: 16/6: (Dummy Bombing run Orfordness) 18/6 (to Le Bourget Paris Air Show Demonstration and return): 20/6 (HP Radlett to RAE Farnborough): 22/6 (RAE Farnborough to HP Radlett): 23/6(two) (Handling Flights): 27/6:28/6:29/6(two) 30/6: 1/7 (PEs at High and Low level at AAEE Boscombe Down): (4/7 Bomb door Vibration test): 5/7 (Demonstration Flight 2): 6/7 (Handling Flight): 7/7, 8/7, 9/7 (RAE Farnborough Demonstration and return): 27/7, 28/7 (two) 2/8, 7/8, 8/8, 10/8, 12/8, 16/6, 17/85 (Handling Flight): 17/8 (Elevator Load Test): 19/8 (Demonstration Flight): 19/8, 22/8, (Buffett Boundary test): 24/8, (two) (Tail Strain and Buffett Boundary test): 25/8 (Stalls and thrust drag levels): 1/9, (Air Test): 3/9 (HP Radlett to RAE Farnborough SBAC Show Demonstrations Painted Curellian Blue): 5/9, 6/9, 7/9, 8/9(two): 9/9, 10/9, 11/9, 12/9 (RAE Farnborough to HP Radlett): 5/10, 14/10, 18/10 (four), 4/10, 26/10, 23/11(two), 24/11: (Handling Flight), 18/12, 21/12, (Handling Flight Flutter): Flying hours at 31/12 133.05hrs.

1956: 11/1: (two) (Flutter) 5/1: 16/1: 18/1 (three): 21/1:22/1:24/1(three): 27/1: (Flutter and to RAE Farnborough) 27/1:1/2 (RAE Farnborough to HP Radlett) 2/2: 25/2: 29/2: 4/3: 5/3: 7/3: (two):8/3 (two): 9/3: 10/3: 12/3: 13/3: 14/3: 15/3: (Flutter) 21/3 (HP Radlett to RAE Farnborough) 22/3 (Air test): 23/3 (RAE Farnborough to HP, Radlett): 26/3 (HP Radlett to RAE Farnborough): 28/3: 3/4: 4/4 (two): 5/4 (two) (Bombing trials from RAE Farnborough (Return to HP Radlett 3/4: 5/4): 7/4: 10/4: 12/4: 15/5: 17/5: 23/5: (Auto Pilot Test): 25/5: 30/5: 1/6:4/6: 13/6 (two): 21/6: 22/6: 23/6: 24/6: 28/6: 29/6: 30/6: 2/7: 3/7: 6/7: 7/7: 10/7: (Flutter) 4/7: 11/7 (Demonstration Flights):13/7: 22/7: (Flutter: 24/7:25/7: 27/7 (Aileron Measurement Tests): 26/7: 2/8: 9/8: 14/8: 17/8:1/9: 3/9: 4/9: 6/9: 18/9 19/9: 20/9: 24/9: 25/9: 27/9: 29/9: 3/10: 4/10: 6/10: 9/19: 11/10: 12/10: 17/10: 19/10: 20/10: 22/10: 29/10: (Flight Flutter): 18/9 (Familiarisation) (248.21Hrs).

1957: 16/4 (Air test) 29/4: 30/4: 1/5(2): 3/5: 4/5: 7/5: 8/5: 10/5: 11/5: 13/5: 14/5: 15/5: 20/5(2): 21/5: 22/5: 23/5: 28/5: 29/5 30/5: 31/5: 1/6: 5/6 (two) 7/6: 11/6: 17/6: 21/6: 26/6: 1/7: 3/7: 4/7: 8/7: 23/7: 24/7: (Flutter): 30/7 (two) (Flight For MPs): 26/9: 1/10: 4/10: 6/10: 9/10:

6/11: 7/11: 14/11 (Flutter) 28/11 (Trim Curves) (297.32hrs)
1958: 20/1 (Air Test): 24/1: 27/1: 3/2: 4/2: 11/2: 14/2: 18/2: 20/2: 28/2: 3/3: 4/3 (RCM Trials) (Mr Burton): 9/6: (Handling Flight): 13/6: 16/618/6 (two): 26/6: 15/8: 19/8: 25/8: 29/8: 9/9: 24/9: 30/9: 1/10: 14/10: 17/10: 21/10: 27/10: 3/11: (RAT Tests): 30/10(PEs)
1959: 10/1: 6/1:19/1:21/1:23/1:3/2:21/2:2/3:11/3: (Drooped Leading Edge trials): 7/4: 10/4: (Trim Curves) (W.R. Burton)
Last Flight 10/4/59 Total Time 366 hrs Grounded: Damaged Flap Gear.
Dismantled 1959 main components to RAE to assist in XH668 crash investigation/(Water Tank).

The following Test Pilots flew the two Victor prototypes
In preparation for the first flight of the HP80/Victor. Sdn/Ldr Hazelden undertook the following flights to familiarise himself with the Armstrong Siddeley Sapphire engines. All these flights were undertaken from HP Radlett. It is possible further flights were undertaken from other locations but no records are available to the author.
Hastings TG 583 fitted with two Sapphire SA 2 engines in the outboard position.
13/11/50   20mins
6/2/51   45mins
12/3/51   2hr 05mins
22/3/51   1hr 15mins
25/5/51   45mins
30/5/51   Aircraft to The NGTE

Canberra WD 933 fitted with two Sapphire SA6 engines 100 Series.
17/7/52   25mins Familiarisation
23/7/52   1hr 10 min with Dalton Goulding

Sdn/Ldr H Hazelden   24/12/52- 14/7/54   53(WB771) Test Flights
WB771, WB775   42(WB775) Test Flights
Mr Dalton-Goulding   22/2/53-25/2/54   29 Test Flights
WB771
Killed in Canberra B2 WJ 622 Crash 25/2/54 Radlett
Mr R Ecclestone   28/6/54-14/7/54   8 Test Flights
WB771
Killed in WB771 crash 14/7/54 Cranfield
Mr J Still   26/10/55-7/57   105 Test Flights
WB775
Mr J W Allam   28/9/54-10/4/59   112 Test Flights
WB775,
Mr W R Burton   10/1/57-10/4/59   46 Test Flights
WB775
Mr P Murphy   9/58-10/4/59   3 Test Flights
WB775
Total Test Flights   WB771   90   86hrs 10 mins
                          WB775   308   366hrs
                          Total   398   452hrs 10mins

A&AEE Assessment of WB775 March 1955

1st Part of Report No. A.A.E.E./915
8th June, 1955.

AEROPLANE AND ARMAMENT EXPERIMENTAL ESTABLISHMENT
BOSCOMBE DOWN

Victor WB.775 (2nd prototype)
(4 x Sa.6)

Preview Assessment

A.& A.E.E. Ref: AAEE/5701,o/1
Period of Test: 14th – 31st March, 1955

Summary

A preview assessment has been made on the second prototype Victor, flying at an intermediate c.g. position and light weight (~ 100,000 lb.). This aircraft was restricted to 248 knots I.A.S. and 2.25g, whereas production aircraft are designed for 415 knots E.A.S. and 2.7g with an operational take-off weight of about 165,000 lb. The prototype was also non-representative of production aircraft in respect of engine thrust, keel surface geometry and cockpit layout.

As tested the aircraft was easy and pleasant to fly and appeared to have a high potential as a bomber aircraft. No adverse features were encountered up to the maximum true Mach number attained (0.95), which was reached with no rapid increase of drag being apparent, and it is considered that, if possible, the transonic potentiality should be exploited.

The aircraft appeared to be a satisfactory bombing platform, but failure of the auto-stabiliser would seriously impair the accuracy of bomb-aiming. The Mach number/buffet threshold is believed to be adequate for the bombing needs of initial production aircraft, but may not be adequate for increased operating altitudes made possible by the introduction of more powerful engines.

Very severe buffet was encountered near the straight stall, causing concern for structural safety. Although the stall has no operational significance the buffet level should be reduced, if possible, lest it incur embarrassing speed restrictions at higher weights. Flexing of the airframe was apparent in manoeuvres at high Mach number and, in the light of recent experience on other aircraft, the structural consequences of high Mach number buffet should be investigated.

Particularly commendable features were the light and effective controls, the aircraft response to control movement, the excellent infinitely variable airbrakes and the small changes of trim with speed and change in configuration.

Various aspects of the cockpit layout were unsatisfactory, in particular crew comfort and power control safeguards. The field of view was restricted and was felt to be inadequate in conditions of poor visibility. Some concern was also felt for possible external reflections in the windscreen at night.

Certain features mentioned within the report should be investigated.

This report is issued with the authority of

[signature]

Air Commodore
Commanding A.& A.E.E.

1. Introduction

At the request of Handley Page Ltd., a preliminary flight assessment has been made on the second prototype Victor WB.775, the aircraft being serviced at and flown from the Firm's airfield at Radlett.

Following the loss of the first prototype, due to tail flutter, the limiting airspeeds had been restricted to 248 knots I.A.S. at sea level and 0.9 I.M.N. above 45,000 ft. pending further ground tests and structural modifications. This necessarily limited the scope of the tests but sufficient experience was gained within these flight limitations to permit a general assessment of the aircraft's potentialities.

At the commencement of these tests the Firm had completed a total of 126 hours development flying. In all, a further 14½ hours were obtained by three A.& A.E.E. pilots, including 2½ hours spent on familiarisation.

2. Details of aircraft relevant to tests

Victor WB.775 was the second prototype Handley Page 80, a heavy/medium bomber designed to Specification B35/46. It was a mid-wing monoplane of conventional layout having a crescent wing planform and swept tail surfaces. The power units were Armstrong Siddeley Sa.6 turbo-jet engines, having a static thrust rating of 8150 lb. (each engine) at I.C.A.N. sea level conditions and take-off engine speed.

During these tests the aircraft was flown at an intermediate c.g. position of 38% S.M.C., undercarriage up, at take-off weights between 92,000 lb. and 104,000 lb. Take-off weight of production aircraft with full internal fuel and 10,000 lb. bomb load is estimated to be 167,000 lb.

Details of the aircraft, the flight limitations and other data relevant to these tests are given in Appendix 1.

The main differences between the prototype and production aircraft are listed below.

(a) The fuselage nose section will be extended by 42 inches on the latter.

(b) The fin and rudder will be cropped by 20 inches and the dorsal fillet deleted on production aircraft.

(c) Production power units will be Armstrong Siddeley Sa.7 engines (static thrust 10,200 lb.).

3. Scope of tests

The test programme was based on the requirements of Instruction 317 of the A.& A.E.E. Handbook of Test Methods, modified to conform with the flight limitations imposed. The main object of the tests was to assess the aircraft's flying qualities with reference to the bomber role. Within the scope of these tests it was not possible to investigate the characteristics in flight with asymmetric thrust, extreme sideslips and reduced power control output.

4. Results of tests

The results of the tests, based on detailed flight reports and analysis of quantitative flight records, are given in Appendices 2 to 10[*]. The salient features are discussed below. Mach numbers quoted are true values, except where otherwise stated.

4.1 General appreciation. Production aircraft will have an operational take-off weight of about 167,000 lb. and are designed for the following conditions; V_D 415 knots E.A.S., M 0.95, and n_1 2.7. As flown at a maximum
/weight.....

[*] Limited circulation only.

weight of only 104,000 lb., restricted to 248 knots I.A.S. and 2.25g and
differing from production aircraft in respect of engine thrust and certain
geometric aspects, the Victor possessed easy and pleasant flying qualities and
appeared to have a high potential as a bomber aircraft. It is emphasized that
this Establishment is not in a position to estimate fully the effects of the
very large weight increase to production aircraft although this has been taken
into account as far as possible.

All controls were light and effective, response to control movement was
good and changes of trim with speed or configuration were small. The power
controls appeared to be very satisfactory and to have adequate response rate
within the flight limitations quoted. No adverse features such as nosing down,
wing dropping or noticeable buffeting were encountered up to 0.95 Mach number,
which was reached without any apparent rapid increase of drag. The aircraft
was considered to have transonic potentialities worthy of exploitation.

As far as could be judged the aircraft appeared to be a satisfactory
bombing platform; failure of the auto-stabiliser would however seriously impair
ability for accurate bomb-aiming. It is believed that the Mach number/buffet
threshold will permit adequate manoeuvring for the bombing needs of initial
production aircraft. The adequacy of the buffet threshold determined in these
tests should be considered against the possible introduction of more powerful
engines and consequent higher operating altitudes.

Extremely severe buffet was encountered during the approach to the
straight stall, causing concern for the safety of the structure under such
conditions. The stall is of no operational significance on this class of
aircraft but, if possible, the buffet level should be reduced lest it result
in embarrassing restrictions of minimum airspeed at operational weights. The
flexible nature of the airframe was apparent to the crew in manoeuvres and the
consequences of high Mach number buffet should be investigated as soon as
possible in the light of recent experience on other aircraft in this class.
It should be noted that it was not possible to assess the aileron and rudder
control forces in relation to the strength limitations of the airframe.

The "self-landing" characteristic was considered to be of no especial
advantage, though with the light and sensitive elevator control it resulted
in only small control forces and movements during landing, which was a
pleasant departure from the characteristics of previous heavy aircraft. The
infinitely variable air brakes were found to be a most effective means of
controlling the approach path.

Due to the wide differences in engine thrust and aircraft weight between
the aircraft as flown and the production version it was not possible to make
a valid assessment of the performance capabilities. It can however be said
that 48,000 ft. was attained with comparative ease, and a Mach number of 0.915
was reached in level flight.

Various aspects of the cockpit layout were unsatisfactory, in particular
crew comfort and power control safeguards. The field of view was restricted
and felt to be inadequate in conditions of poor visibility. Concern was also
felt for the possibility of external windscreen reflections at night (to be
tested shortly at A.& A.E.E.).

4.2 Aerodynamic qualities

4.2.1 Ground handling, take-off and landing. It was necessary
for the power control units to be switched off during taxying to prevent
overheating, and, apart from pre take-off cockpit drill, there were no positive
means of preventing take-off with the units still switched off. It is strongly
recommended that a mechanical lock, or similar device, be incorporated to
prevent the throttles being opened for take-off under these conditions. Ground
handling was satisfactory though the nose wheel steering control requires
improvements to eliminate a "dead-spot" and/to make it more accessible to short
pilots.

/The.......

The view during taxying was not good but was considered to be adequate. In the air the field of view was poor, particularly during the circuit and approach. Under conditions of poor visibility the view was considered to be inadequate and it was easy to misjudge turning points in the circuit.

The handling characteristics during take-off and landing presented no difficulties once pilots had accustomed themselves to the light and sensitive elevator control characteristics and the automatic flare-out on entering the ground effect. This "self-landing" characteristic was not felt to be of particular advantage, apart from reducing the level of control forces, and pilots preferred to follow normal flying techniques. In order to achieve smooth "self-landings" the engines are not throttled until after touch down, contrary to normal practice where thrust is reduced over the runway threshold. The infinitely variable air brakes were found to be a most effective control over the approach path and were highly praised by the pilots. Aileron control on the approach was good and "side-step" manoeuvres could be made with ease. Trim changes were commendably small throughout take-off, landing and the overshoot.

4.2.2 Behaviour near the stall. Full stalling tests had not been carried out by the Firm at the time of these trials and the aircraft was restricted to a minimum speed of 95 knots I.A.S. in all configurations, with an over-riding limitation that the nose flaps were to be down, from considerations of longitudinal stability at all speeds below 130 knots I.A.S.

At the test weights (90-93,000 lb.) light airframe buffeting began in the region of 125 knots I.A.S. in all configurations, and increased in intensity with reduction of speed until a heavy shuddering began in the region of 100 knots I.A.S. This shudder was so severe as to cause concern for structural safety. All controls remained effective down to the minimum speed attained and no instability tendencies could be detected.

The risk of damage to the structure and electronic equipment, incurred by flight under conditions of heavy and sustained buffet, is unacceptable and although the straight stall has little or no significance on this class of aircraft the level of buffeting should, if possible, be reduced. It is possible that the present buffet characteristics might dictate an excessive approach speed at the higher landing weights of production aircraft, particularly in the case of an immediate re-land after take-off at maximum weight. In any case it is considered that for purposes of pilot familiarisation with the low speed flying characteristics the aircraft should be restricted to a minimum speed corresponding to the onset of heavy shuddering. There is adequate warning, by progressive buffeting, of the approach to this condition.

4.2.3 Longitudinal characteristics

(a) Static stability was assessed as positive throughout the permitted speed and altitude range, though accurate assessment at the extremes of the speed range was made difficult by the severe shuddering near the stall and the transient conditions at maximum Mach number. Elevator control forces to change speed were light and response to control movement was very good apart from the expected deterioration at high Mach number which was, however, slight.

(b) The longitudinal short period oscillation was generally well damped, though at high altitudes a poorly damped pitching oscillation, which was not apparent to the pilots, was noted on the trace records of turns and pull-outs at high Mach number, persisting until normal 1g flight was resumed (see Fig.A6/1). This characteristic will require further investigation, particularly with increase of aircraft weight and any extension of maximum Mach number.

(c) The longitudinal trim changes with change of configuration were:-

Lowering undercarriage   Slight nose up
Extending nose flaps   Slight nose down

/Extending.....

Extending main flaps	
To take-off setting	Slight nose down.
Take-off to full flap	Moderate nose down.
Extending air brakes	Momentary slight nose down followed by slight nose up.
Opening bomb doors	Slight nose up.

(d) Specific stick force per 'g' measurements were not made, but its value was estimated to be about 40 lb. between 0.80 and 0.90 I.M.N. at 45,000 ft. This value was considered to be satisfactory, but final judgement must be reserved until tests have been made over a representative range of altitude and aircraft loading; it may be noted that it is within the limits proposed in J.A.C. Paper 626, i.e. 63 to 27 lb.

4.2.4 Lateral stability and control characteristics

(a) The damping of the lateral oscillation without auto-stabilisation was inadequate. At 10,000 ft. the oscillation was poorly damped and did not fulfil A.P.970 requirements (that it shall damp to half amplitude in one cycle); above 40,000 ft. the oscillation was divergent (see Fig.A7/1).

The periodic time of the oscillation was of the order of 4 seconds and with practice and a high degree of concentration a pilot could control and eliminate the oscillation for limited periods in straight flight. Dutch rolling occurred in turns.

The auto-stabiliser installation was not in its finalised form, nor were its settings necessarily those for optimum damping, but even so it enabled the lateral oscillation to be well damped.

It is to be expected that the damping of the oscillation will be less on production aircraft due to the reduction in effective fin area and increase in aircraft inertia. Auto-stabilisation will be essential at all times if the aircraft is to fulfil its operational role effectively. Without auto-stabilisation prolonged flight at high altitude would prove tiring, a bombing run would require a high degree of concentration and it is doubtful if a successful attack would result. Serious consideration should be given to the practicability of duplicating the auto-stabiliser in production aircraft (see para. 4.2.7 for further comments on bombing platform characteristics).

(b) The ailerons were light and effective at all speeds. The aircraft's response to control movements was immediate at the higher speeds but deteriorated at low speeds, the response being rated as moderate but adequate on the approach. Similar control characteristics were noted for the rudder.

The rolling performance was impressive for the size of aircraft, particularly at high altitude where steady rates of roll of 25 degrees/sec. were achieved with only about one third aileron displacement (see Fig.A7/2).

(c) The aircraft was easy to trim laterally but the aileron break-out forces proved disconcerting for small corrections under instrument flying conditions. Coupled with the aileron break-out forces was a dead spot in the centre of the control travel. This feature should be remedied and the break-out forces reduced.

(d) The aileron/rudder interconnection setting of 0.35:1 would appear to be adequate for all normal conditions of flight. Slight adverse yaw was only noted when specifically looked for at low indicated airspeeds. It is for consideration whether the intended complication of varying the aileron/rudder interconnection ratio automatically with airspeed is justified.

4.2.5 High Mach number characteristics

(a) A true Mach number of 0.915 (0.90 I.M.N.)[*] was attained in level flight at 46,000 ft. with no marked compressibility effects, and the

/case......

---

[*]Pressure error corrections based on firm's report FTR O/Victor/X/35.

case with which the aircraft could be manoeuvred was impressive. The maximum permitted speed was inadvertently exceeded on several occasions and 0.95 M (0.95 I.M.N.) was reached with ease. At 0.95 M no adverse effects such as buffeting (though it should be borne in mind that the aircraft weight was low), wing dropping or longitudinal instability were encountered and all controls were effective. Changes of longitudinal trim with Mach number were very small and manoeuvre stability, as far as could be assessed, was positive, though the characteristics of the longitudinal short period oscillation (see para. 4.2.3) require special consideration.

(b)   It is evident that the maximum Mach number of 0.95 required by Spec. B128P covering production Victor aircraft can easily be exceeded, and it is strongly recommended that the aircraft's capabilities for so doing be investigated as a matter of urgency in order to obtain the obvious advantages of the highest possible Mach number. It is considered that, when possible from structural considerations, the maximum Mach number of an aircraft should be set by some natural barrier, preferably a marked drag rise. Should it prove impossible to increase the allowable Mach number to such a drag rise it will be necessary to limit the aircraft to the selected maximum Mach number by some automatic device, preferably air brake extension. The Firm are understood to be investigating the possibility of increasing the design Mach number.

(c)   The threshold for the onset of buffet is shown in Fig.A8/2 and it should be noted that, as far as could be investigated, there was only a gradual increase in buffet intensity above the threshold. It is evident from the figure that while no buffet occurred in these tests in straight flight at 0.95 M, some buffet is to be expected at 1g at higher weights at the higher altitudes, and this is one aspect to be considered in connection with (b) above.

When applied to initial production aircraft, Fig.A8/2 indicates that at the specification cruising speed (500 knots T.A.S., 0.873 M) at 47,500 ft. and 120,000 lb. weight (predicted optimum range target conditions with 10,000 lb. bomb on) the aircraft should be capable of a turn at 1.3g ($39\frac{1}{2}^{\circ}$ angle of bank, 4.37 nautical miles radius) before buffet commences. It is believed that this degree of manoeuvrability will be adequate for bombing but consideration must be given to the following factors:

(i.)   The adequacy of the manoeuvrability available for evasive action.
(ii.)   The ability to maintain speed and height when turning at high altitude
(iii.) The consequences of buffet on the aircraft structure and equipment.

In view of recent experiences on other aircraft of this class (iii.) should be investigated at an early date.

The adequacy of the buffet threshold to permit the use of more powerful engines and raise the operating height of the aircraft must also be considered.

4.2.6 Airbrake characteristics

(a)   Pilots were eulogistic in their comments on the airbrakes, which were an effective means of speed control and did not produce any marked trim changes or appreciable buffet within the speed and height ranges tested. Although the overall deceleration was not outstanding (see App. 9), it can be considered adequate for the needs of a bomber aircraft.

(b)   The infinitely variable selection was well liked and proved an invaluable aid in the circuit and final approach, where the flight path could be controlled more easily by the airbrakes than by the throttles.

(c)   Without auto-stabilisation, extension of the airbrakes appeared to cause a deterioration in the lateral damping, aggravating the Dutch roll tendencies.

4.2.7 Assessment as a bombing platform

(a)   With auto-stabilisation the aircraft was qualitatively assessed as an adequate bombing platform at high altitudes (about 46,000 ft.) up to the maximum Mach number achieved in level flight (0.915 M). Manoeuvrability was thought to be adequate (see para. 4.2.5).

(b) Without auto-stabilisation a normal bombing run could be made on this aircraft, including the normal rate turns required to align the aircraft for the final run in. This, however, required a high degree of concentration and should the auto-stabilisation fail at an early phase in an operational sortie there is some doubt if a successful attack would result (see para. 4.2.4).

(c) Trim changes on opening the bomb doors onto an empty bomb bay were very mild and the mean deceleration over a period of 10 secs from the selection of bomb doors open, assuming no change of drag with stores in the bay, is estimated to be about 0.8 ft/sec^2 at cruising Mach number at target weight (120,000 lb.). The maximum permissible deceleration over a like period proposed in J.A.C. Paper No.602 is 0.6 ft/sec^2.

(d) Buffeting with bomb doors open was moderate at 10,000 ft. With increase in altitude and Mach number the degree of buffeting decreased until it was rated as light at 0.90 I.M.N. at 46,000 ft. The effect of this buffet on the bomb sight and associated equipment should be determined as soon as possible.

4.3 Cockpit layout and crew comfort

(a) The cockpit layout of this prototype was largely non-representative of production aircraft. An assessment of the production layout was made on a mock-up, and the results, together with comments on relevant features noted in flight on the prototype, will be given in a separate report. It can however be stated that the production layout is considered unsatisfactory and will require considerable modification in order to reach the standard expected in this class of aircraft. In particular the layout of the flying instruments made accurate flight difficult.

(b) The lack of comfort in the ejection seats was severely criticised, and the intrinsic seat discomfort was aggravated by the seat and parachute harness complexities, restricted leg room, inadequate rudder pedal adjustment, short arm rests and the sloping floor of the cockpit.

(c) Cabin heating appeared to be adequate. It should be noted that the cabin differential pressure was restricted to 5 lb./sq.in.; production aircraft will be pressurised to 9 lb./sq.in. No misting was encountered during the tests.

(d) The unusual noises, which appeared to emanate from the N.A.C.A. type nose intakes, should be eliminated. These consisted of a roaring above 200 knots I.A.S., with a superimposed rythmic clanking at altitudes above 25,000 ft.

(e) Separate pitot-static sources should be provided for the 1st and 2nd pilots.

5. Conclusions

Although tested within severe limitations of weight and airspeed, and in several respects non-representative of production aircraft, the second prototype Victor showed the type to have a high potential as a medium bomber. It is considered that these potentialities should be exploited with the minimum delay.

Consideration should be given to the following and, where possible, action taken.

(i) Possible extension of the design Mach number for transonic flight.

(ii) Possible reduction of buffet level near the stall.

(iii) Structural consequences of buffet in high Mach number manoeuvres.

(iv)   Adequacy of the buffet boundary for evasive manoeuvres.

(v)   Adequacy of the buffet threshold for use of more powerful engines and higher operating altitudes.

(vi)   Effect of buffet with bomb doors open on sighting equipment.

(vii) Ability to maintain speed and height in turns at high altitude.

(viii) Damping of the longitudinal short period oscillation in manoeuvres at high Mach number at high altitude.

(ix)   Duplication of the auto-stabiliser.

(x)   Reduction of aileron break-out forces and neutral dead-spot.

(xi)   Deletion of/the proposed variable gearing in the aileron/rudder interconnection.

(xii) Accessibility of the nose-wheel steering control and elimination of dead-spot.

(xiii) Mechanical link between power control switches and throttles to prevent take-off with controls switched off.

(xiv) Possibility of serious external reflections in the windscreen at night.

(xv)   Unsatisfactory cockpit layout and field of view, particularly in poor visibility.

(xvi) Serious lack of pilot comfort.

(xvii) Elimination of noises from nose intakes.

(xviii) Provision of separate pitot-static sources for 1st and 2nd pilots.

5.   Further developments

The results of a cockpit assessment related to production aircraft will be given in a further part of the Report.

Early H.P.80 Models

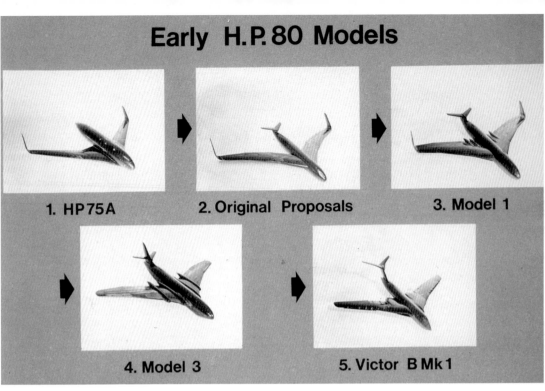

1. HP75A

2. Original Proposals

3. Model 1

4. Model 3

5. Victor B Mk1

Early HP 80 Models. HP-HPA

HP 80 WB771 A&AEE 12-52

HP80 WB775 Second Prototype in Curelian Blue. HP-HPA.

HP 80 WB775 in original Colours. HP-HPA

HP 80 WB771 SBAC 9 53. HP-HPA

HP 80 WB771 Prior to First Flight Signed by Sdn Ldr Hedley Hazelden

The Production Specification B128P Victor B Mk 1

MINISTRY OF SUPPLY

AIRCRAFT SPECIFICATION
No. B. 128 P

VICTOR B. MK. 1

This reprint dated 1st September 1954 incorporates amendment Nos 1 - 6
inclusive of this specification

NOTE

This reprint dated 1st September, 1954, incorporates amendments
Nos. 1 - 6 to this specification.

Amendment No. 6 introduces OR.229 Issue 3 which is for Information
Only.

AIRCRAFT SPECIFICATION

B.128.P

VICTOR B MK. 1

INDEX	Pages

Prepared by: R.D.T.2

Reference: 7/Aircraft/9955

Approved by: G. SILYN ROBERTS

for Director General of Technical
            Development (Air)

Date: 25.9.52

PREFACE

    This specification is issued to cover production of the Handley Page
Victor B Mk.I crescent wing bomber for use by the Royal Air Force.

1 - GENERAL

1.01 This Specification and its Appendix A (No. 2038) forms part of the Contrac
Agreement and are subject to the same conditions. It neither cancels or superse
Specification No. B.35/46 which was based on OR.229.

1.02 Operational Requirement No. 229/Issue 3 forms the Appendix B, which is non
contractural and for information only.

1.03 The aircraft shall be designed and constructed in accordance with the
drawings and schedules comprising the Master Record for the second Prototype
aircraft built to Specfn. B.35/46 up to and including A.L. No.6 except where
changes are necessary to meet the requirements of this Specfn. B.128.P.

1.04 "Technical Procedure Requirements for Service Aircraft" with amendments up
to and including No.29 are applicable.

2 - GENERAL DESIGN REQUIREMENTS

Air Publication 970

2.01 The requirements of A.P.970 Vol.1 (Restricted Edition) with amendments up
to and including No.53 except as specifically agreed by P.D.R.D. (Aircraft) or
his authorised representative.

2.02 The recommendations of A.P.970 Vol.2 where applicable should be considered

Aircraft Design Memoranda

2.03 A.D.M. current on 1st October, 1952, shall be met.

Air Service Standardisation Design Memoranda and Standard Instruction Sheets

2.04 S.D.M.(A) and SIS current on 1st October, 1952 are applicable.

Deviations from and Concessions against the Design Requirements

2.05 Deviations from and concessions against the Design Requirements of this
specification as agreed by P.D.R.D.(Aircraft) or his authorised representative
are recorded in Table 1.

3 - STRENGTH AND STIFFNESS

Maximum Design Take-off Weight

3.01 When applying requirements based on the Maximum Design Take-off Weight
(W_T of Chap. 304 para. 1.4) the value assumed shall be 160,000 lb. made up of:-

(a) The tare weight items shown in column 10 of the Appendix "A".

(b) Such removable non standard parts as will be necessary for the
contractor to supply and fit in order that the military load may be
carried.

(c) The normal military load defined in the Appendix "A".

(d) Fuel and oil required to give the range specified in paragraph
4.03(ii).

Maximum Design Weight for Landing

3.02 The Maximum Design Weight for Landing (W_L of Chap. 304 para. 1.4) shall
be:-

(a) One half of the total fuel remaining for the 3,350 nautical miles
case, no bomb. This value will be used for undercarriage stressing.

(b) For all other stressing dependent on the Maximum Weight for Landing
a value of 115,000 lb. shall be used which is equivalent to half fuel
remaining for the 5,000 nautical miles case.

Flight Envelope

3.03 (i) For the general flight envelope of Chap. 201 para. 3, the following
values shall be assumed.

n_1 = 2.7

V_D = 415 knots E.A.S. at altitudes from sea level to a height where
this speed corresponds to M = 0.90 reducing to 385 knots E.A.S.
and M = 0.95 at 25,000 feet, and at higher altitudes by speeds
corresponding to M = 0.95

V_B = The maximum speed in level flight or 0.9 V_D whichever is the
lesser, provided that in any case it is not less than 0.8 V_D.

(ii) These requirements shall be satisfied at the Maximum Design Take-off
Weight.

3.04 The design shall be such that following take-off the above value of n_1 will
increase to at least 3.0 by the time one quarter of the still air range specified
in paragraph 4.03 (i) has been achieved, and will not subsequently fall below
this value.

Gust Loads

3.05 The gust cases of Chapter 203 may be reduced in severity as follows:-

(a) Cases 1 and 2 of Table I of Chapter 203 to a gust speed of 36 f.p.s.
E.A.S. from sea level to 43,000 ft. followed by a linear drop to
30 f.p.s. at 50,000 ft. The aircraft speed should be the design
cruising speed (500 knots true) but need not exceed 332 knots E.A.S.
(0.8 V_D Max. E.A.S.).

(b) Cases 3 and 4 of Table I of Chapter 203 to a gust speed of 18 f.p.s.
E.A.S. from sea level to 43,000 ft. followed by a linear drop to
15 f.p.s. E.A.S. at 50,000 feet. The aircraft speed should be the
speed for which M = 0.90 V_D E.A.S. Value).

Undercarriage Energy Absorption

3.06 The Design Vertical Velocity of Descent (V) of Chapter 304 para. 2.2 shall
be not less than 12 ft./sec. at the Landing Weight of para. 3.02(a).

4 - PARTICULAR DESIGN REQUIREMENTS

Engine

4.01 The aircraft shall be fitted with four Sapphire Engine Change Units MK.20001.

Undercarriage and configuration

4.02 The aircraft shall be suitable for operation from permanent airfields
having a Load Classification Number of 55.

Range

4.03 (i) With a 10,000 lb. bomb the still air range must not be less than
3,350 nautical miles.

(ii) Additional range up to 5,000 (approx.) nautical miles with the same
bomb load is required, as long as this does not involve a weight
penalty to the permanent structure required for case (i) above equivalent
to a loss in height over the target of greater than 300 ft. in case (ii).
External tanks may be used to achieve this additional range.

/(iii)

(iii) Cases (i) and (ii) above must be obtained with the full specification factors, nevertheless provision shall be made for additional range to case (ii) above, which can be obtained with an $n_1 = 2.5$ at take-off, bearing in mind the maximum permanent structural penalty of (ii) above.

Take-off

4.04 Under A.P.970 Chap. 105 Fig. 1 maximum temperature, the aircraft must clear a 50 ft. screen in 2,400 yds., from rest in still air or with a cross wind of up to 20 knots at right angles to the take-off path. If necessary, rocket assisted take-off equipment shall be used.

Landing

4.05 The aircraft must be capable of landing in cross winds of up to 20 knots. It must be capable of coming to rest within 1,400 yds. after crossing a 50 ft. screen in still air at the maximum landing weight under the Maximum Design Temperature conditions as shown in Fig.1 Chap. 105 A.P.970. For this, tail parachute (s) may be used.

Bomb Loads

4.06 In addition to the normal bomb loads provision shall be made for the maximum bomb load, for which a value of $n_1 = 2.5$ at take-off may be used but any weight penalty to the permanent structure (required for 4.03(i)) must be included in the maximum referred to in 4.03(ii) which gives a 300 ft. loss in height. Wing bomb nacelles may be used. All bomb loads are detailed in the Appendix "A" to this specification.

Tail Armament

4.07 Deleted by Amendment No.4.

Emergency Exits

4.08 The emergency exits shall be as in the 2nd prototype aircraft.

Maintenance

4.09 Provision shall be made for as much in-flight inspection as possible to assist maintenance, but without prejudicing the pressure cabin layout.

Engine failure at Take-off

4.10 In amplification of A.P.970, Chap. 104 para.3, in the case where the pilot decides to pull up safely without damage, the total length available from the start of run-way will be 3,100 yards.

Tail parachute(s)

4.11 If tail parachute(s) is/are used, then the system must be easily refurled from the cabin, or easily replaced by a freshly packed installation.

Window Launching

4.12 Provision shall be made for launching Window.

5 - GENERAL CONDITIONS

Equipment

5.01 The equipment detailed in the Appendix A shall be installed to the satisfaction of AD/ARDQ or his authorised representative.

TABLE 1

The following A.P.970 requirements do not apply to aircraft designed to this specification. It is not proposed to amend A.P.970 to make these concessions generally applicable.

Chap. No.	Para. No.	Subject
207	10.1	Duplication of push-pull control rods not provided.
103	3.3	Pilot's head room. Clearance not fully met
100	2.1	Crew entrance door opens outwards and is not jettisonable.
709	3.11	Requirements for number of earthing points not met.
SDM.	120	Aircraft Jacking Pads
SDM.	232	Aircraft tank manhole covers

PART TWO

The Victor Mk 1 Series

or

Into Production

The Victor and its Structure

AAlthough it is some time ago that the Victors wing and its highflying tail unit first caught the public imagination it is only now that the primary characteristics of their construction can be revealed. Mr Sandifer does this. He gives the reasons behind the choice of their structural features and tells of the great efforts that have been made to ensure adequate safety an aspect of supreme importance.

The structural features of the Victor are not that well known to the variety of aviation historians and enthusiasts and the easiest way I have found to let you know all about them to hand you over to R. H Sandifer the Assistant Chief Designer (Structures) back in the 1950's when the Victor production was at its height. This was written back in mid 1958 to bring the correct facts regarding the construction of the Victor for the use of the aviation press of the day and other interested individuals. It is for that reason that I am using his article in total. And it will still after all this time [nearly 50 years] disprove some of the myths of the Victors basic construction. [It was the only V bomber that was designed and built in such a way as to allow it to be transported by road and easily resembled. This was done with three aircraft apart from WB771, XA919, XH672, and XL164, a truly large "Airfix Kit" after all the major components were made for all production Victors at the HP factory in Crinklewood North London and transported to the production line in the Colney Street factory on Radlett Airfield near St Albans]

Interior of the Crescent

A successful aircraft structure combines essential features. It is strong enough to withstand all loading conditions. Stiffness is sufficient to prevent flutter and other adverse aero elastic effects and to maintain aerodynamic form. External surfaces remain smooth and free from waving under normal flying loads. Adequately safe life against fatigue is provided and the structure possesses fail safe characteristics. Its weight is as low as possible. Manufacture and maintenance are straightforward and simple, consistent with other design requirements.

To satisfy any one or even two of these features simultaneously is a simple engineering exercise; to satisfy all of them in one design is a supreme art.

Although it would be foolish to claim complete success, the Handley Page design organisation can justifiably claim to have continuously held this target in view and achieved a substantial measure of success. Clearly the solution has been one of optimisation and teamwork, not only within the design office but also between that office and other departments, such as those concerned with testing and production.

To show the degree to which the Victor design requirements have been satisfied, it is essential to describe briefly the loads which the different parts of that bomber's structure have to carry and to note the primary elements of each component's structure.

VICTOR: *Its Structure at a Glance*

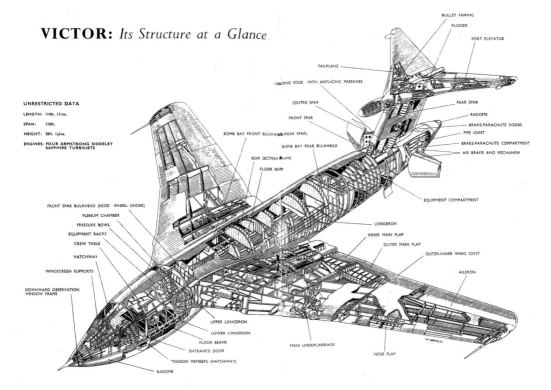

UNRESTRICTED DATA
LENGTH: 114ft. 11ins.
SPAN: 110ft.
HEIGHT: 28ft. 1½ins.
ENGINES: FOUR ARMSTRONG SIDDELEY SAPPHIRE TURBOJETS

Wing

In designing the wing consideration had to be given to satisfying several sets of flight conditions such as symmetric and asymmetric manoeuvres, gust loading and many others which, although requiring less extensive calculations, nevertheless were important. These included aero elastic and dynamic effects where appropriate.

Simultaneously, numerous ground loads such a bending, manoeuvring and taxiing for the aircraft as a whole and the wing in particular were evaluated. Further loads of a special nature arise from the carriage of fuel that, apart from its inertia loads during various manoeuvres, needs to be pressurised to prevent boiling at altitude.

All these calculations lead to systems of loads along the wings in the form of bending moments, shear forces and torques, with superimposed pressures in the fuel tank cells.

Choice of Structure

The structure is required to carry these loads in a span-wise direction to the wing root. This primary requirement is best met by providing a majority of span-wise webs, capped by reinforced end-load carrying skins thus forming multiple torsion boxes. It soon became evident that maximum structural and aerodynamic efficiency together with minimum weight would be achieved if the skins possessed some inherent bending and shear stiffness in both directions. This quality would not only stabilise the skins for the carriage of span-wise compressive loads without the addition of frequent full depth ribs, but would also provide a chord-wise load path for the effects of fuel tank pressures (and incidentally for aerodynamic loads). The fuel tank pressures arising from both inertial and superimposed pressures were found to be as high as 20lb/sq.in ultimate. The answer to this was, of course, sandwich panels for both the top and bottom skins with span-wise corrugated cores.

Thus was developed the primary wing structure shown in the illustration, these being the general arrangement of the inner and outer wings respectively. Across the centre fuselage, and for approximately half of the inner wing, there are three main webs and two torsion boxes; outboard of the undercarriage there are four main webs and three torsion boxes. These webs or spars have structural 'kinks' in plan view at the same stations along the wing as those at which sweep back changes. In this way the well-known crescent shaped aerodynamic wing form is produced. The spars and torsion boxes across the centre fuselage are at right angles to the fore and aft axis of the aircraft and so create a major 'kink' at the fuselage side where there is a transport joint similar to that between the inner and outer wings.

There are as few as eight ribs on each side of the fuselage in the whole wing and only six of these are of major importance. Their chief function is to interchange bending moments and torsion moments at the 'kinks' and to distribute into the primary structure such concentrated loads as arise from the presence of engines and undercarriage which are buried in the inner wing behind the torsion boxes.

A chord-wise corrugated sheet stiffens the top surface of the wing in this region. The bottom surface comprises undercarriage doors of full sandwich construction and engine access doors stiffened by span-wise corrugated sheeting. These features are chosen deliberately.

Corrugated sheet stiffening eliminates the tendency (so prevalent in conventional skin panels) for permanent shear waves to form in service due to 'sympathetic strains' in secondary structure less heavily loaded than the adjacent primary structure. The corrugations in the top skin are placed chord-wise to minimise the picking up of span-wise end loads in this secondary structure. In the case of the bottom surface underneath the engines the span-wise direction is justified because the panels as a whole are curves in a span-wise direction and so already have some flexibility that enables them to avoid sympathetic span-wise strains. Moreover the manufacture problems of these curved panels are eased by this choice.

Spot Welding and Chord-wise Joints
Perhaps the most significant feature of the detail design of the Victor wing is the use of electric resistance spot welding. The primary application of this method of attachment is to the assembly of the sandwich panels. The need for maintaining a smooth aerodynamic surface is most economically and efficiently met by attaching the outer faceplate of the sandwich to the corrugated core by spot welding.

The use of a comparatively large diameter electrode on the outside surface of the skin ensures a smooth external wing surface of such high quality that it is often difficult to discern the exact location of a line of spot welds either by sight or touch. Local indentations are virtually eliminated; so also is skin panel creep along a line of attachments and exceptional accuracy of aerodynamic finish is thereby achieved.

A standard form of blind rivet attaches the inner faceplates of the sandwich panels

Sandwich panels are also used for many of the rib webs and for intermediate span-wise webs. The reason for this choice is partly to provide a web of significant lateral bending stiffness under the action of tank pressures and partly to ensure a smooth supporting surface for flexible bag tanks.

Chord-wise joints in the sandwich panels are another special feature of detail design. They are commonly known as pipe joints. A similar one exists at the fuselage side. It is achieved by butting edge-on two approximately rectangular cross sectional forgings that run the full chord length of the primary wing box. These long forgings are inserted between the face plates of the sandwich panels and attached to them by suitably arranged groups of bolts, countersunk where necessary, to give a flush surface. The corrugated core is cut back to allow the entry of the forged joint members and its load transferred to the forgings by local doubling plates.

These in the case of early production Victors take the form of fingerplates; in later aircraft they were improved by tapering the thickness to avoid concentrated fingers and by engineering a corresponding taper locally in the depth of the corrugation.

The two forgings are joined together by a series of tension bolts virtually buried in the slots in the forgings. Careful detail design and testing have progressively evolved the proportions and features of these joints to meet all design requirements including those of fatigue endurance.

Manufacturing Problems

The inner-wing spar webs merit special mention because of the large holes incorporated for the engine intakes. In the foremost spar there is one large elliptical hole to provide for common entry for the intakes of both engines. Behind it, the other two spares each have twin elliptical holes for the new separated air intakes of the inner and outer engines.

Because these holes eliminate a very large portion of the spar web, considerable reinforcement has been necessary. Correct proportioning of this material round the holes in conjunction with the spar booms and remaining web, led to elaborate calculations. The results of these tests were checked in critical cases by photo elastic model tests. In addition major stiffness tests on the completed wing provided a final confirmation that adequate stiffness had been achieved.

Webs of the first and third spars are made from rolled plate that in the interests of economy is subsequently machined all over to graduate the thickness according to the intensity of the load. One-piece forged rings reinforce the inner edges of the holes in these plates. Later models achieved even greater weight economy by using one piece-forged plates incorporating the inner forged rings.

The middle spar, having a significantly lower load, is of sandwich construction with suitable forged rings around the inner peripheries of the holes. Adequate heat treatment in relation to machining operations has been followed for all these heavy web plates in order to minimise distortion and residual stress.

When the Victor was in the early stages of development examples of stress cracking were experienced both at Handley Page and elsewhere. It became evident that the occurrence of residual stress must be avoided or severely minimised in production aircraft.

Numerous precautions have therefore been taken. For example, all large forgings are fully machined or at least rough machined in the annealed condition. Parts manufactured from moderate or large cross-sectioned bars or extrusions are resolution treated before, during or immediately after machining according to the size and shape of the part and the nature (symmetrical or unsymmetrical, deep or shallow) of the machining operation. In an attempt to minimise assembly stress, limits regulating the fit or mating of parts have been closely controlled, shouldered bolts or similar devices have been used where necessary and controlled tightening torques for major bolts have been specified.

Hot air has been used for wing and tail unit de-icing. It is supplied from the power plant through ducting to specially constructed shaped duct forming part of the wing leading edge. From there it is filtered through chord-wise channels. These are made by the use of a comparatively thick inner skin and a thinner outer leading-edge skin.

Grooves machined in the former provide these air channels. The design of this structure has taken due account of temperature and pressure effects caused by the hot air supply, as well as external aerodynamic loads.

Materials

Choice of materials is always a compromise between achievement of minimum structure weight for maximum static strength, on the one hand, and adequate safeguards against stress cracking and premature fatigue failures on the other. The provision of fail-safe characteristics also must be kept continuously in mind.

Nevertheless the role of the bomber does not call for such a long operational life, as does that of a transport. This fact has enabled the designers to take advantage of high strength light alloys for static strength while, at the same time, providing for an adequately safe life. Thus skins of the primary wing structure are of aluminium-zinc-copper alloy of high specific strength (Specification DTD 687) as also are the spar caps and all important forgings and extrusions to (Specification DTD683). Secondary structure is generally of an aluminium -copper alloy, L72 or L73.

Using titanium where appropriate has saved weight. Main-rib webs flanking engine bays must necessarily be fire resisting and these are now made in the highest grade of commercially pure titanium instead of in steel. The Victor thereby weights some 250lb less. In addition a number of bolts have been changed from steel to titanium where weight saving is justified.

Finally, extensive use had been made of magnesium zirconium castings for many detail parts not only in the wings but also the tail fuselage and controls. These castings have a favourable strength-weight ratio compared with those in aluminium alloy and equally good fatigue characteristics.

Fail Safe

In the early stages of design a series of fatigue tests was undertaken to enable safe life calculations to be made for all those critical chord-wise joints on the bottom surface of the wing primarily in tension during flight. Several detail improvements were incorporated as a result. But tests established more than this; they confirmed the belief that the essential structure of the joints in the sandwich panels behaved in a fail-safe manner.

This meant that the first indication of fatigue approach were by small cracks in the faceplates of the sandwich. Almost invariably they were in the outer faceplates that are more easily inspected. It will be remembered that this plate is spot welded to the corrugated core where the inner faceplate is riveted. This difference increases the relative stiffness of the outer plate with a consequent small increase of end load and thus, apart from the natural scatter of such features, there is reason to expect fatigue cracks to appear first in the outer plate. The outer faceplate is also slightly further from the wing's neutral axis. Nevertheless by removing or rolling back the flexible bag tanks in the wing one can inspect the inner faceplate.

The corrugated core is in two pieces with a span-wise joint between spars. This constitutes a fail-safe feature; it would limit the extent of a crack, should one occur, to half the distance between two spars. The difficulty of inspecting the cores makes this a particularly useful feature.

Two other facts should be noted; Firstly failures in the corrugation on test have never been known to occur before the faceplates. Secondly, even if they did and the core failed to the extent of one half of the distance between the two spar webs the residual strength of the wing in bending would still not fall below 90 per cent of the original design value. In torsion the residual strength is even greater because the shear stiffness of the corrugated sheet is less than that of the same area of faceplate.

Tests have shown that the initial small cracks in the faceplate referred to above occur at between 60 and 80 per cent of the total life of the sandwich panel and that they grow slowly at first, so constituting ample warning of final failure. Furthermore, the scatter aspect already mentioned is provided for by a generous safety factor on the number of loading cycles required of the aircraft in service in relation to those achieved on test. Because of this safety factor, it is most unlikely that cracks will occur before the permissible safe life of the structure is reached; but if they should occur, they would give ample warning without danger.

Moreover, the most likely regions for cracks to begin are known from fatigue tests. They invariably appear at the joints. Inspection at reasonable intervals during the later stages of the aircraft's life can be arranged accordingly.

Other Fail-Safe Devices

It is relevant to mention here several other fail-safe features of the Victor wing. Firstly, the primary material resisting bending loads are distributed across a large proportion of the chords rather than being concentrated in one or two extruded members. Actually, the maximum aggregate area of spar booms, occurring near the wing root, is about 30 per cent of the total area of bending material; outboard it is much less. This aggregate is not concentrated in one spar, there being at least three. Further, a multi spar arrangement provides for duplicate or triplicate torsion boxes.

Sandwich panels are not arranged continuously across the chord; at each spar there are complete span-wise joints. These arrest the progress of any chord-wise cracks. Thus a failure in one box or sandwich panel always leaves one or more alternative paths for loads and the residual strength is high.

The Victor wings crescent form is brought about structurally by two major 'kinks' in plan form. At these points and at the root are major ribs that serve to redistribute bending and torsion moments. These ribs have corrugated sandwich webs that again are of a fail-safe nature by virtue of having three sheets instead of one as a path for loads. Moreover, at the transport joint between outer and inner wings, and at the wing root the rib booms are double members and constitute a fail-safe structure.

Finally, the wing control surfaces and leading edge flaps have fail-safe features in as much as they are attached by multi hinges and, the ailerons excepted, are in two parts span wise on each wing.

Tail Unit
The T shaped configuration of the tail is now familiar. Among the reasons for its choice was the need for the tailplane to be reasonably high above the fuselage in order to clear the jet stream. Having achieved this, it was more efficient both aerodynamically and structurally to place the tailplane on top of the fin with a carefully designed bullet-shaped fairing.

In principle the detail design of the tail unit structure is similar to that of the wings and it has, therefore, similar fail-safe characteristics. Several important joints have been selected for fatigue tests that have proved the safe life attributes. The choice of materials as applied to the wings has governed tail unit design as well.

Horizontal Surfaces
Principal structural features of the tailplane and elevators are shown in the illustrations. Aerodynamic and inertial loads resulting from overall balance calculations on the complete aircraft were translated into distributed shear forces, bending moments and torques along both the elevator and tailplane. The method was similar to that employed for the wings.

It was done for both symmetric and asymmetric manoeuvres. Due account was taken of the position of the outer and inner hinges of each elevator and the method of reacting (or applying) elevator torsion moments. This is affected by means of a skew lever whose main shaft is actuated by the power control unit jack in a span-wise direction. The action is converted into rotation in a plane at right angles to the jack axis by virtue of the levers transverse axis being mounted at approximately 45 degrees to the vertical.

In conformity with wing design, the elevator and tailplane have two main shear webs and few ribs. The latter are placed at strategic locations: the twin elevator ribs, for example, at the skew lever and the complete elevator rib at the outer hinge station with a complementary main rib at the tailplane tip

This hinge carries by far the greater portion of the elevator load, and by the same token the hinge load is the major one applied to the tailplane (Illustration No 5). Naturally, therefore the design of these hinge fittings and their associated ribs has been of paramount importance and much testing has been undertaken in order to develop the best structure.

Problems associated with the tailplane were accentuated by the necessary and considerable taper in plan view, of the main box. Theoretical work was made more complex by this feature but a successful design was evolved and has been proved by structural and flight-testing.

The power unit drive shaft for the skew lever is mounted in bearings housed in a special magnesium zirconium casting. This forms an integral part of the tailplane rear spar-web and joins up with another connecting web to the outer hinge housing.

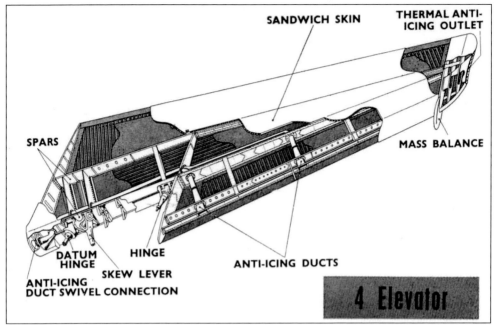

Fin

The anchorage of the tailplane on top of the fin constituted another major problem that has been successfully solved. Here all the loads are taken through a four-point pick up, two forward and two aft, through high-strength light alloy forgings. Stiffness calculations, later confirmed by wear resistance strain gauge checks on the full-scale test structure and by flight tests, were made to determine the true load paths; locations of these forgings are shown (Illustration 5).

The form of construction for the fin and rudder follows that of the wings.

The fin has three main spars of which the centre one is introduced to create torsion boxes of economical size to give adequate support for the sandwich panels and to ensure fail safe characteristics by providing a natural stopper to any chord-wise cracks.

For the root anchorage of the fin to the fuselage, a similar distributed chord-wise joint has been designed on similar lines to the transportation joint on the wing. This also has been fully tested both statically and from the standpoint of fatigue. Beyond it and inside the fuselage are two fore and aft bulkheads of similar design and configuration chord wise curvature corresponding

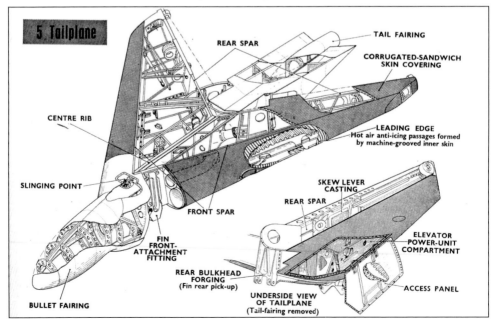

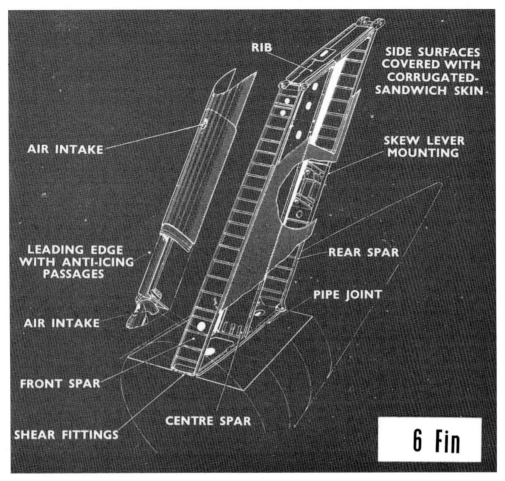

AIR INTAKE

RIB

SIDE SURFACES
COVERED WITH
CORRUGATED-
SANDWICH SKIN

SKEW LEVER
MOUNTING

LEADING EDGE
WITH ANTI-ICING
PASSAGES

REAR SPAR

PIPE JOINT

AIR INTAKE

FRONT SPAR

SHEAR FITTINGS

CENTRE SPAR

6 Fin

to the fins platform. These serve to translate sandwich shear and bending loads applied to two transverse bulkheads. The latter line up with the vertical continuation of the front and rear spars of the fin and extend to the upper skin and lower floor of the rear fuselage. This is a very stiff multiple box structure and is provided for the anchorage of the tail unit to the fuselage.

Rudder

The rudder has three hinges, the bottom one forming the datum. Operation is again by skew lever. The front spar is the primary one; the rear spar serves to stabilise the skin panels and ensure a double torsion box.

Skin panels in the rudder are stiffened by chord-wise corrugated sheet with no inner faceplate. The reason for this choice is similar to that applicable to parts of the rear surface of the wings; loads are so light that a full sandwich construction could not be achieved economically with practical thickness. Also, of course corrugated sheet stiffening attached by spot welding prevents all incidental waving of thin sheet panels and thus gives a better aerodynamic finish. The rearmost portion of the elevator is similarly constructed.

From Nose to Tail - Features and Materials

The front fuselage forms the crew cabin and is the location of most of the operational equipment. Design loads arise chiefly from the pressurisation of this cabin and ground manoeuvres have also been considered.

This component is attached to the centre fuselage by four main pick up points. The reaction from these are diffused into the cabin shell by top and bottom longerons. The pressurised compartment is bounded by the main floor, the shell plating including hatches, doors and windows and the pressure bulkhead at the rear of the crew space. Behind it, and housing important equipment lies a small plenum chamber which is pressurised naturally by ram air introduced for cooling assisted by two pressurisation fans.

The many necessary discontinuities constituted a major problem in the structural design of the crew cabin, not only statically but also from the standpoint of fatigue. Although suitable safety factors on static loads were used, this was no guarantee against fatigue troubles; full scale fatigue tests on the crew cabin and the plenum chamber, therefore have been undertaken. These revealed a number of secondary weaknesses that have been remedied. They also proved that the pressurised compartments have adequate life and that the structure is of a fail-safe character.

The pilots windows comprise a series of long flat panels of strength glass with Vinyl layers capable of holding the cabin pressure should the glass fracture; demisting is effected by a dry air sandwich and warm air jets. These panels conform generally to the cabin shape so that a minimum of drag occurs; yet being long and sloping forward and downward they provide satisfactory vision. Similar panels are provided for the bomb aimer

Pilot ejection was by standard Martin Baker seats with power operated escape hatches immediately above. These hatches also have transparencies incorporated for upward vision. They are fully load carrying, having circumferential tension members with latches mating up with similar tension members in the sides of the shell plating. A fore and aft central spine member provides for the continuity of the longitudinal structure in the hatch region.

The crew entry door is on the port side. Opening upwards, it has load carrying hinges at the top and latches at the bottom and is therefore a circumferential load carrying member. As this door is also the crewmember's emergency exit, protective blinkers are incorporated to prevent danger from the airflow during initial escape. Especially strong frames to carry pressure and shear loads flank this door.

It will be noted that every effort has been made to avoid excessive concentration of load at discontinuities; furthermore adequate local reinforcement has also been incorporated at smaller unavoidable multiple discontinuities. Thus stress intensities have been kept low and stress gradients from points of high stress are as such as to discourage fast crack propagation in the event of local fatigue failure. All of this ensures a fail-safe structure.

The pressure bulkhead is basically spherical in order to minimise stresses due to pressure. However, because the lower boundary of the pressurised compartment is a flat floor, incidental loads arise at the junction of this floor and the bulkhead. Use is made of the navigator's table and its adjacent structure to balance out and redistribute these loads without inconvenience to crewmembers that are just behind the entry door and face aft.

The floor is of conventional design; the covering being metal-faced ply; with the wood uppermost it gives a non-slip and non-buckling surface. This covering is supported by closely spaced transverse I-section beams which transfer loads to the fuselage side below the bottom longeron.

The under floor structure which is not pressurised, carries much equipment; it is designed not only to cater for this but also to absorb incidental loads arising from its attachment to the primary cabin structure. The forward part comprises a large one-piece sandwich radome of glass cloth laminates and foamed rubber filling.

Unlike the remainder of the primary structure, the crew cabin is constructed entirely of aluminium copper alloy sheets. The chief reason for this choice is that skin stresses have been kept low in the interests of fatigue and do not warrant the use of the highest strength light alloy available.

Rear and Centre Fuselage
The function of the rear fuselage is to collect and carry loads from the tail unit and to house and carry loads from stores and equipment. It must, furthermore, possess a reasonable aerodynamic shape. The centre fuselage is even more important in so far as it represents the clearing house

for loads from front and rear fuselage and from wings. The primary box of the inner wing therefore passes through the centre fuselage. It does so at right angles to the fore and aft axis.

Thus at the fuselage side three main centre spars are kinked through approximately 45 degrees and considerable fore and aft loads are thereby introduced. These loads are reacted by the root rib and gradually diffused into the fore and aft structural members of the rear fuselage. This root rib also serves as a transport joint for the wing and is of the same form as that for the joint between the inner and outer wings.

The central box, of standard wing construction form, serves also as the supporting shell of flexible bag fuel tanks, separated transversely by a central fore and aft bulkhead of sandwich construction and otherwise by the central main spar.

The discontinuity created by this deep wing running through the fuselage has been virtually nullified by placing the front fuselage floor and longeron, the bottom wing skin and the main rear fuselage bottom longeron all in the same horizontal plane and thus providing a continuous path for the fore and aft load.

The main portion of the rear fuselage comprises a large bomb bay, completely clear of encumbrances. The roof of this bay is supported by four equally spaced fore and aft girders running the full length with light but strong 'catenary' floor skins between them. These fore and aft girders are attached at suitable intervals to heavy box section frames which provide the main supports for bombs or other military loads.

Two long doors whose double skin construction gives high torsional stiffness close the bomb bay. They are actuated by hydraulic jacks at each end and retract inside the bomb bay.

Behind this bay comes a small equipment compartment and thereafter the box structure, already described picking up the tail unit

The extreme aft end of the fuselage is a detachable tail in which are situated two large clam type air brakes, operated hydraulically, and the housing for the brake parachute

The main shell of the rear and central fuselage is of conventional skin stringer construction supported by bulkheads and heavy frames, as already stated.

In between these is a series of light frames to stabilise the stringers against torsional and flexural instability. These stringers are of 'hat' section and are spot-welded to the skin. Frames are generally attached only to the stringer flanges; but shear plates to provide frame to skin attachment are fitted where loads are high.

In some regions the upper shell has an inner skin with closely spaced stringers; a form of sandwich not needing a continuous corrugated core because of the circular shape of the fuselage cross section. It has the added advantage of permitting stringers to be terminated freely at various stations to suit load grading.

The main bending strength of the fuselage is completed by a substantial longeron of extruded high-strength light alloy; it runs along the upper edge of the bomb bay opening in lieu of stringers. Torsional strength and stiffness of the fuselage in this region is maintained by differential bending of the two sides, supplemented by the torsional contribution of the upper section.

There is considerable interaction between fuselage and rear portion of the wings: the design of this feature has been the subject of extensive stiffness calculations, supported by full scale testing.

Jet efflux effects have been catered for by the use of thicker skins locally on the lower fuselage side, just aft of the bomb bay. Another feature that assists the fuselage to withstand these loads is stringer flanges that face inwards and thus provide a double fixing between stringer and frame.

Materials used in the fuselage primary and secondary structure are the same as those for the wings. Strategic joints in the top shell structure have been tested for fatigue endurance and fail-safe characteristics.

Undercarriage – Main and Nose

The Victors undercarriage has been designed and produced by Electro-Hydraulics Ltd in close collaboration with Handley Page.

Each main unit carries four double wheels whose comparatively small diameter facilitates housing within the inner wing, just outboard of the engines. The runway load from each leg is spread over eight wheels.

They are mounted on a balanced bogie with a pair of high-strength light alloy forgings bolted together along the fore and aft axis. This bogie is pivoted at the bottom of a vertical oleo pneumatic shock absorber leg with adequate sideways and drag bracing. A secondary dashpot connects the leg to the rear of the bogie. Retraction is by hydraulic power.

Great care must be exercised in detail design and choice of materials; high-grade steels and high strength light alloys are used, according to suitability. The result is unit of outstanding strength/weight ratio and one that caters completely for all landing conditions and severe ground manoeuvring, including turning about one leg. Strength tests have fully confirmed design requirements.

The undercarriage nose unit is of twin wheel form. Wheels are mounted independently on a single oleo pneumatic shock absorber leg, castoring through a total angle of 175 degrees. This leg incorporates a yoke forging of light alloy and a separate articulated radius rod upon which the retraction jack operates.

Steering is accomplished by two hydraulic jacks at the top of the leg operating effectively through a total angle of 90 degrees. Structural testing of this unit was completed successfully.

Major Structural Tests

No account of the Victor's structural design would be complete without reference to the part played by major structural testing.

Each component described here and in the preceding account of the aircraft's wing and tail structure was fully tested for the prototype. Then in order to prove thoroughly the latest developments and improvements, a full programme was repeated for production aircraft.

To this end a combined tip-to-tip wing with the centre and rear fuselage structure attached was subjected to a series of major tests representing the most critical landing case and towing conditions, the most severe symmetric flight loading, the maximum asymmetric manoeuvre and the maximum negative acceleration case.

For each of these conditions a complex loading system is arranged to apply distributed forces along wings and fuselage. These are linked together conveniently and culminate in a few selected points at which resultant loads are applied by hydraulically balanced jacks or fixed anchorages in the ground.

For this purpose a very large steel girder frame has been built with a moveable overhead cross gantries and specially reinforced floor. Its overall dimensions are 130ft long by 30ft high by 45ft wide.

Loads are applied in uniform increments as percentages of the ultimate design load, numerous deflections, wire resistance strain gauge readings and general observations of structural behaviour are noted. Most test cases are taken between 85 per cent and 90 per cent of design ultimate conditions. One case is chosen for which the loading factor is increased to produce ultimate failure.

Much valuable data is thus collected and used as a check on calculations. They also provide more realistic information about complex problems of interaction between one part of the structure and another.

This results in a number of improvements to the structure being incorporated at suitable stages as soon as possible either to ensure satisfactory compliance with design requirements or to add still further to the aircrafts capabilities.

A similar but smaller independent test frame was designed and built to enable the complete tail unit and its attachments to the rear fuselage to be tested simultaneously.

At least four major design cases were represented consecutively, together with numerous stiffness test specially undertaken for aero elastic investigation.

As already noted the cabin was tested separately not only for static loads but also for fatigue characteristics. These tests involved the application of cyclic pressure loading and, in the interests of safety and preservation of the specimen, were carried out by completely submerging the cabin in a water tank.

Since this article was written back in the 1950s the restrictions on the materials used in the construction have been lifted and the data that follows is the main materials used in the construction of the airframe structure by Handley Page.
The materials used in this vast and complex aircraft structure cover various types of material and in some cases a special one for a specific purpose.
The Main Materials are:

Aluminium Alloy Sheet
DTD 610/ L72
DTD 546/ L73
DTD 687/ L88

Aluminium Alloy Bar and Extrusion
L40 and L45/L65
L64/L65
DTD683/DTD5054

Titanium Alloy Sheet
Ti 160/DTD 5063. TA6
Ti 314C/DTD 5063.TA6

Steel Bar
S1/S93 for 1in thick and over
S96/S11, S94, S95, S98

Steel Sheet
DTD124 (Soft) S515
S84/S511
S515/S514

Aluminium Alloy Tubing
L54/T9/L56
L56/DTD 310
L62/T4

Stainless Steel Sheet
DTD171/S521
DTD166/S520
S521/S527

Steel Tubing
T35 and T45/T53, T60

These materials are used in a wide variety of locations and the following are a selection of the areas that the various materials are used in.

The Cabin/Rear Fuselage/ Tail Unit
This is constructed mainly of DTD 610 in a variety of thickness from 12 to 22 SWG and DTD 687 from 14 to 22 SWG. The skinning of the cabin being DTD 546, the rear fuselage in DTD 687 and 610 with 546 being used in critical areas such as the nose wheel bay. In addition DTD 683, 213, S 96 are used in various locations.

The Wings
Here again we see the use of DTD 546, 610 and 687 being used for the structure and skinning along with amounts of DTD 5020, 124, The main spars on the Mk 1 and 2 versions were built from DTD 683 The joint between the top and bottom of Spar 3 and the Boom Spar top and bottom [Part of Frame 398 and known as the Ham Bone] was known as the Club Foot Joint. When it came to the K2 conversion both of the Boom Spar in Frame 398 were changed along with Spar 3 in the wings the material remained the same except for the bottom Boom Spar that was manufactured in material to DTD 5104 rather than DTD 683.

Plan For Pruduction

The planning and production of the two prototypes was carried out well away from the main production areas of the Handley Page factories. Therefore when it came to the production of the first twenty-five on order it was down to the Production Control Department to take over. It is here that I let the then Chief Planning and Progress Engineer, J G (Gordon) Roxborough describe how it was carried out back in the early 1950s without the aid of computers.

This article by J G Roxborough AMIMechE AFRAeS, Chief Planning and Progress Engineer was published in the Handley Page Bulletin No 229 Summer 1958.

A modern jet bomber such as the Victor is constructed from as many as 40,000 different detail parts and has 2,200 items of equipment supplied by the government or outside manufacturers.

The complicated task of ensuring that all these parts arrive on schedule and in the right sequence to ensure a smooth production flow falls, in Handley Page Limited, to the Production Planning Department.

The planning of production may be divided into two parts: process planning which deals with methods of manufacture and production control that deals with production schedules and factory capacity.

It is the responsibility of the process planning office to decide on the quickest and best method of manufacturing a part. It produces job cards on which are specified individual operations and any heat treatment that may be required. These cards are issued to the workshop to instruct the operator on the work he is to carry out.

A close liaison is maintained with the jig and tool drawing office. It specifies and designs the jigs, tools and fixtures to build the aircraft.

Not only must manufacturing methods be determined, but also the quantity of material required for each part must be calculated from the drawing. This is the responsibility of the schedules section. A schedule is drawn up for every assembly and sub-assembly, listing all Handley Page parts, bought-out parts, nuts, bolts, rivets and other items that comprise the assembled component. This schedule is then passed to material control office that compiles a

Spar 3 lower

Spar 3 upper

bill of material for the whole aircraft. The responsibility for purchase and supply according to schedule rests with the buying office.

The production control office draws up production programmes and undertakes shop loading. It has a two fold responsibility, advising the management on what facilities, in terms of manpower and plant, are needed to attain a certain rate of production and measuring actual against planned output, thereby ensuring that bottlenecks and delays are avoided.

Long and short-term programmes are drawn up to ensure smooth production. Long-term programmes cover periods of three years or more and very often have to be formulated when the aircraft is still in the design or project stage. Design schemes are examined and wherever possible, a comparison is drawn between them and designs of previous aircraft where production statistics have been recorded, various assumptions being made to allow for the differences between the old and new designs.

Long-range forecasts are exceedingly important because many major decisions must be taken in the early life of a project. Special plant or exceptionally large machine tools may be required and these may take from eighteen months to two and a half years to design and build. Furthermore it may be necessary to increase the factory floor area.

The illustration on page 138 shows a typical long-term programme for the production of an aircraft type. The programme establishes the start and finishing dates for each stage of manufacture, culminating in the flight-testing and delivery of completed aircraft. Estimates are made of the number of men required at each stage and of the plant and tooling required. Particular attention is paid to the early ordering of high-grade alloys, castings and forgings and materials that have a long delivery period. For example some special aircraft steels have to be ordered two years in advance. Orders must be placed at an early date with equipment manufacturers for they, too, face similar problems and it is important that they should be given a clear and definite delivery programme with their order.

The production control office works out a programme for the supply of all the various materials and items of aircraft equipment. It shows when deliveries are to commence and the required rate of delivery. This information is issued to the buying office for inclusion in the order to the supplier the importance of delivery rate cannot be too highly stressed, since early delivery and the consequent embarrassment caused by lack of storage space can be costly and time wasting as the late arrival of parts.

Individual programmes for each section of the factory are derived from the overall production programme, these section or shop programmes are short term and cover a period up to six months ahead.

The next illustration (page 139) shows a typical programme for a shop on batch production. This term is applied to the manufacture of aircraft sets of a given part at any one time. It occurs in the machine and press shops and in other sections of the factory where detail parts are made. Here the time taken to set up a machine or tool is large compared with the actual manufacturing time. It is therefore more economical to produce a batch of parts sufficient for several aircraft at one setting.

The sequence of work fed into the shops is keyed to the assembly line. Thus in this illustration fuselage parts designated "C" with their drawing code are the first to be loaded on to them. Wing or parts "B" are fed into the shops next followed by those for the tail unit, hydraulic system flying controls and miscellaneous equipment F, D, E, H, and L, codes.

Despite the wide divergence in the size and shape of parts it has been found that in shops where the total number of parts produced is large the law of averages comes into play and weekly output varies if capacity does not alter. Totalling the weekly output of parts is thus a simple and convenient way of measuring output.

The Victor is designed for split construction: all major components such as inner and outer wings, front and rear fuselage sections and tail unit are made on the line principle in separate assembly jigs.

The output of each shop is compared week by week with the programme and if output falls behind, the matter is discussed with the supervision of the section concerned so that action can be taken before serious hold ups develops. The solution may be to increase manpower, equipment or tooling or to introduce improved methods. Sub-contracting is sometimes a solution, particularly if there is only a temporary overload.

The Victor contains over 200 different items of equipment and its electrical system is connected by over 40 miles of cable. All this equipment and cabling has to be fitted within confined spaces of wings and fuselage allowing only a few men to work at a time. Careful planning avoids congestion and enables tests of all systems to be carried out at the correct assembly stage.

Since the installation of equipment must proceed in a definite sequence for greatest

ORDER PLACED	FIRST YEAR	SECOND YEAR	THIRD YEAR
STAGE	1 2 3 4 5 6 7 8 9 10 11 12	1 2 3 4 5 6 7 8 9 10 11 12	1 2 3 4 5 6 7 8 9 10 11
Tooling			
Material supply	Raw	Equipment	
Detail parts			
Minor assemblies			
Major assemblies			
Equipping			
Ground testing			
Flight testing			
Delivery			

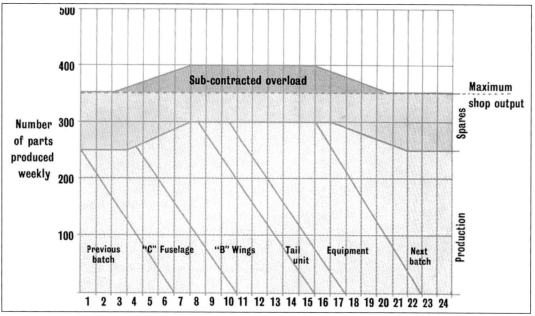

efficiency, delays to one aircraft cause repercussions down the line. It is therefore most important that all equipment is available before the start of each stage. Equipment that is not available at the right time has to be fitted later in the line and will hold up other work scheduled for that stage.

The introduction of stage planning has ensured that all items are available at least a week before they are required and allows the maximum number of men to work on any given part of the aircraft without getting in each others way.

It is of the utmost importance that a substantial backing of spares shall be available before the aircraft enters service. To ensure this spares are provisioned from an early date and manufactured with parts for complete aircraft. This is taken into account when calculating the capacity required in each section of the factory.

The spares and modification office control the supply of spares. It also feeds orders into the factory and is responsible for their meeting delivery dates.

Extensive stocks are held in the stores. Yet there may be a sudden demand for a particular spare necessitating urgent action to get the part manufactured. A section of the spares office is organised to deal with these special requests. On receipt of a telegram or telephone call from the sponsor it has full authority to arrange for the immediate production of the part.

Modifications are fitted in the production line if it does not cause delay or if it is essential to the operation or safety of the aircraft. Less important modifications are supplied as kits to be fitted to aircraft in service at convenient opportunities.

The modern aeroplane needs numerous special items of ground equipment. For example over 250 are used to service the Victor. They range in size from special spanners to large trolleys for jet pipes, from test rigs for the electrical and air conditioning systems to tools for making repairs. All this equipment must be tested and approved by the user before it is delivered.

Closely allied to the spares and modification office is the section that produces the master parts list. These tabulate all the parts that comprise a spare part or modification kit and they are arranged in order of assemblies and sub-assemblies. The master parts list defines the item on order and is used by all departments dealing with spares and modifications. From the list, materials control ascertains materials requirements and the estimating department establishes spares prices. It is used too by the progress department to muster parts.

The attention paid to spares and modifications throughout the programme emphasises the importance of these aspects to routine production. It is accepted, firstly that aircraft must never be grounded for lack of spares if foresight can possibly prevent it and secondly, that the long development schedules characteristic of big modern aeroplanes make modifications during manufacture very desirable from the service or operators point of view.

Victor B1 production. HP-HPA

Corrugated section production. HP-HPA

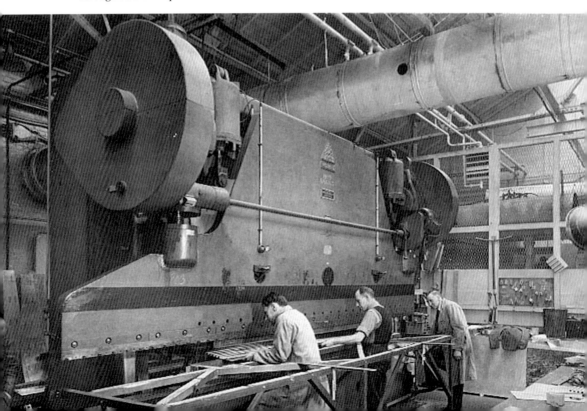

Looking Inside the Victor Mk 1 Series

In this section the parts of the aircraft are examined to see how the various systems were developed and how they worked and enabled the Victor to be such a superb aircraft for its era. A credit to the Handley Page Design and Production teams of years ago.

Access panels and doors

Throughout the aircraft maximum accessibility is given to all services and their associated components.

Panels frequently removed during routine inspections are fitted with quick release fasteners. Screws secure those detached when removing major components such as main planes and tail unit. Special attention has been given to the design and location of easy access panels; every component can easily be reached and serviced through amply sized panels.

Although some of the external quick release panels form part of the primary structure there is no restriction on their removal when the aircraft is stationary. On the main plane there are minor restrictions on a few internal detachable panels that are removed during major servicing as they form part of the main spar structure.

Systems

Aircraft functional systems are arranged to minimise servicing operations without prejudice to maximum efficiency.

Engine and jet pipe installation Mk 1 series aircraft

Large doors in the lower surface of the wing immediately beneath each engine give access to the engine bays for all servicing operations. Installation and removal of the engine is carried out through these doors using a winch mounted on what was called a 'spider' on the top of the wing.

The installation of the four Sapphire SA7 Mark 20201 which are handed port Nos 1&2] and starboard [Nos 3&4] engines is designed to ensure that the engines can be changed with the minimum of effort in the shortest time possible to ensure that the aircraft is returned to the flight line for operations. To quote a time all depends on too many factors and unless all the required manpower and equipment are available and the aircraft in a hangar this task can take some hours when the ground running time is taken into account.

The main attachments for the engine are two trunnions one at each side of the engine. These are held in gate type fixtures on each side of the relevant engine bay. They are called quick release although being torque loaded and split pinned release takes time. A second attachment on the port side of the engine at the forward end is a tubular strut, used for the adjustment of the thrust angle if required. This was originally secured with a nut and bolt and split pinned but this was later changed to a special quick release fitting for ease of access. A central spigot engages with a socket in the wing structure as the central location point.

When replacing an engine, the new engine had to be winched into place by hand. The connections between the engine and its services were quite comprehensive with a variety of electrical connections on a 'quick break' panel. Until the Mk 1A conversion the alternator was mounted on the inboard side wall of the engine bay and driven by a shaft from the engine. The other services to be disconnected and reconnected were the main fuel supply pipe, the fire protection pipe, the hot air pipe for the cabin conditioning and pressurisation along with anti-icing of the leading edges of the wings and tailplane. Also, there was the fuel-tank pressurisation system air-pipe together with

Victor wing panel construction. HP-HPA

various drain and vent pipes that had to be removed. Once the new engine was in place the engine intake extensions had to be refitted (these had to be removed to allow the old engine to be removed), and the throttle/HP cock had to be reconnected. At the very aft end of the engine the jet pipe had to be fitted together with its keep plates and its shroud complete with a drainpipe. After that, the engine fuel system had to be bled to remove the air from the system caused by the removal of the main fuel pipe and then the engine oil system had to be refilled. Finally, the throttle/HP cock was reset.

The B Mk 1A aircraft Serial numbers XH series [except XH617]
With this conversion programme also came a change in engine, it was still the ASSa 7 Sapphire but this time it was the Mark 20701 which was a conversion of the Mark 20201 and was know fitted with the following items: a fuel heater to reduce the chance of ice droplets forming in the fuel going into the engine, an Auto JPT system fitted using additional thermocouples in the jet pipe in order to set up the takeoff, climb and cruise settings without moving the throttle. Finally the alternator was mounted on an intake extension and driven directly from the engine without an external shaft.

The Three Point tankers K1 and K1A
All these aircraft used the ASSa 7 Sapphire Mark 20701 engine, however the K 1 did not have the Auto JPT system. Later in the life of these engines the fuel heater system was no longer used owing to the introduction of FSII [AL48] into the aircrafts fuel AVTUR F34. This being a Fuel System Icing Inhibitor.

Access panels for the jet pipes are from inside the rear engine bay door and the top and bottom of the tail box; these are quick release panels and along with the rear fairing make the changing of the jet pipe quite an easy task although it was time consuming because of the need to refit the rear fairing assembly. The jet pipe was mounted on rollers which helped the fitting.

The Fuel System B Mk 1 Series aircraft. Including the B1A
The fuel system of the production aircraft is a development from that started with the B45/46 submission in 1947 developed and revised for the HP 80 WB771 and WB775. With the production version the basic fuel system of all future Victors was based on this one. All the twenty-nine tanks are bag tanks made of rubber compound (Hycatrol HG.334) of a thickness of between 0.020inch and 0.030 inch and fitted in the bays using metal colleted studs (early ones used rubber studs). There are three basic fuel systems: the fuselage system, and the Port

and Starboard Wing systems. The two wing systems had six tanks each. No. 1 was located in the wing centre section in the fuselage. Tanks 2-5 are located in the inner wing and No. 6 tank is broken down into 6A, 6B, and 6C in the outer wing.

The fuselage system located totally in the rear fuselage being No. 6 is tanks 7-12. There are two 7 tanks designated Port and 7 Starboard and located over the nose-wheel bay and accessible from the plenum chamber, behind them came 1 Port and 1 Starboard. On top of these tanks No. 8 tank was located from the rear of the plenum chamber to the front face of the bomb bay. The next tank No 9 divided into A & B cells and was located up to the equipment bay below the DF loop, from the rear of that bay No. 10 tank divided into A, B & C cells was followed by 11 tank ending at the rear face of the bomb bay. The last two tanks were 12 Port and 12 Starboard located aft of the bomb bay over the old flash bomb bay or where it should have been and nearly up to the rear hatch access panel.

The fuel system is pressure fed at 50 psi from external couplings on the starboard side under the small panel just before the bomb doors. The fuselage refuelling is via a long gallery pipe running the full extent of the bomb bay and into each tank via a solenoid operated refuelling valve. A float switch shuts off fuel contents when the tank is full. The fuselage is fitted with a proportioner: a device to regulate the amount of fuel that is pumped out of the tank when in flight to maintain the aircrafts Centre of Gravity within prescribed limits. The wing systems are rather different to that of the fuselage in that the proportioner is used for both the refuelling and the supply to the engines. This reduced the amount of pipe work required and therefore the space needed for this system. All tanks contain a capacity system, pumps and tank pressurisation equipment. This system was to prove insufficient for some

ferry operations and there was a requirement to increase the capacity by the fitting of two cylindrical tanks in the bomb bay, one forward and one aft, each with a capacity of 8,000lb of AVTUR. In some cases the forward one was permanently fitted and therefore the remainder of the bomb bay could be used for an offensive load. However the fitting of an aft tank required the fitting of an adaptor from which a freight pannier or a spare engine could be carried. This system ruled out the carrying of offensive loads until the aft tank and the adaptor had been removed and the relevant piping had been blanked off. Victor B1 XA930 was used as the trials aircraft for the development of the under wing tanks and flew many sorties with them. However they were never fitted to the Mk 1 fleet operationally and in the late 1960s the attachment points were removed and the pipes blanked off. The trials Victor, XA917, did a few flights with the tanks fitted but this was part of the autopilot trials and they changed the aircraft's flying configuration.

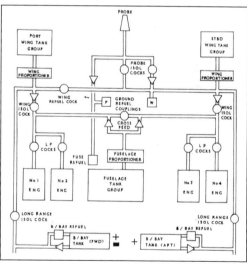

Drawing Mk B1 and B1A Fuel System
Authors Collection

The fuel system for the two-point tanker was essentially the same as the B1A that they were converted from. The two 8,000lb bomb bay tanks were fitted along with the Pannier adaptor to allow the aircraft to carry a freight load as required. As there were only six of these aircraft, the only visible difference externally is the two Mk 20B pods mounted on the outer wing. In the Cabin the fuel control panel 'AT' remains unchanged from the aircraft's time as a bomber. The two pod refuelling cocks that allow fuel to be pumped into the pods are mounted on the coming either side of the Zero Reader on panel 'AW'. The only method of

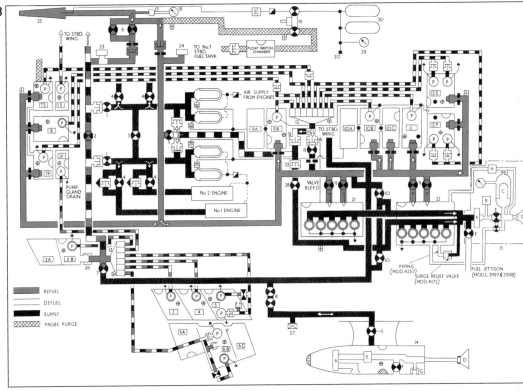

The Fuel System Mk 1 Series Three Point Tankers. Authors Collection

1. Wing isolation cock	13. Main plane fuel proportioner	24. Fuselage refuel coupling
2. Wing refuel/defuel	14. Main plane discharge pod, Mk. 20B	25. Flight refuelling probe
3. Flight crossfeed cock	15. Fuselage hose drum unit, Mk. 17	26. Refuelling surge relief valve
4. Low pressure fuel cock	16. Pressure maintaining valve	27. Underwing tank coupling blank (Mod. 4179)
5. Fuselage defuel cock (inoperative)	17. Flight refuelling pressure transmitter	
6. Probe isolation cocks	18. Flight refuelling pressure gauge (Mod. 4052)	28. Direct cock (Mod. 4501)
7. Long range fuel isolation cock		29. Nitrogen charge pressure gauge
8. Main plane pod isolation cocks	19. Probe purge coupled cocks	30. Nitrogen cylinders
9. Bomb bay tank refuel valve	20. Nitrogen charging point	31. Proportioner protection non-return valve (Mod. 4501)
10. Bomb bay transfer cock	21. Forward bomb bay tank	
11. Fuselage transfer cock	22. Aft bomb bay tank	32. Direct cock protection non-return valve (Mod. 4501)
12. Fuselage fuel proportioner	23. Main plane refuel coupling	

Fuel Discharge Unit Components

A Fuel pump	E Fuel control valve
B Pressure switch	F Fuel jettison cock
C Shock alleviator	G Pod tank relief valve
D Drogue	J Shock alleviator charge point

Symbol Reference

◼	Electrically-actuated non-return valve	Ⓟ	Bottom-mounted pump 9 600 lb./hr.
⊞	Water drain plug	Ⓟ	Side-mounted pump 9 600 lb./hr.
⊕	Fuel/water drain valve	◯	Bottom-mounted pump 29 000 lb./hr.
●	Water drain	⊗	Electrically-actuated cock
	Pressure relief valve	⊢⊗	Manually-operated cock
	Non-return valve	D	High-level float switch
	Solenoid-operated refuel valve	▤	Mid-level float switch
◪	Pressure reducing valve	▨	Low-level float switch
┽	Restrictor plate	⬭	Fuel recuperator

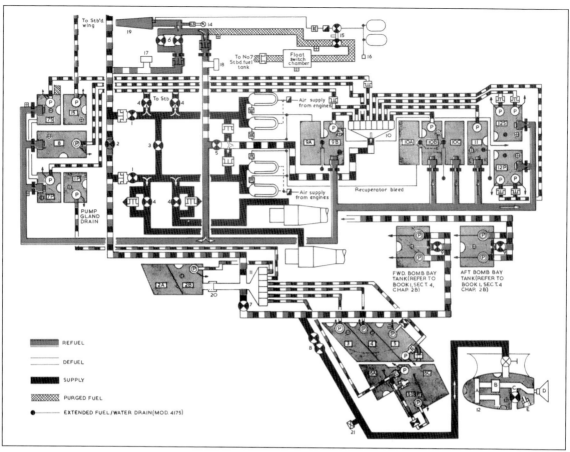

Victor B1A (K2P) Fuel System (Two Pointer)

KEY TO FIG. 1. FUEL SYSTEM DIAGRAM
Fuel System Components

1. Wing isolation cock
2. Wing refuel/defuel cock
3. Flight crossfeed cock
4. Low pressure fuel cock
5. Fuselage defuel cock
6. Probe isolation cocks
7. Long range fuel isolation cock

8. Main plane pod isolation cocks
9. Bomb bay tank refuelling cock
10. Fuselage fuel proportioner
11. Main plane fuel proportioner
12. Main plane discharge pod, Mk.20B
13. Flight refuelling pressure transmitter
14. Flight refuelling pressure gauge

15. Probe purge coupled cocks
16. Nitrogen charging point
17. Main plane refuel coupling
18. Fuselage refuel coupling
19. Flight refuelling probe
20. Refuelling surge relief valve
◀ 21. Coupling blanked after Mod. 4179 ▶

Main Plane Discharge Pod Components

A   Fuel pump
B   Pressure control valve
C   Fuel jettison cock
D   Drogue
E   Pod tank relief valve

Symbol Reference

Symbol	Description
⊠	Electrically-actuated non-return valve
⊞	Water drain plug
⊕	Fuel/water drain valve
●	Water drain
	Pressure relief valve
	Non-return valve
	Solenoid-operated refuel valve
	Pressure reducing valve
	Restrictor plate
◀Ⓟ	Bottom-mounted pump, 9,600 lb./hr.
Ⓟ	Side-mounted pump, 9,600 lb./hr.
Ⓟ	Bottom-mounted pump, 9,600 lb./hr. ▶
⊗	Electrically-actuated cock
⊷⊗	Manually-operated cock
(	High level float switch
◖	Mid level float switch
◖	Low level float switch
⬭	Fuel recuperator

jettisoning fuel on this aircraft is via the two pods. The control panel for the two pods is located adjacent to the Navigator Radar on Panel CI.

The fuel system for the three-pointer tanker was vastly different to that of the bomber. The main fuselage and wing system was retained and only slightly modified. In the bomb bay the doors were removed as well as the 8,000lb tanks and fittings. Into this area were fitted the large two bomb-bay tanks that became of feature of these tankers. Suspended from the fixed suspension points, used to retain the bomb carriers and the two original bomb-bay tank adaptors together with the pannier adaptor, a simple frame was used as the front and aft suspension points for these tanks and they were hoisted in by a winch through a bomb hoist access panel. These tanks were all-metal tanks and profiled at the bottom to fit in with the aircraft's underside curve. Under this curved panel on each tank the five large capacity fuel pumps were located. These tanks had the largest capacity of any on the Victor: 15,300lb, and were to be used as collector tanks to feed the engines and the dispensing equipment. Each tank was fitted with five large capacity pumps. The fuselage and wings feeding into them. The fuel system was modified to accommodate the necessary changes and this ended up in combining all the three systems and in theory you could pump fuel from any tank to any other tank. That being so it was easily possible to dispense virtually all the fuel or to burn it all depending on the task being undertaken and the fuel load on board. This was a very flexible system and this is what made the Victor a flexible tanker. What did hinder the Mk 1 series three pointers was the lack of thrust from the engines particularly when operating in high temperatures. Behind these tanks was the Mk 17 Hose Drum Unit (HDU) with its retractable fairing which contained the jettison system and its discharge pipe protruding from underneath however more on that and the pods later. The control panel for the HDU was located under the pod controls on Panel CI.

Electrical Power supplies Mk 1 series all versions.

The electrical power supplies required by the aircraft were divided into two basic systems. Medium Voltage 112VDC and Low Voltage 28VDC. To provide these requirements the output from the aircraft's alternators had to be transformed and rectified. The alternators driven by each engine had an output of 104 and 208 volts AC frequency wild. However, this type of output was not suitable except for the electrical de-icing equipment. Therefore, the outputs were fed via a Rotax Compounding unit to the Rotax Transformer Rectifier Unit [Located in the Plenum Chamber] where the supply was converted and controlled to that required by the aircraft's services and the relevant outputs then connected to supplying the Port and Starboard MV and LV Bus Bars. In addition there was the emergency backup system of the two 24 volt batteries for the two LV Bus Bars and the eight batteries in two banks of four supplying the two MV bus bars. There were three Type 350 invertors (Located in the Plenum Chamber) that supplied voltages and frequency for the multitude of Avionics and other control equipment and a Type 153 (Located in the Plenum Chamber inverter to supply the Flight Instruments). The system could be very reliable then all could change and it would require a great amount of maintenance. The TRU's were large heavy items and changing them was not a quick task as it involved a lengthy ground run afterwards to set them up. When it came to the Mk 1A and the use of Electronic Counter Measures ECM the two inboard engines were restricted to a certain speed in order to provide a certain power at a certain frequency but this restricted the aircraft's operational ability considerably. All the electrical distribution boards were coded alphabetically starting from the nose. However, due to the changes required by the introduction of the 42 inch extension and the resultant moving of equipment from the rear hatch to the plenum chamber meant that panels coded 'J' broke the sequence, so looking at the aircraft you will find 'J' before 'I'.

Victor Wheel and brake pack initial version.
Author's Collection

Victor Wheel and brake pack improved version from 1961 Modification 545 dated 12/61.

The Hydraulic System

The Victor was a rather unique aircraft for its era in that the hydraulic system's supply pumps were not engine driven like the majority of the aircraft in service at that time.

This aircraft did not need a separate hydraulic supply system external to the aircraft; it had two substantial electrically driven pumps (Operating on 112 VDC for the Mk 1 and 200volt AC for the Mk 2 aircraft) providing the 4000psi required to operate all the following services. Main Undercarriage, Nose Undercarriage, Main Flaps, Airbrakes, Nose flaps, Bomb Doors, Nose wheel Steering and the Braking System. Later in its life the Nose Flaps were deleted and the leading edges fixed. In the tanker role the bomb doors were deleted and that system modified to raise and lower the Mk 17HDU. A change in the brake parachute operating system in the early/mid 1960s led to hydraulic operation. When the Mk 2 came along the Ram Air Turbines (RAT) at the rear of the aircraft required a supply of hydraulic pressure to hold them shut in flight

The operation of the various sub systems is basically the same. The two pumps are located at the rear of the nose wheel bay under the 26-gallon hydraulic tank. They feed the port and starboard Power Panels again in the

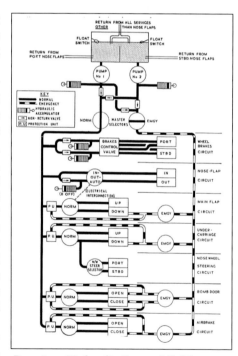

Drawing Hydraulic System Mk B1. Authors Collection

nose-wheel bay. Each panel has a Normal and Emergency Selector and An Automatic Cut out that takes the load off the relevant pump when the system is fully charged, and brings it back on load when operationally required. In addition there are accumulators and a variety of other specialist valves etc. All the hydraulic system operations apart from the brakes are selected electrically by the aircrew in the cabin and indicated in the cabin electrically either by pressure gauges, position indicators of various types or, in the case of the hydraulic pumps, by their ammeters showing the running current.

Apart from the brake system all the other sub-systems use basically the same components, two electro/hydraulic selectors, one normal and the other emergency, a protection unit that changes the pressure supply when emergency is selected, a variety of valves and such as non-return valves, and a stop cock to stop of the service for servicing use when on the ground. Finally, the flaps have a hydraulic motor that drives the flaps up and down. When it comes to the main wheel brakes are operated by 1500psi but the supply pressure remains the same at 4,000psi. Therefore in the system there is a variety of pressure reducing valves, a separate accumulator and a brake-operating valve that allows differential braking as required. The brake units are incorporated into each wheel giving eight sets of brakes that comprise four rows of rotors and eight rows of static brake pads (three double rows and two single rows). These are actuated by hydraulic pistons and use an anti-skid system incorporating a wheel driven Maxaret unit on each brake unit. Operation is by toe brakes on both pilots' rudder pedals via a brake motor system and a hand operated parking brake when required.

Air Conditioning System

Hot air tapped from the outlet from the engine compressors is fed through two cabin air isolation cocks and a pressure control valve and restrictor that will regulate the mass flow of air to the cabin. It is then fed to a temperature control valve that splits the supply: some goes via the cooler and the rest via the Cold Air Unit. The air then passes through the water separator and into the cabin. There are alternatives to this route in that a flow augmenter valve which when open provides an alternative path for the air bypassing the CAU and direct into the cabin. For unpressurised flight ram air is admitted through a Ram Air Valve with the supply taken from the starboard nose intake.

Control of the cabin pressure is by the co-pilot. Two pressure controllers are provided and both are set to 8,000ft conditions. No 2 however has an actuator that can alter the setting of the controller to cause the pressure to maintain 25,000ft conditions. The pressure controllers control the combined valve unit that maintains the pressure in the cabin to the setting selected by the co-pilot. All the controls for this system are operated by the co-pilot and situated on panel 'AD'.

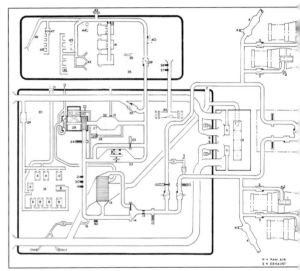

Drawing Airconditioning System Schematic. Authors Colle

AIR CONDITIONING SYSTEM – SCHEMATIC

1. Engine bleed isolation cock	26. 0.085 in. restrictor bleed (Mod. 89
2. High pressure duct test connection	27. Low pressure restrictor
3. Non-return valve	28. Cold air unit
4. Wing anti-icing jet pump	29. Flap-type control valve
5. Transformer rectifier units (4)	30. Bowden cable
6. Inverter	31. 2 in. ground cooling connection
7. Indicator pressure switch	32. Water separator
8. Ground cooling fan	33. Manually operated ram air valve
9. Air supply to windscreen de-icing tank (Mod. 2357)	34. Combined valve unit
10. Cabin air isolation cock	35. Ram air valve operating cable
11. Cabin non-return valve	36. Ram air valve control (Mod. 242)
12. Pressure ratio control valve	37. Temperature bulb
13. Restrictor	38. Cabin sensing element
14. Temperature control valve	39. Cabin air non-return valve
15. Ram air fed cooler	40. Duct relief valve
16. Heated air supply to crew door locks (Mod. 2013)	41. Crew footrests
17. Heated air spray nozzles	42. Ground truck connection
18. Radar equipment	43. Heated air supplies to Pilots' fee
19. Thermal switch A (MAX. HEAT)	44. Pilots' windscreen de-misting co
20. Thermal switch B (OVERHEAT)	45. Pilots' windscreen heating contr
21. Duct sensing element	46. Pilots' windscreen de-misting lo
22. Flow augmentor and flood valve	47. Bomb Aimer's de-misting control
23. Cold air unit by-pass valve (Mod. 908)	48. Bomb Aimer's windscreen de-mis
24. Cold air unit inlet valve (Mod. 908)	49. Bomb Aimer's flexible de-mistin
25. Differential pressure switch	50. Medium pressure duct test connec

Key to Airconditioning System. Authors Collection

Anti-icing System

The basis of this system is that it uses the high-pressure hot air from the engine compressors and mixes it with cold air in a jet pump in each wing's leading edge just outboard of the main intakes. This item is fitted with hot and cold air valves; the cooled air is then fed into a variety of ducts in the leading edge of the wings. A temperature selector sets the temperature and then with a temperature controller opens and shuts the air vales to ensure a correct temperature is maintained. All the controls for this type of anti-icing and the electrical anti-icing of the engine intakes and the Powered Flying Control Unit inlets along with the battery bay heater mats is by the co-pilot from panel 'AD'. There is another jet pump situated in the rear hatch which undertakes the same function and provides air for bomb bay heating and tail anti icing as required.

The Navigator Radar on panel 'CB' carries out the control of the bomb bay heating and tail anti-icing.

The Powered Flying Controls

The flying controls on a Victor are of the conventional variety – ailerons, elevators and a rudder. Handley Page had always been involved with manual controls and manual trimming with trim wheels until the Victor. The Victor was a real change and the flying control system was no different. From the cabin to the relevant control surface this was conventional in that it

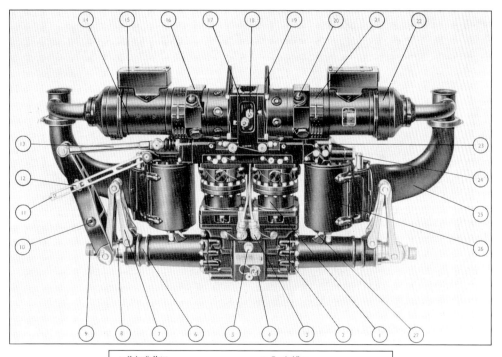

1. Hydraulic Motor.	15. Terminal Box.
2. Gearbox.	16. Hydraulic Pump.
3. Connection for Hydraulic Circuit Filling Valves.	17. Valve Block.
4. Gearbox Oil Level Indicator.	18. Hydraulic Circuit Relief Valves.
5. Gearbox Oil Filler Valve.	19. Mounting Bracket.
6. Mounting Location on Screw Housing.	20. Magnetic Filter.
7. Anti-torsion Link.	21. Flameproof Gauze covering Motor Attachment.
8. Nut.	22. Electric Motor Brush Cover.
9. Jack Output Connection.	23. Pilot's Input Damper Piston.
10. Connection for Auto-Pilot.	24. Thrustat-controlled Cooling Shutter.
11. Jack Stroke Governing Stops.	25. Reservoir Cooling Duct.
12. Pilot's Input Connection.	26. Pressurised Reservoir.
13. Connecting Rod to Relay Valves.	27. Reservoir Contents Indicator.
14. Electric Motor.	28. Mounting Point—Single-ended Jack

was a series of rods and bell cranks to bring the movement from the cabin to the relevant control surface and in order to move this surface with the forces on it a powered method was required. To undertake this task a powered flying control unit that was self contained was required and it was to H.M. Hobson of Wolverhampton that Handley Page turned with excellent results.

The construction of the flying control unit may be described as a screw jack powered by duplicated units disposed around a centre valve block to form a compact self-contained assembly. The weight of the completed unit is around 200lb depending on whether it is a single or double-ended screw jack. The entire hydraulic circuit is contained within the unit casing; the only external piping being for filling and overspill.

Dual Electric motors drive hydraulic pumps which are directly mounted on the valve block. These pumps supply the pressure to hydraulic motors via a control valve system that receives it inputs from the pilot and translates them into the required actions in the valve block. Pressure is then directed to the motors to operate the screw jack via a gearbox assembly and move the control surface in the required direction. Should a sub-unit fail due to the loss of an electric motor or other component then the remaining sub-unit will carry out the control movements as required until the aircraft lands. There is no manual reversion on this type of system, therefore the need for a back-up system. All the three surface units operate in the same way with a single- ended screw jack unit except the aileron that employs a double-ended screw jack.

With a fully powered system the pilot does not feel any of the flying control loads so therefore an artificial feel unit is incorporated and this is fed by ram air from the small intake at the very front of the nose. The unit is situated under the cabin floor adjacent to the H2S Radar Scanner.

Apart from the pilot inputs to the flying control system the autopilot produces inputs as do the yaw and later the roll dampers fitted. The fitting of an auto mach-trim system was later rendered inoperative in some versions. A trimming system was incorporated that was electrically operated from the cabin and increased or decreased the length of the control system depending on the settings made by the pilot to ensure a correct line of flight.

THE HANDLEY PAGE VICTOR Mark 1 Series
TECHNICAL DATA

DIMENSIONS

Span 110ft	**Height** 24ft 9in-28ft 1.5 in	
Length	**Overall** 114ft 11in	**Fuselage** 102ft 5 in
Diameter (Bomb Bay)	10ft	
Track	30ft 2in	
Tail Span	32ft 8in	
Wing Area	2,406 sq ft	2,033 sq ft net
Tail Area	263.6 sq ft	
Air Brakes	29.5 sq ft each	
Tail sweep	56.73deg	
Wing Sweep	47.7/40.5/32.0,deg	

Weight lb	B1	B1A	B1A(K2P)	K1, K1A	Cart Spring
Basic	89,030	90,100	91,740	90,100	90,105
Operating	92,228	94,048	99,310	99,927	99,940
Ramp	170,700	178,700	178,000	186,500	187,500
Take-off	170,000	185,000	178,000	185,000	186,000
Flt Ref.(In flt)		185,000	185,000	185,000	186,000
Emerg Land		125,300	185,000	185,000	185,000
Land	110,000	135,000	135,000	135,000	135,000

Operating Weight for Tankers includes 2,000lb freight
Mk B1 AUW 160,000-170,000 Depending on Modification State
Max. Altitude 49,000ft

Maximum Speed Limitations

Clean Aircraft	330 Knots/0.93M: 415EAS0.95M
Airbrakes	Nil Restriction
Undercarriage	235 Knots
Flaps at Take-off	200 Knots
Flaps Fully Down	180 Knots
Nose Flaps (B1/B1A)	0.75M

Clean Aircraft (Cart Spring) This applies to the following aircraft XA927,XA932,XA939, XH651: 330knots/0.90M
Crosswind Take-off and Landing 25knots
Brake Parachute Limitations   AUW 1600,000lb 158Norm 164 MAX
Cable Trampling   Cleared for CHAG.PUAG. RHAG, SPRAG, Bliss Bak 12, & 500s
Asymmetric Approach Height 1 engine out 150ft true
                                                2 engines out 200ft true

Air To Air Refuelling Limitations

Max Height Hoses Trailed   43,000ft
The Victor Mk K1, K1A and B1A(K2P) are cleared to refuel the following aircraft
Belfast, Buccaneer, CF5, F100, Harrier, Jaguar, Lightning, Phantom,
Sea Vixen, VC10, Victor, Vulcan. Javelin Mk 9

Mk 20B Pods Speed Limitations

Max. Trail and in-flight speed	320Knots/0.88M
Max. in-contact speed	290knots/0.88M
	300knots/0.88M Phantom
Min in-contact speed	230knots

Mk 17 HDU Speed Limitations

Max. trail and in-flight speed	320knots/0.88M
Min. trail and in-flight speed	210knots at Sea Level
	227knots at 43,000ft
Max. in-contact speed	320knots/0.88M
Min. in-contact speed	210-227 knots

Night Dispensing

Victor B1A(K2P) is not cleared for night contacts
Victor K1 and K1A are cleared for night contacts

The Victor is cleared to receive fuel from
KC135 by day only up to 30,000ft 250-260 knots
Victor K1 K1A K2 by Day and Night up to 40,000ft
Victor B1A KB50J 22,000ft 230knots
The Autopilot is cleared for use between 1,500ft and 49,000ft

OPERATING FACTs
Endurance:
160,000lb AUW   220 knots IAS
6.3 NM per 1,000lb fuel or approx 10,000lb per hour
Range Aircraft clean AUW170,000LB
33,000ft 240 knots IAS 8 hours
120,000 AUW
Approach speed   143 knots IAS
Threshold   133 knots IAS
Pattern   153 knots IAS

Descent   From 35,000ft

FAST   Airbrakes out
        Throttles Closed (Idle)
        4.75min 31NM, 320lb fuel

SLOW   Airbrakes In
        Throttles Closed (Idle)
        46min 205NM   3100Lb fuel.

JET   Airbrakes 3/4
        Throttles Closed (Idle)
        10.25min 53nm   920lb fuel

MAX AUW	186,000lb	LCG IV ESWL	33,600lb/ft
LANDING	125,300lb	LCG IV ESWL	20,420lb/ft
Unladen	97,300lb	CG V ESWL	15,600lb/ft

Propulsion and Fuel System
Armstrong Siddeley Sapphire 20201
Armstrong Siddeley Sapphire 20701
Bristol Siddeley Sapphire
Rolls Royce Bristol Sapphire
Starters Rotax C6805 112vDC
Limitations:

	RPM	JPT	Limit
Take-off Special	101.5% (8,729)	685deg C	1.5min
Take-off	100.5% (8,643)	660deg C	10min.
Inter Climb)	98% (8,426)	625deg C	30min
Cont (Cruise)	96% (8,256)	600deg C	No Limit
Approach (Idle)	60% (5,160)		No Limit
Ground Idle	37.5% (3,225)	625deg C	No Limit
Max JPT on Start	875deg C		
100% RPM	8600		
Idle limit	+/-2.5% or +/-215 RPM		

*Armstrong Siddeley
Sapphire 200 Series*
Authors Collection

Oil Pressure	30-38PSI at 96%RPM
Oil Pressure Idle	8 PSI at 37.5%RPM
Min Oil Pressure	25 PSI at 96%RPM

Max sortie 14 hrs on 18 pints oil. Max 1 pint per hour

Aircraft Fuel System cleared to use AVTUR, AVTAG, AVCAT
Based on AVTUR at 8 lbs/Gallon

Fuselage		**Wings Port and Starboard**	
Capacity in Pounds lbs		**Capacity in Pounds lbs**	
7Port	4,712	1P & S	3,736
7Stbd	4,712	2P & S	2,360
8	2,736	3P & S	2,108
9	4,232	4P & S	2,588
10	6,184	5P & S	2,724
11	3,056	6P & S	3,800
12Port	4,196	Total	17,316 each wing
12Stbd	4,196		
Total	34,024		

Bombay Tanks	**B1**	**B1A**	**B1A (K2P)**	**K1 & K1A**
Capacity in Pounds lbs				
Forward	7900	7900	7900	15300
Aft	7900	7900	7900	15300

Mk 20B Pods
Capacity in Pounds lbs
Port and Starboard 1100 each.

Totals   Maximum Capacity Fuel Load in Pounds lbs

B1	84,456 (10,558 Galls)
B1A	84,456 (10,558 Galls)
B1A(K2P)	84,456 (10,558 Galls)
K1 & K1A	101,456 (12,408 Galls)
Max Standard Fuel Load	85,000lb K1 and K1A only
	80,000lb B1A[K2P] only

Victor B1 and B1A Fuel loads
In the Bombing Role the fuel load depends on the bomb load and the distance to the target plus the weather conditions. The requirement to carry a full bomb load would seriously restrict the aircraft's operational range and is based on the basic consumption of 10,000lb in the take-off and climb and 10,000lb an hour after that. This does not give a great range to ensure a return to a friendly airfield, with a load of 50,000lb of fuel.

The aircraft was able to carry 84,456lb of fuel as Maximum Capacity but this did not allow it to carry any bomb load. And with the All Up weight of 180,000lb no bomb load at all. Not exactly an efficient weapon of Strategic Bombing.

Victor K1 and K1A Standard Fuel loads in lb

The fuel loads for the three-point tanker version were set and it was standard procedure to use them depending on the task involved. They ranged from 30,000 lb to 85,000lb and the distribution of this load was to the following table

Total	Wings [P & S]	Fuselage	B, Bays	Pods
85,000	32,000	21,000	30,000	2,000
80,000	32,000	16,000	30,000	2,000
75,000	32,000	11,000	30,000	2,000
70,000	32,000	10,000	26,000	2,000
65,000	32,000	10,000	21,000	2,000
60,000	32,000	10,000	16,000	2,000
55,000	32,000	10,000	11,000	2,000
50,000	32,000	10,000	6,000	2,000
45,000	29,000	10,000	4,000	2,000
40,000	24,000	10,000	4,000	2,000
35,000	19,000	10,000	4,000	2,000
30,000	14,000	10,000	4,000	2,000

Victor B1A (K2P) Standard Fuel loads in lb

The fuel loads for the two-point tanker version were set and it was standard procedure to use them depending on the task involved. They ranged from 45,000 lb to 80,000lb and the distribution of this load was to the following table:

Total	Wings [P & S]	Fuselage	B, Bays	Pods
80,000	31,600	30,700	15,800	2,000
76,400	31,600	27,000	15,800	2,000
73,000	28,000	27,000	15,800	2,000
70,000	28,000	27,000	13,000	2,000
65,000	28,000	27,000	8,000	2,000
55,000	28,000	23,000	2,000	2,000
45,000	25,000	16,000	2,000	2,000

ELECTRICAL SYSTEM
Main Generating System

4 x 208 Volt AC Alternators frequency wild 73KVA
Via 4 Transformer rectifier units (TRU) producing 112VDC and 24VDC
208VAC frequency wild used for airframe anti-icing only
2 Banks of 4 x 24VDC Varley Type J batteries 25amp hour
Supplying 96 V DC to each main bus bar.
1x 24VDC Varley Type J Battery supplying 24VDC to each LV bus bar.

350	Inverters	supplying	115VAc 1600HZ	1 phase
			115VAC 400HZ	3 phase
153A	Inverters	supplying	115VAC 400HZ	3 Phase
108	Inverter	supplying	115VAC 400HZ	1 Phase (TACAN) Tanker Only

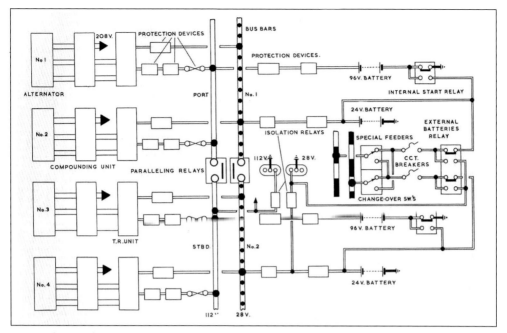

Main Electrical System Mk 1 Series.

AIRCONDITIONING SYSTEMS

Cabin Air Supplies:

This comes from the HP Compressor through dual purpose Engine Bleed Isolation Valves. Then through a combined Dual NRV and Safety Valve before the ducts unite to give Port and Starboard supplies via two Cabin air Isolation Valves. The air then passes via flap type NRVs to the Pressure Ratio Control Valve (PRCV) and the Temperature Control Valve (TCV). Air is then ducted via the medium pressure ducting to various cabin supplies.

Cabin Pressure Control:

This system is duplicated and can maintain the cabin at either the COMBAT (4PSI max at 19,500ft) or CRUISE (8 PSI. At 38,500ft) selection.

Unpressurised Flight

The Starboard ram air intake nostril supplies air for ventilation during un pressurised flight.

Ground Conditioning:

A connector on the starboard side of the nose enables an air-conditioning truck to be connected to the cabin prior to take-off. It is normally more convenient to insert the air-condition trunking through the crew doorway.

HYDRAULIC SYSTEM

Hydraulic power supplied by:

Two electrically driven (112VDC) type BM480 pumps providing 4,000PSI pressure.

Two Main Power Panels supplying pressure to all Normal and Emergency systems via Normal and Emergency Selectors in the panels. Automatic Cut Outs control the pressure in the system and therefore the load on the pumps.

System Limits   Pumps cut in at.   3,600PSI

                    System relief at.   4,800PSI

Systems Operated:

Main Undercarriage	Normal and Emergency Down Only
Nose Undercarriage	Normal and Emergency Down Only
Nose Wheel Steering	Normal
Flaps	Normal and Emergency

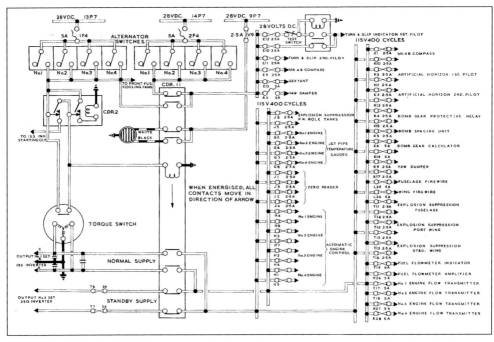

Inverter Supplies Mk 1 Series. Authors Collection

Brakes	Normal
Brake Parachute	Normal and Emergency
Air Brakes	Normal and Emergency Close Only
Bomb Doors (B1,B1A,B1A/K2P)	Normal and Emergency
Mk 17HDU (K1&K1A)	Normal and Emergency

Limiting Speeds of Hydraulically Operated Services

Undercarriage	235 Knots
Flaps T.O.	200 Knots
Flaps Down	185 Knots
Air Brakes	Nil Restriction
Brake Parachute	147-158 Knots depend on landing weight
Bomb Doors	Nil Restriction
Mk 17HDU	320 Knots
Brakes	125 Knots

Tyres	Size	Pressure
Main Undercarriage	27x6.5 X 15	240+/- 5PSI
Nose Undercarriage	30 x 9 x 15	170 PSI
Tail Bumper	7 x 4.5	35 PSI

Accumulator Pressures	Nitrogen
Power	3,000+ 0-200 PSI
Steering	350+/- 35 PSI
Brake	1,625 PSI at 20 deg C
Brake Parachute	1,960 (Temp) PSI

NAVIGATIONAL INSTRUMENTS
Auto Pilot Mk 10
Zero Reader Flight Director

Newmark Yaw Damper
Hobson Yaw Damper
Auto Mach Trim
Ground Position Indicator Mk4
Air Mileage Unit
T4 Bomb Sight (Blue Devil)
GIVB Compass System

ARMAMENT AND SAFETY EQUIPMENT

Ejection Seats	1st Pilot MB 3L/1 (3L/1)
	2nd Pilot MB 3L/2 (3L/2)
Rear Crew Seats	Fixed Seats. All Bomber Versions except XH592-594 when used for crew training in tanker version. Swivel Seats except 6th (Tanker Versions Only)
Parachutes	1st and 2nd Pilots Type B Mk 9 Assembly with ZF Harness Nav P, Nav R,AEO, 6th. Mk 20
Dinghies	Pilots Type Q
	Nav P, Nav R., AEO, 6th Type S or S Mk 2
	Main MS5Mk1
Bomb Load	35x 1,000lb or 1x20,000lb or 7,000lbIWS
Nuclear Weapons	Yellow Sun Mk1 1960-63 7000lb/1/2mt
	Yellow Sun Mk 2 1961-66 7250lb/1/2mt

Bomb Hoisting via hoist holes in fuselage roof using Simons Hoist and RAE Special hoist system.
Very Pistol   1.25in Mk2
Brake Parachute Irvin 45ft Ring Slot LB51Mk2 (159lb +12lb Shackle)
Oxygen System   10 x 250 litre bottles charged to 1800PSI Demand System using
              Mk 17F Regulators.
Emergency Oxygen bottles in all crew parachutes and ejection seats

The Handley Page Victor Mk B1   XA917-941

This initial production batch was ordered under Contract 6/aft/8441/C.B.6 (a) and the production of the main sections was to be carried out at the Cricklewood factory with the final assembly and installation of the services and equipment at the Colney Street factory at Radlett. The completion of the aircraft was to the current production standard. The aircraft was prepared for its Production Test Flights to the agreed schedule and level of testing. The Test Pilots and Flight test crews from HP Radlett carried out these flights. The number of flights required depended on the need to refly because of defects or because the flight had been shortened because of weather conditions. On completion of this Production Flight Test schedule the aircraft would be cleared by the Testing Crew. The aircraft was then prepared for delivery with all outstanding items cleared. The Air Ministry were then advised and details of the delivery flight date advised to HP. Sometimes the delivery was by HP Crew but on most occasions a Crew from the relevant RAF Unit would travel to HP Radlett to collect the aircraft and fly it to its new base.

On arrival from HP Radlett the aircraft would then be taken into the hangars and, under the control of the Aircraft Servicing Flight, undergo the Acceptance Servicing and fitting with the avionics and other equipment that were not supplied through Handley Page. The Squadron markings would be applied to both sides of the tail fin. All the flying controls, hydraulics were

Victor Bomb Bay with 35,000lb bomb load looking forward and aft, Victor Bomb Bay with Baffle, Bomb Carrier. Authors Collection

tested and full engine ground runs were also carried out along with the electrical systems. The aircraft was then handed to the Squadron Crew Chiefs for the Compass Swing to be carried out in conjunction with the Navigators. The Squadron markings would be applied to both sides of the tail fin. The final task was an Air Test by the Squadron QFI or Pilot Leader. The aircraft was then available for operational use in any part of the world.

Aircraft that were to be fitted with test instrumentation and used by initially by Handley Page were moved to the Park Street facility where the relevant test instrumentation and recording equipment were fitted and calibrated before the test flights were undertaken. The following aircraft of this batch went to Park Street after the initial test flights were XA917, XA918 and XA919.

This initial production batch of the B1 aircraft were to be used by a number of trials and testing agencies as well as being the aircraft that were to serve with 232 OCU at RAF Gaydon, the Radar Reconnaissance Flight at RAF Wyton and the first operational Squadrons No. 10 and later No. 15 at RAF Cottesmore.

These aircraft were considerably different to the two prototypes in a number of areas as they were designed and built to the original Specification B35/46 with the changes that were to be introduced by Specification B128/P and this specification led to the following changes some already coming from the problems found in the prototype.

The fuselage was lengthened by forty-two inches with an insert behind the pressurised cabin to accommodate the following equipment that had previously been located in the rear compartment (known as the Back Hatch by the RAF). The four Transformer Rectifier units and the various types of invertors used to supply the various power supplies and their distribution panels complete with the associated control equipment. The five-man dinghy was also located in this area. This helped to reduce the excessive aft centre of gravity problem encountered on the two prototypes. Later, additional radio and other electronic equipment were fitted in this area.

The fuselage fuel system was revised to accommodate all the various fuel tanks as were proposed in the original design and this layout along with a fuel proportioner system, was to remain the basis of the Victor system for the rest of their RAF service.

The fin height was reduced to assist in improving the reduction in the Buffet experienced on the prototypes. In addition the attachment points were

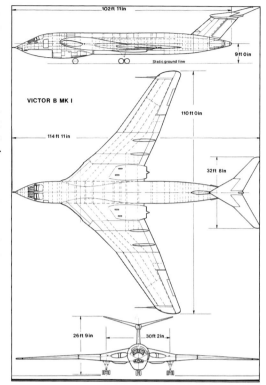

Aircraft 3 View.

improved and strengthened and the structure improved. The extensions to the leading edge of the fin were removed however to return for the Mk 2 version.

The addition of vortex generators to the top of the wing was the only external change. As to the internals of the wing the main improvement was to incorporate a fuel proportioner system to ensure that the fuel to and from the wing tanks was pumped in from the refueller and pumped out in proportion to the tanks contents. This was to aid the maintenance of the centre of gravity position. The tank pressurisation system was changed from the use of nitrogen and a new system developed using air from the aircrafts engines to pressurise the tanks to 3.3/4psi. The fitting of the Armstrong Siddeley ASSa 7 engines known to the RAF as the Sapphire 200 series and those for the Victor Mk 1 as the Sapphire 20201. These gave a superior performance to the ASSa 3 engines used in the HP 80 prototypes. The cabin itself was internally redesigned and the basis of the future layouts started. This was a vast change to the prototype layout which was built as a one pilot operation, however, a second seat was later fitted for the co-pilot with the test crew sitting at the rear table. The new layout at the front and rear was to meet the needs of a five man operating crew and therefore it was to take some drastic changes to implement the Air Ministry requirements.

The Hydraulic System was very similar to that of the HP80 with some minor changes and upgrading for operational use.

The Airconditioning-Pressurisation system was to be improved as the aircraft was developed but remained basically the same as the early version used on this batch of aircraft.

The escape hatches were changed from a solid construction to having two large transparencies fitted to provide the crew with the facility to view above the aircraft. Fixed fittings for future in-flight refuelling were fitted on all production Victors, however, not all were fitted with probes in their service life. The development and fitting in suitable locations took quite a time because the various pieces of communication and navigation equipment needed several trials to ensure that the equipment was installed in its correct location and working to the specification called for. With the Smith's Mk 10 Autopilot there were a number of problems and the need to carry out extensive trials by Handley Page and the A&AEE before it was cleared for use by the RAF meant that quite a few aircraft were delivered without the system complete and in use.

Test and Development Flying

Handley Page retained two aircraft (XA917 and 918) for use on Manufacturers Trials and in conjunction with the A&AEE under the control of Controller of Aircraft [CA] at the Air Ministry. A great deal of test and development flying was carried out covering a great variety of subjects and in a variety of conditions. These ranged from flying at a height in excess of 35,000ft with the door open and on another occasion with the hatches removed. All this just to see what it was like to fly the aircraft in those conditions. And it did happen; on at least one occasion the door was lost in flight and on another flight the hatches were lost. The first instance of a V bomber going supersonic was with XA917 flying from RAF Gaydon under the control of HP Test Pilot John Allam on a Saturday afternoon and it was heard in Watford by Charles Joy the then Chief Designer.

The second aircraft that virtually lived all of its life in trials and testing was XA918 this too undertook a great variety of trials and spent some time at the AAEE. Until 1964 it was designated to be the prototype and development aircraft for the then three point Victor tanker. The same basic system was to be used by the RAF from February 1966 to October 1993

Fuel Control Panel AT   Author's Collection   *Engine Start Panel AT*   Author's Collection

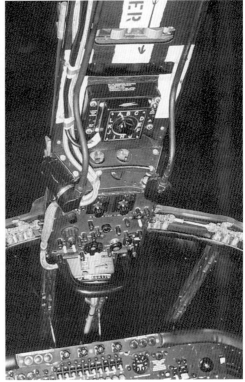

Front Cabin, 1st Pilots Side Panel.

Front Cabin, Co Pilots Side Panel.

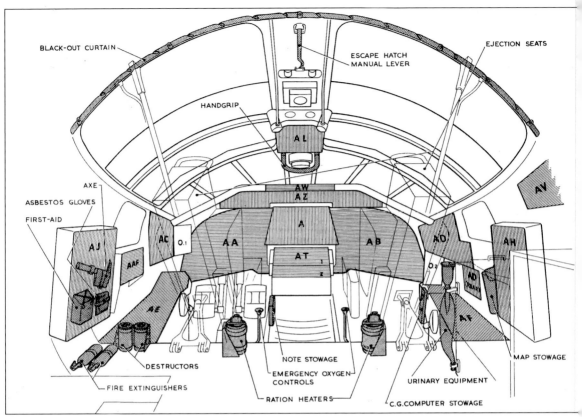

Front Cabin B1

Rear Cabin B1-4

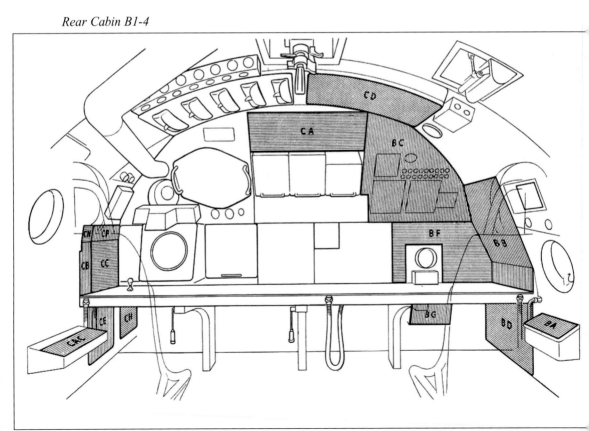

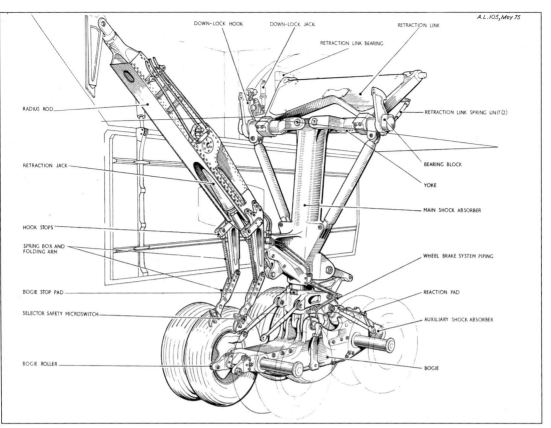

Main Undercarriage

Retraction Sequence

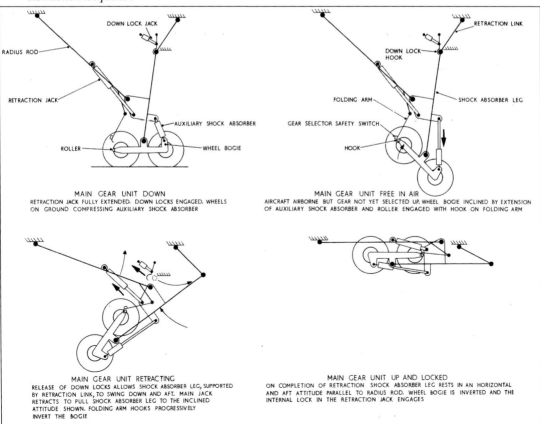

MAIN GEAR UNIT DOWN
RETRACTION JACK FULLY EXTENDED. DOWN LOCKS ENGAGED. WHEELS ON GROUND COMPRESSING AUXILIARY SHOCK ABSORBER

MAIN GEAR UNIT FREE IN AIR
AIRCRAFT AIRBORNE BUT GEAR NOT YET SELECTED UP. WHEEL BOGIE INCLINED BY EXTENSION OF AUXILIARY SHOCK ABSORBER AND ROLLER ENGAGED WITH HOOK ON FOLDING ARM

MAIN GEAR UNIT RETRACTING
RELEASE OF DOWN LOCKS ALLOWS SHOCK ABSORBER LEG, SUPPORTED BY RETRACTION LINK, TO SWING DOWN AND AFT. MAIN JACK RETRACTS TO PULL SHOCK ABSORBER LEG TO THE INCLINED ATTITUDE SHOWN. FOLDING ARM HOOKS PROGRESSIVELY INVERT THE BOGIE

MAIN GEAR UNIT UP AND LOCKED
ON COMPLETION OF RETRACTION SHOCK ABSORBER LEG RESTS IN AN HORIZONTAL AND AFT ATTITUDE PARALLEL TO RADIUS ROD. WHEEL BOGIE IS INVERTED AND THE INTERNAL LOCK IN THE RETRACTION JACK ENGAGES

starting with the Mk 1 and 1A conversions and ending up with the K2 version based on the HP design but converted by HSA, later to be called BAe. The variety of trials carried out by XA917 and 918 can be seen by the length of time they spent on that type of work.

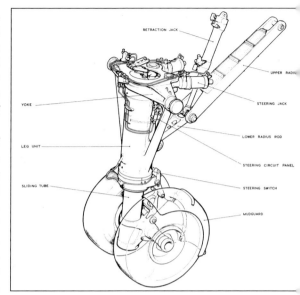

Another two aircraft spent most of their working life at the A&AEE. One was XA919, this aircraft was used by the A&AEE for communications, radar and bombing systems assisted by XA922 from the Handling Squadron (XA919 landed with the starboard brakes on which caused extensive damage and, in addition, this aircraft lost both its escape hatches in early 1959 which caused considerable damage to the rear fuselage). The other main aircraft was

Nose Undercarriage

XA920 which was used extensively for the multitude of trials that were required for the CA release. These concentrated on the operation of the nose flaps when handling problems concerning longitudinal stability became a problem at aft CG. And lateral oscillations that were a problem at CG's. A single channel yaw damper later controlled this but was later duplicated for reliability. There were to be other problems that needed attention including the artificial feel system and the reliability of the braking parachute. Later it was to undertake photo-reconnaissance trials. Aircraft XA 921 was another aircraft that spent a considerable time at RAE Farnborough on ballistic trials before moving on to A&AEE for the acceptance trials of the 35,000lb load and its release. Aircraft XA 922 was the last of the six trials and development aircraft. It was initially used by the Handling Squadron at the A&AEE for the

Victor B1 XA917 Landing with 4 Chutes. HP-HPA.

Handling Flight Production clearance of the Pilots Notes. It then returned to HP Radlett before moving to RAF Farnborough where it carried out further ballistic trials from late 1958 until mid 1966 when it was returned to HP Radlett; to carry out further tests using wing-strain gauges. One other aircraft, XA930, spent a considerable time at A&AEE initially on the intensive flying trials carried out by RAF Bomber Command crews under the control of the A&AEE scientific staff. Then it undertook trials covering the fuel system, underwing tank, refuelling probe and RATOG trials before being delivered to Handley Page Radlett for removal of the trials equipment and it was brought up to production standard and delivered to RAF Cottesmore for use by 10 Squadron.

It is often stated that 10 Squadron was the first Victor unit in the RAF. According to my researches and discussions with AVM John Herring, who, when a Sqn/Ldr was one of the first Victor Captains on the Radar Reconnaissance Flight. They and their crews were trained at RAF Gaydon by 232 OCU on the first Victor Course and proceeded with their three aircraft to RAF Wyton in March and April 1958. This unit was to have an establishment of three aircraft which were fitted with Yellow Aster, a radar equipment that was used in conjunction with the Blue Shadow-NBS/H2S system. The unit was operational until October 1961 when the aircraft were returned to RAF Gaydon for the equipment fit that was required to carry out the training duties with the OCU. All three aircraft also spent some time at RAF Cottesmore before disposal to training schools and specialised trials. The remaining aircraft from the first batch were allocated to 232 OCU for crew training and conversion to the V bomber role along with deliveries to 10 Squadron that re-formed at RAF Cottesmore on the 15 April 1958. They were to receive eight aircraft over the coming months and these were initially used to bring the new crews fresh from the OCU up to operational standard and competent in all aspects of the aircraft's operation within the V Bomber force. The first aircraft actually arrived on 9 April 1958 and the next seven over the next four months. These aircraft were to be the subject of many modifications in their early life to bring them up to the required level of equipment specified. It was a long learning curve, not only for the aircrew but for the ground crew, most of whom had many opportunities to actually find their way round an aircraft at their own pace and trade requirements. (I can well remember my first few weeks at RAF Marham in the Victor Servicing Flight and what it took me to really understand them, and that was in 1966). The crews were to spend a great many hours flying Navigation Exercises, Visual Bombing, Radar Bombing, Competition Bombing and Exercises both home -based and on detachments to various parts of the world. All this training was to bring the crews to the high standard required of them. The second Squadron to be formed was No.15 and this was on the 1 September 1958 again at Cottesmore. Their first aircraft was delivered on 17 September 1958, X941, this being the last of the first-batch. As the deliveries built up there was some movement of aircraft within the two Cottesmore Squadrons to even out the lives of the aircraft as they went through extended servicing due to the modification programmes that were under way at that time.

DEVELOPMENT AIRCRAFT   XA917-XA922
Production: Mk.B1
Contract 6/Acft/8441/C.B.6 (a) 6/52
XA 917 Silver
1956
Taxiing Trials: 29/1, 30/1
First Flight 1634-1639 15 min (J W Allam) (2 HP Test Flights)
HP Park Street 26/3(Silver)
16/4:19/4:3/5:4/5:8/5:17/5: 22/5:24/5:28/5(Handling and Performance Flights): 28/5: 30/5:

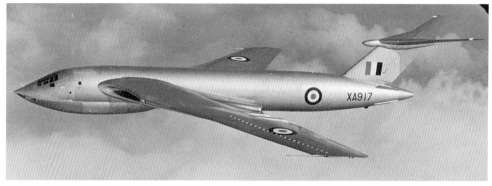

Victor B1 XA917 First Aircraft for Delivery. HP-HPA.

1/6(2) 2/6:3/6:4/6:5/6: (Familiarisation A&AEE Crew): 18/5 (Air to Air Photography): 16/7: 22/7: 23/7; (Handling Flights) 25/7 (High Altitude P/E.) 25/7 (Zone 3 Cooling Tests): 26/7: 27/72/8: 3/8: (Handling and Performance Flights) 8/8: 9/8: (Low Altitude P/E at A&AEE with a Venom): 8/8:9/8: (Return to HP Radlett): 14/8: 20/8: 30/8: 24/9: (With Aft and Ext Aft C of G): 3/9: 5/9: (SBAC Show and return to HP Radlett) (J W Allam: Sdn/Ldr A Ringer: R Williams: G Wass): 15/9: 23/1126/11: 27/11: 5/12: 13/12: (Auto Stabiliser test): 3/11: 8/11: 11/11 (Handling Flights) (91.09hrs)

1957

3/1: 7/1: 17/1: 5/2: (Handling Flight): 10/1: 28/3: (Yaw Damper and Auto Mach Trim): 19/1: 29/4: (Auto Stabilisation and Yaw Damper Test): 13/3: 15/3: 21/3: 29/3: 30/3: 4/4: 6/4: (Engineering Tests): 11/4 HP Radlett to A&AEE Boscombe Down: 11/4 (Performance Test J W Allam 6.47 hrs): 15/4: (Handling Flight A&AEE): 5/4, 16/4, 25/4: (Demonstration Flight): 29/4 (A&AEE Boscombe Down to HP Radlett): 3/5 (Yaw Damper Test): 4/5 (High Mach No test Flaps Down): 8/5 (Nose flaps out at High Mach No): 10/5: 15/5: 22/5: 27/6: 15/7: 18/7: (Engineering Test): 21/5 (Demonstration to BOAC): 29/5 (Cabin Heating Test): 30/5 (Nose Flaps at High Altitude): 1/6 (Longitudinal Stability Test and Broke the Sound Barrier): 3/7 (Handling Flight Sdn/Ldr Moreau): 6/7 (TRU Cooling): 18/12 Air Test: 19/12, 20/12: (Thermal Anti-icing and Nostril Intake Test): 31/12 (Nostril Intake Test): (180.25hrs)

1958

7/1: 8/1: 25/1:4/2: 6/2: (Ant-icing Test): 11/1 (Anti-icing and Handling Nose Flaps Down): 14/1 (Tail Load Test): 20/1 (Handling Nose flaps): 14/2: 17/2: 18/2: (Flood Flow and Thermal De-icing Test): 6/3 (2): 12/3 (Elevator Angles for G Test): 11/3: 13/3: 14/3: 17/3: 19/3: 21/3 23/3:24/3: 28/3: 1/4: 3/4: 8/4: 11/4: 4/4: 21/4: 22/4: 28/4: 1/5: 2/5: 13/5: 15/5: 19/5: 21/5: 23/5: 28/5: 9/6: 17/6: 7/10: 8/10: 11/10: 14/10: 17/10: 23/10: 27/10: 31/10: 1/11: 4/11: 5/11: 1/12: 8/12: 9/12(2) 11/12: 18/12: 20/12: 30/12: (Auto Pilot Test):11/4: (Yaw Damper Test) 3/10 (Air Test): (309.55hrs)

Victor B1 XA917 Landing Radlett End. HP-HPA

Victor B1 XA917 withdrawn from use - Alan Dowsett.

1959
2/1: 8/1: 9/1(2) 16/1: 21/1#: 23/1#: 3/2: 24/2: 26/2: 27/2: 25/3: 31/3: 4/4: 10/4: 17/4: 20/4: 24/4: 28/4: 29/4: 4/5: 12/5: 14/5: 26/5: 27/5: 28/5: 2/9: 5/9: 7/9: 8/9: 10/9: 15/9: 17/9;18/9· 21/9· 8/10· 9/10/14/10ι 22/10. 23/10. 26/10. 28/10: 4/11: 5/11: 12/11: 19/11#: 4/12: 8/12: 31/12: (49 Auto Pilot Tests): 7/4(Anti-icing Test): 27/7(Flood Flow Test): (430.15hrs): # A&AEE Crew Flights

1960
9/1: 11/1: 18/1: 20/1: 3/3: 7/3: 17/3: 7/4: (8 Auto Pilot Test): 28/1: 8/2: 9/2:(Auto Mach Trim Development) 31/3 (Auto Pilot Test with Underwing Tanks): 8/4: (Auto Pilot and Elevator angle for G test): 12/4: (Auto Pilot Test Landed A&AEE Boscombe Down): 13/4: 14/4: 21/4: (3 Auto Pilot Test At A&AEE Boscombe Down): 1/6 (Stability Test Landed HP Radlett): (469.40)

1961
20/2 (Air Test): 2/3 (Radio Trials): Last Flight under HP Test Programme
Total Flying Hours 473.30   222 Test Flights by HP Test Pilots and Flight Test Crews.
Misc notes not all verified
8/12/59 Damaged Rear End on Landing W Burton:
3/60: Mach Comp Test formatting on XH668 P Murphy 10/4/59
HP Park Street Partly Dismantled 8/62
Cat 5 Training 7827M 13/12/63. SOC 1/64.
Crew Drill Trainer. RAF Wittering, Wyton, Marham (1971-93)
Tender February 94 Crowland Lincs. /94: Guardbridge Fife 8/95

XA 918   Silver
1956:
First Flight 21/3/56 1247-1302 15 min (J W Allam) (five HP Test Flights) AwC 29/3/56
HP Park Street for Development Flying: 29/3: 31/10: 8/11(2): 18/12 (Air Test): 6/12 (Fuel Assessment): 29/12 (Flight Flutter Test)
1957
12/1: 18/1: 20/1: 20/2: 21/2: 25/2: 1/3: 13/3: 14/3: 15/3: 28/5: 6/6: 13/6: 15/6 (Landed A&AEE Boscombe Down): 3/1: 28/6: 1/7: 4/7: 20/7: 22/7: 29/7(2): 31/7 (2) 17/9(3): (Flight Flutter Test) 8/1 (Photography and Familiarisation): 10/1: 23/1: 4/2 (2) 5/2: 11/2: 13/2: 12/3: 11/6: 26/6; (Aileron Load Test): 22/2: 2/5: (Open Door in Flight): 1/5 (Air Test): 6/5 (Nostril noise Test): 7/5: 15/5 (RAF Marham Flypast Rehearsal): 8/5 HP Radlett to A&AEE Boscombe Down) 8/5 (2) (Brake Parachute Deployment at High Speed) 8/5 (Rtn A&AEE Boscombe Down to HP Radlett):11/5: 11/6: 12/6: (Bomb Bay Heating test): 13/5: 16/5: 17/5: (TRU Vibration test): 15/5 (RAF Marham Flypast) (J Still: Sdn/Ldr A Ringer: J Ogilvie: P/O Williams): 15/5 (HP Park Street Silver): 16/6 (A&AEE Boscombe Down to HP Radlett): 20/6 HP Radlett to RAF Coningsby Flight Flutter and return): 20/6 (Flight with Hatches removed): 24/6 (HP Radlett to A&AEE Boscombe Down) 24/6: (Flight With Hatches Removed at A&AEE): 24/6 (Rtn to HP Radlett): 5/7 (Demonstration to NATO at DH Hatfield and Flight Flutter Test): 18/7: 19/7: (Maxaret Brake Test): 24/7 (Aileron Rod Load Test

*Victor BI XA 918 Landing at SBAC Show 1957.*HP-HPA.

Landed A&AEE Boscombe Down): 25/7 (Aileron Rod Load Test Landed HP Radlett): 26/7 (HP Radlett to A&AEE Boscombe Down and return after Aileron Rod Load Test): 28/7 (Rudder Kicks): 2/8: 7/8 (Crew door opening): 7/8 (Zone 3 Cooling): 28/8: 29/8 (Air Test): 31/8 HP Radlett to RAE Farnborough and photography SBAC Show) 2/9: 3/9: 4/9: 5/9: 6/9:7/9: 8/9: (Demonstrations at SBAC 1957: 9/9 (RAE Farnborough to HP Radlett): 13/9 (Elevator and Aileron Rod Measurements): 14/10: 17/10: 17/10: 19/10: (Power Off Brake Test): 23/10: 24/10: 30/10: 1/11: 13/11: 14/11: (Yaw Damper Test): 25/10: 1/11 (Pressure of Brake test): 22/11: 26/11: (RCM Vibration Test): 30/11: 9/12: 14/12: 21/12 (Crew Door Opening and Hatches off in Flight) (Electrical Over volting Test): (109.25hrs).

1958

3/1: 23/6: 26/6: (To A&AEE Boscombe Down Brake Parachute Streaming at High Speed and Rtn to HP Radlett): 9/1: 11/1: (Tail Load test): 14/1 (Nose Flaps down at High Speed): 20/1: 13/2; 14/2 (Rudder Hinge Movement Test): 24/1: 15/2: 18/2: (Yaw Damper Test): 13/2 (Fuel Pressure Test): 20/2 (Brake Capacity Test A&AEE Boscombe Down and Rtn to HP Radlett): 2/5 (Air Test): 12/5: 13/5: 15/5: 19/5 (2) 20/5: 27/5: 28/5 (Flight Flutter Test): 21/5: 30/5: 3/6: 9/6: (RCM Trials): 13/6: 16/6: (Air Brake Instrumentation): 18/6 (2) (Escape Door Opening Trials) 30/6: 3/7: (Air Brake Load Test): 4/7; 14/7: 17/7: 18/7: 21/7: 23/7: 24/7: (PFCU Test): 8/12: 9/12: 11/12: 19/12: 30/12: (Vortex Generator Development):(166.35hrs).

1959

2/1: 21/1: 22/1: 24/1: 3/2: 20/2: 23/2: 4/3: 7/3: 11/3: 13/3: 17/3: 26/3:(Vortex Generator Development): 2/4: 3/4: (HP Radlett to A&AEE Boscombe Down, Aileron Load Test) 6/4: (A&AEE Boscombe Down to HP Radlett): 17/4: 21/4: (Flight with Door Open): 24/4 (Vibration Test): 25/4: 28/4: 4/5: (Engineering Test Landings at RAE Bedford): 9/6: 15/6 : (Drooped Leading Edge N/F List) 16/6 (Stalling Test): 19/6: 26/6:(Trim Curves): 2/7: (Handling Flight): 7/7: 8/7: 27/11: 12/12: 16/12: 18/12/ (Performance Test): 13/7: 22/7: 23/7: (Cruise Climb): 30/7: 26/11: (Buffet Boundary): 6/8 (HP Radlett to A&AEE Boscombe Down and Return Pegs at A&AEE with Javelin at 40,000ft): 11/8: 12/8: (General Handling and Drooped Leading Edges): 2/12 (Bomb Bay Temperatures): (244.55hrs):

1960

22/1: 25/1: 10/5: (Trim Curves): 29/1: 15/2: 16/2: 10/3: 2/4: 7/4: 8/4: 13/4: 21/4: 25/4: 12/9: 13/9: (Bomb Bay Vibration): 5/2 (Trim Curves and Wing Tuft Observation): 9/2: 13/6: (Vortex Generator Development): 8/3: (Pitch-up Boundary Measurements): 28/4 (Performance Test): 3/5: 5/5: 24/5: (Bomb Bay Heating/Cooling): 5/5 (Drag M/S): 11/5: 30/5: 1/6: 4/7: 8/7: 20/7: 29/7: 9/8: 23/9: (Buffet Boundary Test): 4/7 (De-icing Test): 9/9: (Vibration Test) 4/10: (Mach Trim Runaway): 14/10: 4/11: 14/11: (Instability Boundary Turns): 27/10 (Windscreen De-icing Test): (308.35hrs): 21/4 (P Murphy 2 Barrel Rolls)

Victor B1 XA 918 on Flight Test Duties with HP and A&AEE. HP-HPA.

1961
12/5: 16/5: (Continuous running Hydraulic Pumps Test): 24/5: 25/5:30/5:23/6:23/8: (X Band Radio Trials): 2/6: 6/6: 9/6: 14/6: 21/6: 26/6: (Plenum Chamber Hatch off Trials at LL 20k and 34k ft): 16/6 (Crew Door Opening in flight): 1/9: 22/9: (Leading Edge Stagnation point): 26/9: (Dorsal Fin Intake Efficiency M/S) (344.05hrs)

1962
24/1: 2/2: 8/2: 9/2: (Red Neck Trials): 19/2 (HP Radlett to RAE Bedford and Return):13/3 (Trim Curves Braking Parachute Test Landed RAE Bedford and Run): 26/3: (Formation with Lightnings pre-Flight Refuelling Trials): 12/10 (Air Test and Trim Curves): 2/11 (Levels and High Speed Brake Parachute Stream Landed RAE Bedford) 5/11: (RAE Bedford to HP Radlett): 14/11 (Quasi Levels): 30/11 (Performance Test): 21/12 (Buffet Boundary Test) (371.10hrs)

1963
8/3: (Trim Slots etc. Delivery to A&AEE Boscombe Down); 5/12 (Air Test) (373.40hrs)

Victor B1 XA918 Red Neck Fitted and ECM tail aerials. Alan Dowsett

Victor B1 XA918 Red Neck. Alan Dowsett

XA 919 Silver
First Flight 13/3/57 1154-1244 50 min (J W Allam) (four HP Test Flights) AwC 28/3/57:
HP Park Street 11/4/56-26/3/57 (Conference Aircraft)
Delivered to A&AEE Boscombe Down 28/3/57(J W Allam):
A&AEE Boscombe Down 19/9/57: Nose undercarriage retracted on ground A&AEE 9/1/58 rebuilt: by HP Working Party: Minor Servicing 100hr at A&AEE by HP 23/4/59 :(219.5hrs)
Flying Accident 3/9/59 Hatches came off in flight damage to rear fuselage rebuilt by HP Working Party: Minor Servicing 200hr at A&AEE 22/9/59 :(265.10hrs)
RAF Locking No 1 Radio School Instructional 7724M 15/16/5/61 -10/4/64
Returned to HP Radlett by road 9/66 for fatigue testing duties. Scrapped 1970:

Victor B1 XA919. Author's Collection

Victor B1 XA919 at Park Street Test House. HP-HPA.

Victor B1 XA919 Valiant Vulcan Flypast A&AEE. Author's Collection

XA 920 Silver
1956
First Flight 12/5/56 1529-1547 18 min (J W Allam)

14/6(2): 15/6:(Production Test and Handling): 13/12(Air Test) 14/12:(HP Radlett to A&AEE Boscombe Down) 18/12:29/12:(Handling and Stability Test):(7.05hrs)

1957
1/1: 3/1: 6/1: (Handling and Stability Test) 3/1 :(Performance Test): 14/1 (Handling forward C of G): 16/1: (Handling Aft C of G): 16/1 (Flapless Landing): 16/1 (2) (Familiarisation):-/- (Rtn to HP Radlett) (90.20hrs): 9/9 (Air Test): 11/9: (JPT Controller and Fuel Flow Test): 13/9:19/9: (Performance Cruise Checks): 26/9: 27/9: 9/10 (Yaw Damper Test): 26/9 (JPT Controller Test): 22/10: 23/10 (2) (105.10hrs): 25/10 (HP Radlett to A&AEE Boscombe Down)

1958
At A&AEE Boscombe Down: 17/2 Repair to starboard Bomb door, starboard Inner Flaps etc (117.20hrs): Repair by HP Radlett and CAT 3 by 49MU: Repair to airbrakes by HP 5/58:

1959
At A&AEE Boscombe Down until return to HP Radlett: 22/5: 28/5: 11/6: 12/6: 16/6 : (Air Test) 16/6: 27/6: (Bomb Bay Heating): 29/6: (PR Roll Test): 7/7: 5/12 (Vibration Tests): 8/7 (HP Radlett to A&AEE Boscombe Down)8/7: 14/7: 22/7: 23/7: 27/7: 31/8: 2/9: 3/9: 8/9: 10/9: 28/9: 29/9: 30/9: 5/10: 6/10: (Night Flying at A&AEE) 17/7: (PR Heating Trials Ldg. to HP Radlett): 21/7 (HP Radlett to A&AEE Boscombe Down) 30/7 (Rtn to HP Radlett) 29/8: 16/10: (PR Heating Trials): 31/8: (HP Radlett to A&AEE Boscombe down): 11/9: (Rtn to HP Radlett): 18/9: 20/11 (Handling Flight): 21/9: (HP Radlett to A&AEE Boscombe Down): 23/9, 24/9, 28/9, 29/9, 30/9, 5/10, (Handling Flight at A&AEE and PR Tests at 45,000ft):8/10(Day Photography and Landing HP Radlett):6/12(PR Vibration Test):17/12(Vibration and Leak rate test):21/12:(Camera Vibration Test)

1960
5/1: 22/1, 25/1, 5/22 6/2: 4/3: 5/8: 18/8: 25/8: 29/8: 7/9: 4/10: 28/10: (Camera Vibration Test at 45,000ft M.985) 9/1: 21/4: 22/4: 23/4: 25/4: 29/4 :(PR Trials) 19/1: 22/1: 25/1: 3/2: 5/2: 15/2: 8/3 (BD): (PR Vibration Test): 7/3: (HP Radlett to A&AEE Boscombe Down): 21/3: 23/3 (PR day Photography at A&AEE): 22/3: 23/9: (PR Night Photography at A&AEE): 1/4 (Rtn to HP Radlett): 10/5: 15/8: 22/8: (Camera Heating Trials): 5/8 (Air Test): 17/8: (HP Radlett to A&AEE Boscombe Down):
26/9: (Camera Trials): 4/10: 28/10: (Night Vibration Test)
1961
9/2· 6/6 · (Night PR Vibration Test).
Delivered to MOA Fire School Stinted 25/9/63 from A&AEE Boscombe Down
SOC 9/63 to Foulness
Misc Note not all verified
Cabin Leak rate 28/5/59: Air Brakes Broken at 390 Kts 28/5/59 W Burton:
29/6/59 Bomb Doors Damaged by Camera Crate 29/6/59 P Murphy:
23/9-6/10: PR Tests at 45,000ft (J Rudeforth)
21/1/61 2 Barrel rolls at 1.015M P Murphy J Rudeforth: SBAC
CAT 3-49MU/ HP Repair 17/2/58-23/6/58 at A&AEE Boscombe Down
107 HP Test Flights

XA 921 White
1956
First Flight 20/6/56 1945-2009 24 mins (J W Allam) (five HP Test Flights) AwC 12/7/56
17/7: (Handling Flight): 19/7: (HP Radlett to RAF Marham): 23/7 Queens Review Bomber Command: 23/7 (RAF Marham to HP Radlett:):
1957
18/7: 22/7: 23/7: 26/7: 29/7: 16/9 (Air Test) 27/7: (Parachute Doors): 31/7: 2/8: 7/8: (HP Radlett to RAE Farnborough) 31/7: 2/8: 7/8: 19/8 (RAE Farnborough to Bombing Range to HP Radlett): 15/8: 16/8: (HP Radlett to RAE Farnborough and Rtn): 16/8 (Bomb Carriage Assessment): 18/9 (HP Radlett to A&AEE Boscombe Down):
1958
8/9: 10/9: 11/9: 17/9: (Test Flying at A&AEE): Repair to Bulkhead 804 by HP at A&AEE;
1959
28/10: 2/11: 5/11: (Test Flying at A&AEE) Minor Servicing 200hr by HP at A&AEE 12/8/59: (127.10hrs)

Victor B1 XA921A&AEE 6-5-63. HPA.

Victor B1 XA921 A&AEE 7-5-63. HPA

1960
At A&AEE Boscombe Down returned to HP Radlett date unknown
1961
19/1: 21/1: 24/1: (Production Standard Test Flight): 24/1: (HP Radlett to A&AEE Boscombe Down) Scrapped at A&AEE Boscombe Down 1963
Misc Notes not all verified
RAE 6/59 RAE Dropped 35K 6/59: Trials continued until 24/1/61
At RAE until 12/61 35K Trials.
Max Overload Trials, Initial Probe Trials:
Damaged A&AEE Boscombe Down 23/4/58 repaired by HP Working party at A&AEE
Returned to RAF disposal 14/10/62 Dismantled A&AEE Boscombe Down 5/63 SOC 17/10/64
(39 HP Test Flights) Long Range Tank and Leaflet Container Clearance date not known

XA 922 White
1956
First Flight 12/9/56 12130-1245 15 min (J W Allam) (1 HP Test Flights)
1957
8/6 (Production Test Flight) 3/7: (HP Radlett to A&AEE Boscombe Down): 4/7: (Rtn HP

Radlett): 28/9: 4/10: Alternator Coupling shaft seized (J Allam) 20/10: 23/10: 26/10: 30/10: (Production Test Flight): AwC 30/10: 27/11(Production Test Flight) AWC 27/11/57: 29/11: (HP Radlett to A&AEE Boscombe Down Handling Squadron):

1958
19/4/58 A&AEE Handling Squadron Returned to HP Radlett
9/9: 10/9: 11/9: 13/9: 16/9: 17/9: 19/9: 23/9 :(Handling Flight Production Clearance)
26/9: (HP Radlett to RAE Farnborough): 14/11 (Crew Training at RAE):

1959-1966
At RAE Farnborough on RAE Ballistic Trials: Repair to damage caused by Buffeting in Bomb Bay whilst conducting special RAE Test by HP Working Party 15/5/61-(320.40hrs) Stored in open 1 year for corrosion trials MOA 11/60:

1966
3/5 (Ferry Flight RAE Farnborough to HP Radlett 3 crew U/C down Flaps TO avoiding large towns 25mins. Crew P1 A.J.Camp, P 2 M.Thompson, AEO R.A. Funnell)

1967
8/8: 10/8: 19/9 :(Air Test): 29/9:5/10:24/10:(Wing-Strain Gauging Test)

1968
17/1: 23/2: 6/3: 7/3: 25/3: 5/4: 30/4: 4/6: 10/6: 14/6: 27/8: 5/9: 19/9(Wing Strength Test) 8/2: 9/5: 21/8: (Air Test)

1969
25/3: (Main ARC Roller Testing): 16/10(Air Test)

1970
Stored at HP Radlett
To HSA Woodford 8/4/70 (J W Allam: B S Grieve: RA Funnell): SOC 9/8/73
Cannibalised and scrapped last section left 9/3/73
41HP Test Flights

PRODUCTION AIRCRAFT DELIVERED TO THE ROYAL AIR FORCE
XA 923 Blue Shadow/Yellow Aster
First Flight 24/8/56 1623-1706 43 min (J W Allam) (11 HP Test Flights) AwC 31/1/58
1st and 2nd Pilots Windscreen split 28,000ft (J Allam)
RAF Gaydon 232 OCU 4/2/58: RAF Wyton RRF 14/4/58
232 OCU RAF Gaydon 16/10/61: HP Radlett 22/10/63 (2): RAF Cottesmore 4/64 to RAF Cosford 27/5/64: HP Test Crew (E R Gordon, M Thompson, J Tank) (1200-1225 0.25hrs)
RAF Cosford Inst 7850M 27/5/64-29/4/70-9/73: RAF Museum Cosford 9/73-3/85
Scrap 3/85

Victor B2 XA923 RAF Museum Cosford, 1983. Author's Collection

Victor B1 XA922 Handling Squadron A&AEE. Author's Collection

XA 924 Blue Shadow/Yellow Aster
First Flight 28/9/56   1430-1450 20 min (J Still) (8 HP Test Flights) AwC 24/1/58
RAF Gaydon 232 OCU 27/1/58: RAF Wyton RRF 20/3/58 RAF Gaydon 232OCU 9/10/61:
HP Radlett 24/7/62: RAF Gaydon 232OCU 11/2/63: 6/63:10 Squadron 28/6/63
No 4 S of T T RAF St Athan 7844M 20/4/64, 14/9/67.
SOC 12/68 Scrap 69

XA 925 Blue Shadow/Yellow Aster
First Flight 27/10/56 1215-1230 15 min (J Still) (five HP Test Flights) AwC 28/2/58
RAF Gaydon 232 OCU 4/3/58: RAF Wyton RRF 16/4/58:RAF Gaydon 232 OCU
15/9/61:5/63:
HP Radlett 3/9/62: RAF Cottesmore 15 Squadron 26/6/63: 7/63: 8/63: 10/63: 11/63: 1/64:
2/64: MOA/HP Radlett 20/4/64: Stored in open 4/64-3/67: Bird Strike Test 6/65: HP
Specialised Corrosion Test and Inspection 3/67:
Dismantled HP Radlett /67:
SOC 7/66.

Victor B1 XA924 No 4 S of TT RAF St Athan 1965. Author's Collection

Victor B1 XA925 232OCU RAF Gaydon 1963. Author's Collection

XA 926

First Flight 25/11/56 1300-1325 25 min (J Still) (6 HP Test Flights) AwC 14/3/58
RAF Gaydon 232 OCU 27/1/58(17/3/58) 13/6/58: Western Ranger Offutt AFB 8/5/59: 6/63:
232 OCU 2/3/61 CAT 3 by 71MU: HP Repair to cabin floor by step (689.0hrs)
RAF Cottesmore 15 Squadron 9/63:
HP for Conversion to K1 17/9/64:

Victor B1 XA926 1963 232OCU. Author's Collection

XA 927

First Flight 29/12/56 1105-1130 25 min (J Still) (11 HP Test Flights) AwC 15/4/58
Used at HP Radlett for Familiarisation by Sdn/Ldr Ringer and RAF Crew 3/1/57-12/1/57:
RAF Cottesmore 10 Squadron 15/4/58; (Major Service. 3/7/62-18/10/62): 15 Squadron
20/5/64: VS. RAF Cottesmore 8/64 ex 10 Squadron:
HP for Conversion to K1 17/9/64:

Victor B1 XA927 Crew Boarding 1962. HPA

XA 928
First Flight 8/2/57 1545-1555 10 min (J W Allam) (22 HP Test Flights) AwC 25/3/57: 6/3/57: 18/5/57: 25/5/57: 30/5/57 :(Fuel Tank Pressurisation Test): 20/3/57: (Air Test): 12/6/57: 14/6/57: (Cabin Pressurisation Test): First Flight Production: 15/4/58: 16.25-1640 P Murphy) 16/4: 17/4: 18/4: 19/4: 21/4: 22/4: 23/4: 24/; 25/4 (2) AwC Collection 26/4: RAF Cottesmore 10 Squadron 5/5/58: VSF RAF Cottesmore to 8/64 ex 10 Squadron:
HP for Conversion to K1 10/9/64:
Notes not Verified A&AEE29/3/57:Nostril Noise 4/58:

XA 929
First Flight 28/2/57 1505-1515 10 min (J Still) (five HP Test Flights) AwC 23/6/58
RAF Cottesmore 10 Squadron 23/6/58: RAF Gaydon 232 OCU 8/4/59:
RAF Cottesmore 10 Squadron 6/6/60(6/1/60): 9/5/61 Cat 3 Repair to cabin after door failed during pressure test early 1961(71MU): Major Serv.14/8/61-30/1/62:
Destroyed Flying Accident RAF Akrotiri on Take-off 16/6/62
Flap Failure incorrect setting and indication: six Killed
F/t/Lt GA Goatham (Captain) F/O AW Mitchell (Co Pilot)
Flt/Lt DC Brown (Nav) Flt/Lt J Gray (Nav) F/O AP Pace (AEO) M/Tech DA Smith ASC (Crew Chief.) 103MU 16/6/62 SOC 2/8/62

XA 930
First Flight 30/8/57 1525-1535 10 min (J W Allam) (106 HP Test Flights) Arc 30/9/57
1957
9/10: (HP Radlett to A&AEE Boscombe Down): 7/11 (AVTUR Test at A&AEE)
12/57 Operational Reliability Trials at A&AEE started. Bomber Command Crews using a total of 187.5 hours:

Victor B1 XA930 without underwing tanks 1959. Author's Collection

1958
1/2-7/2(MOD 814 Lengthened Probe at A&AEE by HP) (Dry Contacts only) (Max Cabin Pressure 2.3/4 PSI during Contacts) 3/6: (Handling Flight at A&AEE):/...(Rtn to HP Radlett): 27/8 (2): 29/8: (Handling Flight with Probe and Drop Tanks): 30/8: (HP Radlett to RAE Farnborough SBAC Show): 1/9:2/9: 3/9: 4/9: 5/9: 6/9: 7/9:8/9: (RAE Farnborough to HP Radlett): 10/9: 12/9 (Windscreen Demisting – Anti Flash):
1959
24/3:25/3: (Air Test): 7/4: 8/4: 15/4: 22/4: 25/5: (Handling with Drop Tanks and Probe): 10/4: 11/4 (5) 13/4: 14/4 (2) 20/4: 23/4: 1/5: 8/5: 22/5: 3/6: (RATO Development): 6/5(2): (Drop Tank Performance Test): 14/5: 20/5: 27/5 (2) 29/5: 1/6: (Power unit Control Test); 2/6: 4/6: 5/6

Victor B1 XA930 Leaving DH Hatfield. Alan Dowsett Collection

(2): (Performance Test): 15/6: (HP Radlett to A&AEE Boscombe Down): 16/6: 17/6(2) (T/O and Ldg at High Load A&AEE): 18/6 (Port Drop Tank Drop A&AEE): 19/6: (Starboard Drop Tank Drop A&AEE): 19/6 (A&AEE Boscombe Down to HP Radlett): 23/6: (Performance Test Landing at RAE Bedford and Rtn.): 26/6 (Performance Test): 7/7: (RATO Trials): 9/7: 14/7: 17/7:
(Cruise Climb): 9/9: (Drag Measurements with Probe):14/9: (Drag Measurements without Probe): 24/9: 26/9: 29/9: 30/9: (Probe Vibration Test): 2/10: (Vibration Test with Tanks): 6/10: (Vortex Generator & Probe Vibration Test): 8/10: (Probe Vibration with tanks):
1960
22/2: (Flight Refuelling Development): 23/2 (Drop Tank Development): 26/2: (HP Radlett To A&AEE Boscombe Down and Rtn 3/6: 3/3 (HP Radlett to A&AEE Boscombe Down FR Development Trials and Rtn to HP Radlett): 15/3: (Fuel Tank Pressure Test): 17/3 (Trim Curve Measurement): 18/3 (Buffet Boundary Test): 25/3: (HP Radlett to A&AEE Boscombe Down): 25/3 (Flight Refuelling DRY Contacts at A&AEE): 5/5: 6/5 (Tank Dropping Test A&AEE): 31/5 :(Flight Refuelling WET Contacts at A&AEE): 22/6 (A&AEE Boscombe Down to HP Radlett): 11/7: (HP Radlett to DH Hatfield): 14/7: (RATO DH Hatfield to HP Radlett) 15/11 (Handling Flight A&AEE Crew):
1961
17/3: (Flight Refuelling At A&AEE): 20/6: (Handling at Max AUW at A&AEE)
23/6 A&AEE Boscombe Down to HP Radlett
1963-1966:
4/9/63: (Production Air Test) 0850-1025. 1.35hrs (J W Allam) AwC 6/9/63:
5/9/63:6/9/63: (Production Test Flights)
Delivered to RAF Cottesmore 30/9/63: 10 Squadron: 21/2/64-13/5/64 60MU Repairs:
RAF Gaydon 232OCU 15/9/64: RAF Honington Wing 18/3/65: MOA 1/9/65-6/10/65: 57 Sdn 1/11/65: RAF Marham 57 Squadron 12/65:4/66: RAF Honington to A&AEE Boscombe Down 10/65: Flight Refuelling Development Flights at A&AEE: 13/10/65:19/10/65: Rtn to RAF Honington late 10/65:Delivered to HP Radlett for Conversion to K1 10/5/66:
Misc Data Not all Verified
23/9/57(Door Open): 10/4/59 Spray Test RATOG N/F down U/C and Flaps down P Murphy: 20/4/59 Spectre Drop 200ft at 220Kts P Murphy: 23/4/59 Spectre Drop 240ft at 250Kts P Murphy: 7/4/59 Spin at 105 Kts Incipient P Murphy: 22/5/59 Metal Nacelle Drop 22ft at 250Kts P Murphy: 3/6/59 Pod drop 240ft at 250kts P Murphy: 30/5/59 Probe Vibration 45000ft P Murphy: Operational Reliability Trial A&AEE 12/57 21/1/58 ORT Radar Flt/Lt C Painting (232OCU Staff Crew): SBAC 9/58: 3/9/58 J Allam two Barrel Rolls and Roll of Top(6) and 6/9/58;Probe 9/9/59: RATOG Trials 10/4/59: HTP Jettison 10/4/59: :Drop

RATOG at 220 Kts 24/5/59: Max brake Landing 116,000lb 1,115 yds 19/6/59:13/4/59 A&AEE Boscombe Down Pilot Check probe: Trim Curves with RATOG 4/59: Bomb Bay tanks 5/59:11/7/60 HP Radlett to DH Hatfield: 14/7/60 RATOG TO. DH Hatfield to HP Radlett (P Murphy 1420-1430 10mins): FR Development 2/60-5/60-3/61: Fuel Tank Press Test.3/60: FR Dev A&AEE Boscombe Down 10/60 Night Refuelling 13/10/60 Flt/Lt Gibson: Report by Mike Wilson Flight Test Engineer. Flew with XA930 to Hatfield as Starboard Nav (Radar) was AEO on return flight. It was a gloomy day with 8/8 stratus at about 2,000ft. We lined up, 'Spud' opened up the Sapphires and away we went. At about the moment the RATO button was pressed there seemed to be a long pause – probably about one second in retrospect. Then a most terrible noise occurred which Alan Turner had overstated. The aircraft lifted off very quickly and we held a steep angle. The Spectres cut in after 60 seconds. I think by this time we were at 2,000ft the cloud base. The RATO units were not jettisoned this time. After a beat up at Hatfield which allegedly made the official photographer fling himself full length on the ground. We landed safely at HP Radlett.

XA 931
First Flight 27/9/57 1730-1750 20 min (J Still) (7 HP Test Flights)) AwC 28/11/57
RAF Gaydon 232 OCU 28/11/57: Ex 415 Trial 27/4/58: IF Trial 10/5/58: Major Service At RAF Gaydon 3/61 (Repairs by 71MU and HP) RAF Cottesmore 10 Squadron 14/12/61: RAF Gaydon 232 OCU 30/8/63:
To RAF St Athan 26/6/64: SOC 30/4/74

Victor B1 XA931 232 OCU RAF Gaydon 1960. Author's Collection

XA 932
First Flight 22/12/57 1045-1140 55 min (J W Allam) (14 HP Test Flights) AwC 11/2/58
RAF Gaydon 232 OCU 13/2/58: IF Trial 26/4/58: RAF Cottesmore 10 Squadron 4/58: CAP Cottesmore 8/5/59 Ret. 24/7/59: Cat3. RAF Cottesmore 10 Squadron /RAF Bicester 71MU 2110/60-11/60 540 Hrs: HP Radlett 14/11/61-18/6/62:Production Test at RAF Cottesmore ferry to HP Radlett 5/3/64(1300-1415 1.15hrs) (J W Allam): MOA/ Tanker Radio Trials 5/11/64:19/11/64:2/12/64: HP Radlett to A&AEE Boscombe Down 18/12/64(J W Allam) Tanker Radio Trials 11/64: A&AEE Boscombe Down to HP Radlett: 3/2/66:
HP for Conversion to K1 2/9/66.

Victor B1 XA932 arriving RAF Luqa after record breaking flight 14/10/58 Farnborough to Luqa, Captain Wg Cdr Iveson Time 2hr 0min 655MPH 1,310 miles. Tony Cunnane Collection

XA 933

First Flight 18/1/58 1305-1355 50 min (J W Allam) (15 HP Test Flights) AwC 25/2/58
RAF Gaydon 232 OCU 3/3/58:Ex 415 Trial 27/4/58: 5/63:6/63: Handling Flight at RAF Gaydon by HP Crew J W Allam: Wheels up Landing RAF Gaydon 24/2/59: repaired by HP (double fuse failure in U/C system)(Flt/Lt D Bryan Captain) (Flt/Lt K Hanscomb Co-Pilot) (Flt/Lt J Churchill Nav Rad)(Flt/Lt J Chaloner Nav Plot) (P/O B Anderson AEO):
Major Service by HP at Cottesmore 27/3/62-25/7/62: RAF Cottesmore 15 Squadron 12/63:MOA 22/5/64:A&AEE Boscombe Down Low level Radar TI under port Wing RATOG Point: TFR Trials 17/8/64-25/8/64: HP Radlett to A&AEE Boscombe Down 27/8/64: TFR Trials: A&AEE Boscombe Down to HP Radlett 19/11/64:Production Test Flights 24/4/65:26/4/65: AWC 26/4/65:RAF Honington Wing 26(29) /4/65:57Sdn: 6/65:10/65:RAF Marham 55 Squadron 12/65 57 Squadron 2/66:3/66: 5/66 7/66: TTF 23/8/66-25/6/67:
To RAF St Athan 26/6/67: SOC 1/10/71.

XA 934

First Flight 3/3/58 1045-1155 1:10Hrs (J W Allam) (3 HP Test Flights) AwC 21/3/58
RAF Gaydon 232 OCU 25/3/58 10/6. /58: CAT 3 Repairs by 71MU and HP /104/61 Corrosion Rudder datum hinge: Flying Accident: 2/10/62 near RAF Gaydon engine failure centre line closure 3 Killed. Flt/Lt N E Cooke (Captain), P/O J A Cotteridege, F/O D F Haynes.
Flt/Lt E BC Gwinnel (Co-Pilot) Survived
SOC 3/10/62

Victor B1 XA934 232 OCU RAF Gaydon 1962 Steve Mills Collection

XA 935

First Flight 18/3/58 0940-0945 5 min (J W Allam) (six HP Test Flights) AwC 2/4/58
RAF Cottesmore 10 Squadron 9/4/58: RAF Gaydon 232 OCU 29/10/58: RAF Wyton RRF 11/5/59: RAF Cottesmore 15 Squadron 1/3/60: RAF Gaydon 232 OCU 9/5/61: RAF Cottesmore 10 Squadron 1/11/61: RAF Gaydon 232 OCU 14/12/61: Repaired on site by 71MU 7/6/62-17/7/62: 232 OCU 18/7/62: 6/63:
Investigation at RAE Bedford (Undercarriage) by HP Crew 25/10/62:
To RAF St Athan (14) 17/6/64: NEA 6/4/70: SOC 30/7/74.

Victor B1 XA935 10 Squadron RAF Cottesmore 1961. Author's Collection

XA 936

First Flight 3/5/58 1110-1200 50 min (P Murphy)(7 HP Test Flights) AwC 23/5/58
RAF Cottesmore 10 Squadron 28/5/58: SBAC 9/58: RAF Gaydon 232 OCU 27/2/59: 5/63:6/63:13/5/59&14/5/59 Barrel Roll P Murphy/J Rudforth Major Service by HP on site 31/1/62-28/6/62: 232OCU 29/6/62:
HP for Conversion to K1. 11/1/65:

XA 937

First Flight 16/5/58 1635-1725 50 min (P Murphy) (5 HP Test Flights) AwC 31/5/58
RAF Cottesmore 10 Squadron 4/6/58: Flying Accident 30/11/59 Engine Fire (Hot Air Duct Leaking?) Emergency Landing RAF Gaydon CAT 3 Rebuilt by HP: HP Radlett 18/8/61-28/8/61: 10 Squadron RAF Cottesmore 1/9/61: Major Service by HP on site 15/5/62-30/8/62: 10Squadron RAF Cottesmore 1/9/62: 15 Squadron RAF Cottesmore 2/3/64: Sdn/Ldr Young: Bombed China Rock on Detachment to FEAF 2/3/64 Exercise Profiteer:
HP for conversion to K1 30/4/64: Prod TI Aircraft

Victor B1 XA937 landing RAAF Butterworth, Malaysia. Author's Collection

XA 938

First Flight 26/6/58 1505-1605 1.00hr (J W Allam) (four HP Test Flights) AwC 22/7/58:
RAF Cottesmore 10 Squadron 28/7/58: 15 Squadron 2/3/64:
HP for Conversion to K1 30/4/64 :(12/10/64)

XA 939

First Flight 14/7/58 1910-1955 45 min (J W Allam) (four HP Test Flights) AwC 27/8/58
RAF Cottesmore 10 Squadron 27/8/58: 19/9/59:15 Squadron Ret Ex Profiteer 1/3/62 RAAF
Butterworth to RAF Gan (3.45) 2/3/62 RAF Gan to RAF Eastleigh (Kenya) (4.20): 3/3/62
RAF Eastleigh to RAF Akrotiri (5.40): 4/4/62 RAF Akrotiri to RAF Cottesmore (4.35). RAF
Cottesmore 15 Squadron 2/3//64 Returned ex RAAF Butterworth 6/10/64:
HP for Conversion to K1 8/10/64

Victor B1 XA940 ex TTF at HP Radlett for Min Tech Trials Duty 1968. HPA

XA 940

First Flight 29/7/58 1755-1805 10 min (J W Allam) (28 HP Test Flights) Awc 9/9/58
RAF Cottesmore 10 Squadron 10/9/58: Flying Accident Starboard Undercarriage failed to
lower after the door had opened (Failure of the sequence valve operating striker rods)
19/12/61 680hrs:Cat 4 RAF Wittering starboard wing damaged Repaired by 71 MU and HP.
RAF Gaydon 232 OCU 7/11/62: RAF Cottesmore 10 Squadron 11/1/63:
15 Squadron 2/3/64:6/64 Returned ex RAAF Butterworth 10/10/64:RAF Gaydon 232 OCU
15/10/64:RAF Honington Wing: 9/3/65:57Squadron1/12/65:6/65:8/65:10/65:11/65:RAF
Marham 3/66: 32MU Major Repair by HP CWP for Corrosion 6/6/67. Repaint in Camouflage
only Mk1 in Camouflage. RAF Marham 14/12/66: TTF 1/1/67: Not up to the required mod
standard for use by TTF so transferred to MIN TECH A&AEE Boscombe Down 8/6/67:
29/11/67-4/7/68 Engine Strain Gauge Test BSEL Thompson/Misc:
RAF St Athan 25/7/68: 9/4/70 (ex TTF) SOC 31/8/73:
Nose to RAF Marham 5/74:

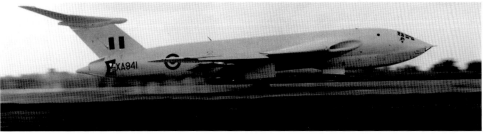

*Victor B1 XA941 first aircraft for 15 Squadron flown in by Wg Cdr Green and Flt Lt D Bywater 17
September 1958.* Gordon Stringer

XA 941

First Flight 27/8/58 1140-1255 1.15 Hrs (W R Burton) (three HP Test Flights) AwC 11/9/58
RAF Cottesmore 15 Squadron 17/9/58: 10 Squadron 25/1/59: RAF Honington 55 Squadron
8/9/60: RAF Gaydon 232 OCU 23/3/61:5/63:6/63: RAF Cottesmore 10 Squadron 3/9/63: 15
Squadron 2/3/64:5/64:4/65: Flying Accident 2/9/64 Centre Line Closure on TO from RAAF
Butterworth one engine exploded. Repaired on site RAAF Butterworth 11/9/64-10/12/64
390MU: RAF Honington Wing 2/2/65: HP 13/5/64 MOA A&AEE Boscombe Down
27/10/65: HP for Conversion to K1 20/12/65:

Handley Page Victors Mk B1 with the Radar Reconnaissance Flight
Based on data from Air Vice Marshall John Herrington
XA923, XA924, XA925 and on loan XA935

This unit was to have an establishment of three aircraft which were fitted with Yellow Aster, a radar equipment that was used in conjunction with the NBS/H2S system. Their own crews delivered the aircraft to RAF Wyton from RAF Gaydon after conversion training at the OCU. The unit was operational until October 1961 when the aircraft were returned to RAF Gaydon and converted to the equipment fit that was required to carry out the training duties with the OCU. All three aircraft also spent some time at RAF Cottesmore before disposal to training schools and specialised trials.

The RRF was the first operational unit to receive the Victor Mk1, ahead of 10 Squadron, the first Bomber Squadron. The high priority for high-level strategic reconnaissance originated from President Eisenhower's proposal for 'Open Skies' for flights over the USSR and the USA to ease tension and hence promote more friendly relations. The Soviets refused and so overt reconnaissance was replaced by overt over flights and the use of the U2 (of the 22 U2s built the RAF acquired five which operated from bases in Cyprus and Turkey). After Gary Powers was shot down the US introduced satellites and NATO became involved in intelligence-gathering flights around the Soviet Union, hence the activities of the RRF and 51 Squadron.

United Kingdom priorities began to focus more on maritime reconnaissance in the late 50s and 60s. Because of the expansion of the Soviet Navy the Royal Navy and NATO demanded more intelligence on the Soviet Navy's whereabouts, activities and tactics. These tasks were progressively taken up by 543 Squadron's HP Victor B (SR) 2 aircraft with its range of cameras and immense radius of action.

The Radar Reconnaissance Flight was formed in the early 1950s at RAF Wyton.

Its tasking was the development of radar reconnaissance equipment and tactics. Priority - side scan radar using the H2S scanner locked to port or starboard producing line-scans images, and Blue Shadow. This was a five foot rigid aerial mounted on the forward side of a Canberra fuselage and inside the front radome of a Victor on the port and starboard side between the H2S scanner and the radome. Simultaneously the RRE at Malvern were testing the line-scan capabilities of a 15ft rigid aerial mounted in the bomb bay of a Canberra.

Trials involved ship measurement to determine size and type of vessel, high and low level coverage of airfields and other tactical and strategic targets (using line-scan it was possible to identify aircraft types on airfields not possible with radial scan) target analysis and prediction in various geographical areas. There then followed proving trials on the modified radars and Photographic Reconnaissance crates to be used in the Victor B (SR) 2 destined for 543 Squadron.

RAF Aircraft Inventory 1958

Two Avro Lincolns	phased out when the Victors arrived
Canberra B2 WJ712	
Canberra B6 WJ770	Both fitted with Blue Shadow side-scan radar feeding into Yellow Aster
Victor B1 XA923	H2S rotating and side-scan, two Blue Shadow aerials
Victor B1 XA924	mounted in the nose radome feeding into a rapid processor
Victor B1 XA925	and Yellow Aster

To exploit the aircraft's capability the RRF Victors flew a number of sorties over the

Eastern Baltic and the Northern Black Sea to establish accurate fix points for V Force mission planning. Interestingly, these flights were sometimes accompanied at a discreet distance by one of 51 Squadron's aircraft, presumably recording the activity stirred up by the presence of a potential intruder flying close to the Soviet border. For the Black Sea operations, for instance, I recall the RRF Victors operated from RAF Akrotiri while the Comets were based at RAF Nicosia.

Another device that the RRF tried out on the Victor, in conjunction with the RRE Malvern was Red Neck, which involved fitting an aerial under each wing. Since these aerials were some 40ft long, the system promised very high-definition SLAR capability. Unfortunately the aerials tended to flex in flight and this corrupted the resolution of the picture. As a result Red Neck never realised its full potential. It never became operation and the programme was cancelled in 1962. (The only flights made with Red Neck were on XA918 and the problems found before the RAF were equipped with this equipment).

The Handley Page Victor B Mk 1   XH587-667
Contract 6/Acft/11303/C.B.6 (a) Dtd 5/58

The second batch was originally to be for thirty-three aircraft, however, before the production was completed the development of the Mk2 aircraft was under way and the last eight were built as the Mk 2 version (XH668-675).

Of these twenty-five Mk B1 aircraft the initial part of the batch was built alongside the latter half of the first batch and the delivery schedule was not interrupted.

The initial deliveries were to No.15 Squadron at RAF Cottesmore. These aircraft were identical to those of the original batch XA serials and as such they were issued to 15 Squadron and later in the basic B1 form to No.57 Squadron   With deliveries to RAF Honington starting in early 1959 for service with 57 Squadron and later 55 Squadron. Over the next five years the basic B1 aircraft were to serve with all the four squadrons at one time or another. With the development of electronic warfare in the fifties after having been neglected since World War II it was decided to fit the Mk 1 Victors with the latest ECM equipment. These aircraft from the second batch once modified are known, as B1A and 15 Squadron became the first to operate them when XH613 was delivered the 18/7/60.

The first aircraft of this batch XH587 was returned to HP Radlett from 15 Squadron for use as the ECM trials aircraft. This was to be the Mk B1A programme, in order to get this programme underway a number of Mk B1 aircraft were retained by Handley Page for this purpose and never saw service with the RAF as B Mk 1. The remainder of the batch were returned for this conversion process and delivered to the Honington Wing with a few going to 15 Squadron at RAF Cottesmore. During the period of RAF service for the second batch only one was lost due to a flying accident this being XH617 in 1960.

The basic B Mk 1 aircraft served with all four Squadrons and the OCU at one time or another over the period from 1958-1966 at various locations.

XH 587
First Flight 1/10/58 1010-1115 1.05 (J W Allam) (six HP Test Flights) AwC 17/10/58
17/10/58 Controller (Aircraft): RAF Cottesmore 15 Squadron 17/11/58:
HP for ECM Trials and [Conversion B1A 6/4/61].
XH 588
First Flight 14/10/58 1545-1655 1.10 (W R Burton)(three HP Test Flights) AwC 28/10/58
RAF Cottesmore 15 Squadron 30/10/58: 1/8/61
HP for Conversion to B1A 2/8/61.

Victor B1 XH587 15 Squadron RAF Cottesmore.. Author's Collection

Victor B1 XH 588 15 Squadron RAF Cottesmore. Author's Collection

XH 589
First Flight 5/11/58 1245-1335 .50 (J W Allam) (five HP Test Flights) AwC 21/11/58
RAF Cottesmore15 Squadron 1/12/58-5/11/61:
HP for Conversion to B1A 6/11/61.

Victor B1 XH 589 15 Squadron RAF Cottesmore at Farnborough 1960. Author's Collection

XH 590
First Flight 12/11/58 1515-1555 .40 (P Murphy) (three HP Test Flights) AwC 26/11/58
RAF Cottesmore: 15 Squadron 1/12/58:
HP for conversion to B1A 3/10/61.

XH 591
First Flight 5/12/58 1250-1355 1.05 (W R Burton) (six HP Test Flights) AwC 7/1/59
RAF Cottesmore: 15 Squadron 20/1/59: 3 Engine Take off 28/11/61 Flt/Lt K Handscomb
HP for conversion to B1A 16/1/62

Victor B1 XH 591 15 Squadron RAF Cottesmore at Farnborough 1960 note Simstart Trolley under Port Wing. Author's Collection

XH 592
First Flight 20/12/58 1045-1140 0.55 (J W Allam)(two HP Test Flights) AwC 31/12/58
RAF Cottesmore: 15 Squadron 2/2/59(2/1/59).
HP for conversion to B1A 1/9/61.

Victor B1 XH592 15 Squadron RAF Cottesmore 1960. Author's Collection

XH 593
First Flight 8/1/59 1100-1155 .55 (W R Burton) (three HP Test Flights) AwC 26/1/59
RAF Cottesmore: 15 Squadron 4 /2/59:(28/1/59).
HP for conversion to B1A   29/7/60:(18/8/60).

XH 594
First Flight 21/1/59 0940-1025 .45 (J W Allam) (three HP Test Flights) AwC 31/1/59
RAF Cottesmore: 15 Squadron 3/2/59:
HP for conversion to B1A 22/7/60.

XH 613
First Flight 20/2/59 1430-1515 .45 (P Murphy)(six HP Test Flights) AwC 27/2/59
Retained by HP for conversion to 1st B1A.

XH 614

First Flight 26/2/59 1645-1655 .10 (P Murphy) (eight HP Test Flights) AwC 18/3/59
RAF Honington: 57 Squadron 23/3/59:
HP for conversion to B1A 30/9/60.

Victor B1 XH614 57 Squadron RAF Honington 1959. Author's Collection

XH 615

First Flight 17/3/59 1505-1540 0.45 (P Murphy)(five HP Test Flights) AwC 7/4/59
RAF Gaydon: 232 OCU 8/4/59:
Demonstration Flight Over HP Radlett 20/6/59 50th Anniversary of Handley Page Ltd
HP for conversion to B1A 11/1/61.

XH 616

First Flight 2/4/59 1405-1455 0.50 (J W Allam)(four HP Test Flights) AwC 21/4/59
RAF Honington: 57 Squadron 23/4/59:
HP for conversion to B1A 6/4/61.

XH 617

First Flight 1/5/59 1625-1705 0.40 (P Murphy) (seven HP Test Flights) AwC 19/5/59
Landing Accident 6/5/59 off runway onto grass B/chute failed P Murphy; 2/5/59
two Barrel rolls R.A. Funnell (Flight Test Engineer) in BA Position (P Murphy):
RAF Honington: 57 Squadron 25/5/59.Flying accident 19/7/60 No.2 Alternator drive bearing
failed, drive shaft fractured and broke fuel line to the No.4 engine causing fire. Aircraft
Crashed 19/7/60 Oakley Norfolk. Wreckage to 71 MU Bicester :SOC (29) 20/7/60: Flt/Lt J
Munford (Captain): F/O G C Stewart (AEO) Survived.
Flt/Lt JBP Wilding (Nav Rad): Flt/Lt RS Bristow (Nav Plot): F/O MJ Wilkes (Co Pilot)
Killed.

XH 618

First Flight 28/5/59 0900-1005 1.05 (J W Allam) (two HP Test Flights) AwC 3/6/59
Retained by HP for conversion to B1A

XH 619

First Flight 9/6/59 1325-1400 .35 (P Murphy) (five HP Test Flights) AwC 24/6/59
RAF Honington: 57 Squadron 25/6/59:
HP for conversion to B1A 28/11/60:

XH 620

First Flight 6/7/59 1540-1640 1.0 (W R Burton)(three HP Test Flights) AwC 20/7/59
RAF Honington: 57 Squadron 21/7/59: Flying accident 16/10/59 Cabin Door opened in flight
Repaired by HP CWP RAF Honington: 23/10/59-4/12/59:
HP for conversion to B1A 19/4/61.

Victor B1 XH619 Awaiting Delivery at HP Radlett Colney Street. HPA

Victor B1 XH620 15 Squadron RAF Cottesmore. Author's Collection

XH 621
First Flight 27/7/59 1505-1605 1.0 (J W Allam) (three HP Test Flights) AwC 31/7/59
Retained by HP for conversion to B1A.
XH 645
First Flight 2/9/59 0845-1010 1.25 (P. P. Baker) (nine HP Test Flights) AwC 25/9/59
RAF Honington: 57 Squadron 28/9/59:
HP Radlett for conversion to B1A 27/1/61.

Victor B1 XH645 57 Squadron RAF Honington 1960. Author's Collection

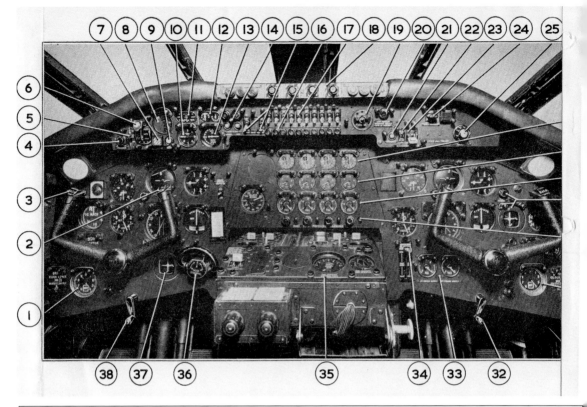

Key to Fig. A

1. Dimmer switch for panel AC and AE lighting
2. Throttle lever gate release switch
3. Jpt. OFF – NORMAL isolation switches
4. Fuel vent pressure NORMAL – ISOLATE switches
5. Nosewheel steering ground test switch
6. Bomb door emergency test switch
7. Undercarriage test switch
8. Drop tank release circuit test push switch
9. Drop tank release test switch
10. Fuel vent pressure gauges
11. Fuel vent temperature gauge
12. Landing lamps switch
13. Emergency decompression switch
14. I.L.S. switch
15. Emergency bomb jettison switch
16. Lower carriers jettison switch
17. Navigation lights switch
18. Landing and taxy lamps circuit breakers
19. Downward ident. lights switch
20. Windscreen heating switches and indicator
21. Cabin pressure warning light
22. RATO controls
23. 1st pilot's oxygen regulator
24. "Abandon aircraft" switch
25. Nose flaps control switch
26. Parking brake
27. Flaps selector switch
28. Undercarriage selector switch
29. Flaps emergency control
30. Undercarriage emergency lowering control
31. Throttle friction lever
32. Hatch jettison lever
33. Airbrakes selector lever
34. Throttles
35. Brake parachute switch
36. Radio altimeter selector switch
37. Aileron/rudder trimmer
38. R.T. selector switch
39. Drop tank release switch

Victor B1 Front Cabin for both XA and XH Series Aircraft HP-HPA

XH 646
First Flight 26/9/59 0900-1010 1.10 (P P Baker)(three HP Test Flights) AwC 30/9/59
Retained by HP for Conversion to B1A

XH 647
First Flight 10/11/59 1055-1210 1.15 (W R Burton)(three HP Test Flights) AwC 19/11/59
Retained by HP Radlett for conversion to B1A

XH 648

First Flight 27/11/59 11.15-1155 0.40 (P Murphy) (six HP Test Flights) AwC 21/12/59
Delivered 21/12/59: RAF Honington (3.45hrs): 57 Squadron 22/12/59:
HP Radlett for Conversion to B1A 24/10/60 (183.25hrs)

XH 649

First Flight 31/12/59 1035-1145 1.10 (P P Baker)(three HP Test Flights) AwC 8/1/60
Retained by HP Radlett for conversion to B1A 20/1/60

XH650

First Flight 29/1/60 1130-1205 0.35 (P Murphy) (three HP Test Flights) AwC 5/2/60
Retained by HP Radlett for conversion to B1A.

XH 651

First Flight 26/2/60 1055-1155 1.0 (W R Burton) (ten HP Test Flights) AwC 31/3/60
First Aircraft with Pale Roundels etc 22/3/60: RAF Honington: 57 Squadron 1/4/60:
HP Radlett for conversion to B1A 13/2/61:

XH 667

First Flight 28/3/60 1045-1145 1.0 (P P Baker)(one HP Test Flight) AwC 31/3/60
Retained by HP Radlett for Conversion to B1A.

Victor Mk B1A   XH587-667

This conversion programme was to upgrade twenty-four aircraft from the second batch of Mk 1 aircraft [XH Serials] with a variety of additional services and facilities including a strengthened pressure cabin to take an 8-PSI differential. Changes were also made to the external panels on both sides of the under floor compartment to allow easier access for the routine servicing task and component replacement of the ECM and other services. Vastly improved ECM with 3 units positioned in the under floor compartment and six units in the rear hatch. By using an enlarged tail cone the Rear Warning Radar was updated to Red Steer. The Vapour Cycle Cooling pack was installed in the old flash bomb-bay on the port side and its heat exchanger in the fairing below along with a vast length of clad glycol piping travelling through the aircraft from front to rear to provide cooling for the ECM cans. To enable the three units to be fitted into the under floor compartment of the nose it was necessary to move the Green Satin Doppler radar equipment to the rear of the aircraft and locate it in the 'Back Hatch'. There were, in addition, changes to the cabin instrument layout to facilitate better crew operations and ease of operating the aircraft.

The Flap and Undercarriage controls were moved from the 1st pilot's side panel [Panel AE] to the revised Panel A that held the engine instrumentation in a revised layout automatic brake application prior to retraction be introduced. The engines were changed to the Sapphire 20701 that incorporated a fuel filter de-icing system and an Auto JPT control system that required four additional thermocouples in the Jet Pipe. The engine driven alternators were mounted on an intake extension and therefore removing them from the engine bay wall and their driving shaft. A Rapid Start System called the Simstart was developed by Sqn/Ldr Dixon using a Trolley of Batteries to allow all four Sapphire's to be started at once from the outside by the Crew Chief.[Some of the XH series Mk B1 had been modified as well]. Changes to the fuel system included the addition of one more fuel pump in each twelve tank and the interconnection of the 7P and 7S tanks. Slight changes to Panel AT were the removal of the Tanker Master Switch and the deletion of the Fuel Reserve Warning light. The Proportioner Indicators were repositioned, the outer wings were to have fixed leading edge droops and the refuelling probe and the Mk 6 nozzle, later changed to the Mk 8 universal nozzle, was fitted. Modifications to the Anti-Icing, Airconditioning and the Crew Door emergency opening systems were incorporated. With changes to the avionics fit including fitting a UHF [ARC 52 Set] and a variety of other modifications the Mk B1A was introduced under cover of Modification Nos 660, 1000, 591,596.

With all the required conversion work and the embodiment of the various modifications being completed. The aircraft was prepared for its Production Test Flights to the agreed schedule and level of testing.

In the aftermath of the Gary Powers incident it was decided that the V Force aircraft would revert to the Low Level bombing method to ensure that they came in under the early warning radars. For this reason aircraft were camouflaged and the crew started to undertake the process of learning low level flying. A structural design/feasibility study was undertaken and completed in August 1963 by Handley Page into this type of operation for both the Mk 1A and the B2 aircraft in great depth and this showed that there would be increased fatigue on the aircraft structure and this would result in a structural repair programme in due course. By late 1964 15 Squadron had disbanded and their aircraft moved to Radlett for conversion to the tanker role or to RAF Honington for use by 55 and 57 Squadron with the remaining twenty-three of the batch involved in the tanker programme.

XH 587
17/11/58 Controller (Aircraft)
HP for ECM fitting and Trials:
First Flight 21/12/59 1455-1550 0.55 (W R Burton) (forty-one HP Test Flights)
(Air Test) 4/1/60:6/1/60:29/1/60:HP Radlett to RAE Bedford 2/2/60: 15/2/60: 22/2/60: 29/2/60: 24/5/60: RCM Trials Landed HP Radlett 4/2/60:16/2/60:23/2/60: 1/3/60: 24/5/60: ECM Cooling Trials 8/3/60: 21/4/60: 26/4/60: ECM Trials 21/3/60: 24/3/60: 7/4/60: 13/4/60: 25/5/60: 31/5/60: 8/6/60: 13/6/60: Anti-Flash Screen 4/4/60: 21/4/60 HP Radlett to RAE Bedford and Rtn 17/5/60: HP Radlett to A&AEE Boscombe Down 19/8/60: A&AEE Boscombe Down to HP Radlett 5/6/61.
HP for B1A Conversion to Production Standard:
Production Test Flight: 24/11/61: 12.10-13.45 1.35(H W Rayner) (five HP Test Flights) AWC 30/11/61:
Delivered to RAF Cottesmore: 15 Squadron 16/8/62:
Trial 457 (Joint ECM Trial with USAF at Seymour Johnson AFB.73 BS, 4241 St Wing:
Flt/Lt K Hanscomb   Captain. Flt/Lt C. H Painting Nav Rad
28/3/63 RAF Cottesmore to RAF Goose Bay   (5.00)
29/3/63 RAF Goose Bay to USAF Seymour Johnson AFB (3.40)

2/4/63	Blank Stare 1	14 Runs High Level	(5.20)
4/4/63	Blank Stare 2	12 Runs High Level	(4.35)
6/4/63	Blank Stare 3	4 Runs Low Level	(3.20)
11/4/63	Blank Stare 4	12 Runs High Level	(4.20)
13/4/63	Blank Stare 5	8 Runs Low Level	(3.45)
16/4/63	Blank Stare 6	9 Runs Low Level	(3.40)
18/4/63	Blank Stare 7	10 Runs High Level	(4.40)
20/4/63	Blank Stare 8	9 Runs Low Level	(3.40)
22/4/63	Blank Stare 9	14 Runs High Level	(4.40)
24/4/63	Blank Stare 10	9 Runs High Level	(3.45)
26/4/63	Blank Stare 11	9 Runs Low Level	(3.20)

27/4/63 Blank Stare 12   15 Runs High Level (4.15)
3/5/63 USAF Seymour Johnson To RAF Goose Bay (3.15)
4/5/63 RAF Goose Bay to RAF Cottesmore (4.20)
15 Squadron 1/64:4/64:6/64:9/64: Camouflage finish by 15/7/64:
HP for conversion to BK1A 6/10/64.

XH 588
HP for Conversion to B1A 2/8/61.
First Flight 19/4/62 1015-1135 1.20 (P P Baker) (eight HP Test Flights)
RAF Honington 55 Squadron 1/6/62:RAF Honington Wing: 57Sdn: 1/65:3/65:9/65:
10/65:11/65;27/5/64-1/6/64 Repair by 71MU on site.
HP for conversion to BK1A 25/11/65.

Victor B1A XH588 RAF Honington Wing Over Malaya 1965. Author's Collection

XH 589
HP for Conversion to B1A 6/11/61
First Flight 3/10/62 1420-1430 0.10 (J W Allam)(eight HP Test Flights)
RAF Honington 55 Squadron 6/11/62:RAF Honington Wing: 57Sdn: 4/65:5/65:
RAF Marham TTF 12/7/65:57Squadron 6/66:
HP for Conversion to BK1A 12/7/66:

XH 590
HP for conversion to B1A 3/10/61
First Flight 21/8/62 1320-1430 1.10 (A J Camp) (four HP Test Flights)
RAF Honington: 57 Squadron 14/9/62: RAF Honington Wing: 57 Sdn: 11/64:1/65:9/65:
HP for conversion to BK1A 1/12/65

XH 591
HP for conversion to B1A 16/1/62
First Flight 17/12/62 0940-1100 1.25 (A J Camp) (two HP Test Flights)
RAF Honington: 55 Squadron 6/2/63:RAF Honington Wing: 11/64:3/65:9/65:12/65:
RAF Marham: 57 Squadron 1/12/65,4/66:5/66:6/66: HP for Conversion to BK1A 13/7/66.

Victor B1A XH590 57 Squadron. Author's Collection

Victor B1A XH591 RAF Honington Wing at RAF Luqa Malta 1965.

XH 592
HP for conversion to B1A 1/9/61
First Flight 15/6/62 0950-1105 1.15 (H W Rayner) (four HP Test Flights)
RAF Honington 57 Squadron 5/7/62: RAF Honington Wing 11/64:12/64:1/65:4/65
RAF Gaydon 232 OCU 11/3/65: RAF Marham TTF 23/6/65: A&AEE Test Flight (CA) Release for FR from KC135: FR with KC135 3623 17 Dry Contacts 1 Wet Contact (CA) Release Approved 1/7/65[KC135 Captained By Capt Harmon.] XH592 Captained by Flt/Lt A Fisher A&AEE Test Pilot. HP Radlett 12/10/66-1/11/66: TTF 2/11/66: Flying Accident Bomb door lost in flight 15/1/68: CAT 3 Repaired by HP CWP at RAF Marham.19/6/68 TTF 19/6/68: HP for repaint 21/6/68-13/8/68: 232 OCU 1/5/70: Repaired by HSA CWP 5/11/71-18/1/72: 232OCU:
RAF Cosford No 2 S of TT 16/10/74 8429M.
Aerospace Museum 13/12/83 Scrapped Sept/Oct 94 Nose to Bruntingthorpe.

Victor B1A XH592 Tanking from a USAF KC135. Tim Mason

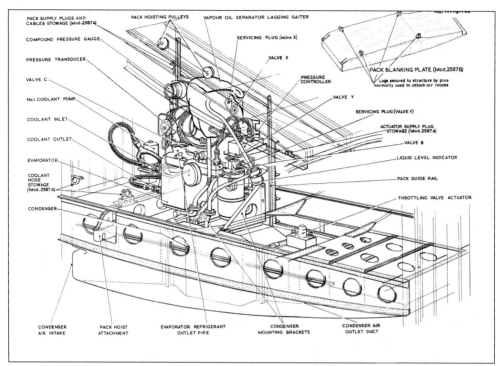

Vapour Cycle Cooling Pack. Author's Collection

Victor B1A Fuel System.   Author's Collection

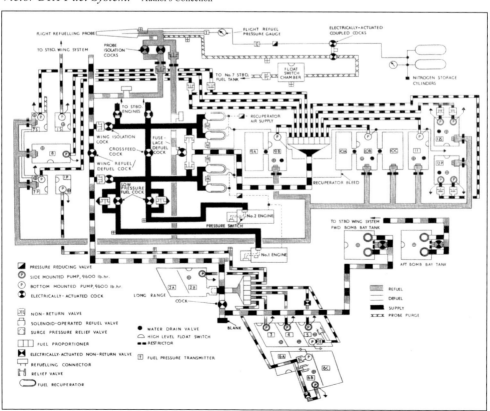

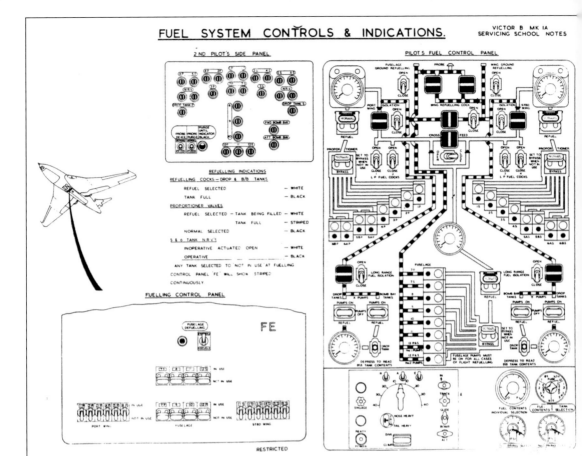

FUEL SYSTEM CONTROLS & INDICATIONS.

VICTOR B MK IA
SERVICING SCHOOL NOTES

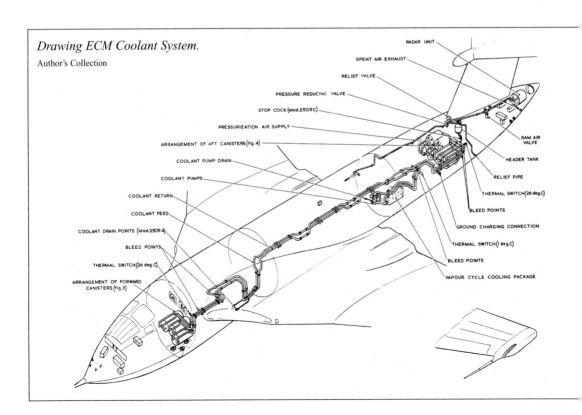

Drawing ECM Coolant System.

Author's Collection

XH 593

HP for conversion to B1A   29/7/60:(18/8/60)
First Flight 10/3/61 1540-1625 0.45 (H W Rayner)(eight HP Test Flights)
RAF Honington 57 Squadron: 29/3/61(17/4/61): RAF Honington Wing: 12/64:1/65:
RAF Marham: TTF 14/7/65: 232OCU 1/5/70:HP for Mods 19/1/67-14/3/67:
RAF Cosford No 2 S of TT 16/10/74 8428M: SOC 18/4/85:

Victor B1A XH593 TTF RAF Marham 1966. Author's Collection

XH 594

HP for conversion to B1A 22/7/60
First Flight 20/2/61 1040-1210 1.30 (P P Baker)(five HP Test Flights)
RAF Honington 57 Squadron: 23/3/61(27/3/61): RAF Honington Wing 1/64:Repaired on site
by HP CWP/71MU 23/9/63-5/12/63: Flying accident in flight refuelling pipe fractured
flooding cabin 24/1/64 (1180.40hrs) CAT 3 Repair by 71MU and HP CWP: .RAF Gaydon
232 OCU 9/3/65: RAF Marham TTF 22/6/65(23/6/65): HP for Mods 16/11/67:
232 OCU: 1/5/70:
Cat 3 to RAF St Athan 19/2/74. SOC 31/5/74.

Victor B1A XH594 232OCU 1973. Authors Collection

XH 613

First Flight 20/2/59 1430-1515 0.45 (P Murphy) (six HP Test Flights) AwC 27/2/59
HP for conversion to 1st B1A (Retained by HP)
First Flight 30/5/60 1610-1715 1.05 (J W Allam) (five HP Test Flights)
Delivered to 15 Squadron 18/7/60: HP Radlett for repaint 9/11/61:Flying accident 14/6/62:
Fuel failure to all four engines on final approach. SOC 15/6/62. Panel AT Plug failure;
Crew: -Wng/Cdr JG Matthews (Capt): F/O WB Lowther (Co-Pilot): Flt/Lt GB Spencer (Nav
Plot): Flt/Lt BH Stubbs (Nav Rad): Flt/Lt EW Anstead (AEO): Survived.

Victor B1A showing Ground Power and Simstart plugs points. Author's Collection

XH 614
HP for conversion to B1A 30/9/60:
First Flight 6/4/61 1310-1410 1.0 (W R Burton)(seven HP Test Flights)
RAF Honington 55 Squadron 28/4/61: RAF Honington Wing: Flying accident RAF Tengah 24/11/64 Centre Line Closure on Two engines Captain Flt/Lt T Filling. Repaired on site by 390MU ex site 2/4/65: RAF Marham TTF 18/8/65
HP for conversion to BK1A 6/10/66

XH 615
HP for conversion to B1A 11/1/61
First Flight 6/6/61 0855-0900 0.5 (J W Allam) (five HP Test Flights)
RAF Cottesmore: 15 Squadron 29/6/61:8/63:10/63:11/63:2/64:3/64:4/64:6/64:7/64:
RAAF Butterworth 2/64: White finish 17/7/64:
RAF Honington Wing 6/10/64:12/64: 2/65:
HP for conversion to BK1A later B1A (K2P) 10/3/65.

XH 616
HP for conversion to B1A 6/4/61
First Flight 31/8/61 1020-1145 1.25 (H W Rayner)(four HP Test Flights)
RAF Cottesmore: 15 Squadron 19/9/61: Flying accident cabin door came away (14) 24/10/62: Repaired by HP CWP: 15 Squadron: 28/11/62: 15/1/63 To Goose Bay: 16/1/63 Diverted into Niagara Falls Airfield with Electrical Emergency. Departed 22/1/63 To Goose Bay Captain Flt/Lt K Handscomb: 15 Squadron 7/63:8/63:11/63:3/64:4/64:5/64:6/64:8/64:9/64:
RAAF Butterworth 2/64: White Finish 27/7/64:
RAF Honington Wing 22/9/64: RAF Gaydon 232OCU 18/3/65:
RAF Gaydon to RAF Marham: 22/6/65: 57Squadron 8/65: 2/66:
HP for Conversion to BK1A 16/8/66.

XH 618

First Flight 21/7/60 1610-1735 1.25 (H W Rayner)(ten HP Test Flights)
RAF Cottesmore: 15 Squadron 15/8/60: CAT 3 Damage to No.3 Engine Bay hot air leak repaired by 71MU HP and RAE Farnborough.15/4/61- 29/1/61: Flying Accident 4/2/63 Brake fire while taxiing: 15 Squadron 4/3/63:7/63: Low level trials HP Radlett and A&AEE Boscombe Down;(16) 19/9/63-11/5/64: RAF Cottesmore 15 Squadron 10/8/64
HP for conversion to BK1A 14/8/64 Prod TI Aircraft:

XH 619

HP for conversion to B1A 28/11/60:
First Flight 16/5/61 1055-1235 1.40 (P Murphy) (four HP Test Flights)
RAF Honington: 57 Squadron 1/6/61: RAF Honington Wing 12/64-12/65(57 Squadron):
57 Squadron RAF Marham 1/12/65-9/6/66.
HP Radlett for conversion to BK1A 9/6/66.

XH 620

HP for conversion to B1A 19/4/61
First Flight 10/10/61 0945-1110 1.25 (J W Allam)(four HP Test Flights)
RAF Cottesmore: 15 Squadron 27/10/61:10/63: Probe and Drop LE Fit 3/62. :
RAF Honington Wing 4/3/64: Cam 9/64:
HP Radlett for conversion to BK1A later B1A (K2P) 11/2/65

XH 621

First Flight 27/7/59 1505-1605 1.0 (J W Allam) (three HP Test Flights) AwC 31/7/59
Retained by HP for conversion to B1A
First Flight 8/9/60 10.15-11.30 1.15 (H W Rayner) (five HP Test Flights)
RAF Mildenhall 26/9/60 (Delivery By J W Allam and HP Crew)
RAF Honington: 57 Squadron 27/9/60:RAF Honington Wing: 57Sdn: 1/65:2/65:3/65:
Flying accident RAF Tengah-bomb bay tank became detached and burst bomb bay open 10/8/65
4/9/65: CAT3 repaired by HP CWP RAF Honington: 57 Squadron 24/9/65:
HP Radlett for conversion to BK1A 6/10/65:

Layout of A.R.I. 5919 - Red Steer

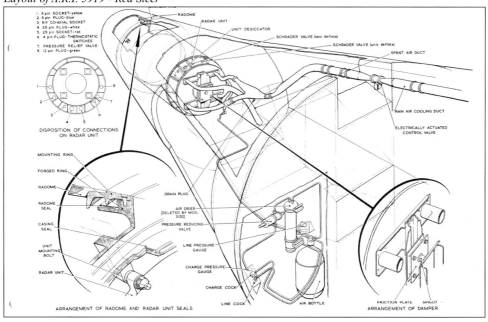

XH 645

HP Radlett for conversion to B1A 27/1/61

First Flight 24/6/61 0845-0930 0.45 (P Murphy) (four HP Test Flights)

RAF Honington: 55 Squadron 12/7/61:RAF Honington Wing: 10/64-11/65 57Sdn:

HP Radlett for conversion to BK1A 1/12/65.

XH 646

First Flight 26/9/59 09.00-10.10 1.10(P.P.Baker)(three HP Test Flights) AwC30/9/59

Retained by HP for Conversion to B1A

First Flight 4/10/60 1605-1720 1.15 (W R Burton) (three HP Test Flights)

RAF Honington: 55 Squadron 24/10/60: RAF Honington Wing 4/64-12/65

HP Radlett for Conversion to BK1A later B1A (K2P) 19/3/65.

Victor B1A XH646 57 Squadron refuelling from a 90 Squadron Valiant 1964. Author's Collection

XH647

First Flight 10/11/59 1055-1210 1.15 (W R Burton)(three HP Test Flights) AwC 19/11/59

Retained by HP Radlett for conversion to B1A

First Flight 3/11/60 1015-1140 1.25 (H W Rayner) (five HP Test Flights) (H W Rayner)

RAF Honington: 57 Squadron 29/11/60: RAF Honington Wing 4/64-1/65:

HP Radlett for conversion to BK1A later B1A (K2P) 16/2/65.

XH648

HP Radlett for Conversion to B1A 24/10/60 (183.25hrs)

First Flight 26/4/61 0910-1040 1.30 (P.P. Baker) (5 HP Test Flights)

RAF Cottesmore 15 Squadron 11/5/61(189.10hrs): 19/7/62 On Air Test U/C U/S (1.05) lost port wing tip landed safely Captain Flt/Lt Keith Hanscomb: 1st Major Servicing RAF Honington 17/9/63 (Due at 800hrs Carried out at 731.45hrs);

RAF Honington Wing 55 Squadron 3/4/64(983.05hrs):

HP Radlett for conversion to BK1A Later B1A (K2P) 15/2/65 (1256.10hrs)

XH649

First Flight 31/12/59 1035-1145 1.10 (P P Baker)(3 HP Test Flights) AwC 8/1/60
Retained by HP Radlett for conversion to B1A 20/1/60
First Flight 28/11/60 1120-1245 1.25 (H W Rayner)(13 HP Test Flights)
RAF Honington 57 Squadron 20/1/61: RAF Honington Wing 2/64-11/64
HP Radlett for conversion to BK1A 5/11/64.

XH 650

First Flight 29/1/60 1130-1205 .35 (P Murphy) (3 HP Test Flights) AwC 5/2/60
Retained by HP Radlett for conversion to B1A
First Flight 29/12/60 1120-1300 1.40 (H W Rayner)(4 HP Test Flights)
RAF Honington 55 Squadron 14/1/61: Ran off Runway at RAF Gaydon 9/62 Cam 9/64: RAF
Honington Wing 2/64-9/64.
HP Radlett for conversion to BK1A 24/9/64.

XH651

HP Radlett for conversion to B1A 13/2/61:
First Flight 18/7/61 0925-1020 .55 (P Murphy) (four HP Test Flights)
RAF Cottesmore: 15 Squadron 10/8/61: 2/62: 1/64:2/64:3/64:4/64:5/64:7/64:8/64:
RAAF Butterworth 2/64: Rtd ex HP Radlett 8/8/64 Camouflage finish:
HP Radlett for conversion to BK1A 9/10/64 MOA 9/1/65-30/6/65.

XH 667

First Flight 28/3/60 1045-1145 1.0 (P P Baker)(one HP Test Flight) AwC 31/3/60
Retained by HP Radlett for Conversion to B1A
First Flight 12/1/61 1200-1400 2.0 (P P Baker)(4 HP Test Flights)
RAF Honington: 57 Squadron 3/2/61: Damage to cables under cabin floor by heat from Hot
Air Ducting Cat 3 Repair by 71MU/HP CWP 19/2/62: RAF Honington Wing: 3/64-1/65:
HP Radlett for conversion to BK1A later B1A (K2P) 11/2/65.

Victor B1A XH620 15 Sdn RAF Cottesmore.

Handley Page Victor Mk BK1A-B1A (K2P) XH615-667

With the demise of the Vickers Valiant Tanker fleet in late December 1964 and January 1965. The Royal Air Force was suddenly left without a Tanker Force to support the Lightnings and the Javelins still in service with the then Fighter Command. There were a number of Victor Mk B1 and B1A aircraft at Handley Page Radlett in the process of being stripped down for conversion to the three-point tanker after the prototype XA918 had flown and completed initial trials. What the RAF needed quickly was an easily converted Tanker that could be produced very quickly and without too many changes that would require a long period of trials at the A&AEE. On 11 February 1965 XH620 and XH667 were delivered to HP Radlett from the RAF Honington Wing to be followed on the 15th by XH648 and on the 16th by XH647. The last two aircraft XH615 and XH646 arrived on the 10 March and the 19th respectively.

The conversion was to consist of fitting two Mark 20B Flight Refuelling Pods under the Port and Starboard wing on Standard RAE 2000lb pylons together with all associated additional piping and electrical services. The fitting of the two control panels and additional instrumentation in Panel C I at the Navigator oblique Radar position. A new VHF/UHF radio, the PTR 175, was fitted to replace the previous VHF installation and the ARC 52 UHF set was retained. Most of the ECM system was removed leaving just the racking cabling and the coolant pipes. Finally the Red Steer installation was removed in total. Two bomb bay tanks and their associated piping were fitted as permanent fittings allowing the aircraft to carry an extra 16,000lb of fuel along with the pannier adaptor in the centre of the bomb bay. The Pod Isolation Cock Control Switches and Indicators were mounted on the top of Panel AW These six aircraft were the only tankers to retain their bomb doors. The bombsight was removed but all the cables stayed for the time being. Finally swivel seats were fitted for the rear crew replacing the original seats that only moved fore and aft. With the swivel seats came the original combined Oxygen/Intercom/Static line system that was to feature in all the Tanker versions of the Victor.

With the CA Release trials being carried out by XA918 in the two-pointer configuration and so obtaining the CA release for these six aircraft meant that there was no need for one initially to spend time at the A&AEE.

The urgent need for a tanker squadron was soon a reality with the first two aircraft delivered to the RAF in April 1965. These aircraft alleviated along with the other four, served the RAF extremely well until the squadron converted to the three-point version in 1967. Once the three pointers had all been delivered these aircraft reverted to the training role with the TTF/OCU usually without pods fitted [XH615, 646 and 647]. Each of the three squadrons was issued with one Victor for day and tanking only Continuation Training and was also used for Lone Ranger training exercises. Victor XH648 went to 55 Squadron, XH620 to 57 Squadron replaced later by XH648 from 55 and XH667 to 214 Squadron. With the change from Mk 1 to Mk 2 conversion training by 232 OCU in 1974 the three squadrons used XH615 and XH647 as required to meet operational tasking. One of the disadvantages of this version was the lack of a night-tanking capability and not being able to refuel other Victors leading to the need to put up two tankers on most occasions as the capacity was also less than the three pointers which were to follow them into service.

Mark BK1A later B1A (K2P) two-point Tankers
XH 615
HP for conversion to BK1A later B1A (K2P) 10/3/65:
First Flight 17/6/65 1445-1610 1.25 (A J Camp) (one HP Test Flight) AwC 18/6/65
RAF Marham: 55 Squadron 21/6/65:HP Radlett for Mods 23/2/67: TTF 16/3/67: 232OCU 1/5/70. Repaired on site by HSA CWP 31/3/71-26/5/71: 23/11/73-12/12/73: 55 Squadron 3/6/74: 232OCU 14/6/74: 55Squadron 23/7/74:214 Squadron 6/9/74:

Station Bull Badge/74
RAF Leeming Fire/Rescue 4/10/74:SOC 5/10/74.
XH 620
HP Radlett for conversion to BK1A later B1A (K2P) 11/2/65
First Flight 15/4/65 1450-1715 1.25 (H W Rayner)(2 HP Test Flights)
RAF Honington 55 Squadron 21/4/65: To RAF Marham 55 Squadron 25/5/65:
HP Radlett 2/67-4/4/67: 57 Squadron 1/5/67: TTF 23/8/67:57 Squadron 25/10/67:
Min Tech/ A&AEE Boscombe Down (5) 8/12/67(Acting as receiver for Tanker Autopilot malfunction while in contact trials):
RAF Marham 57 Squadron 11/12/67: Repaired on site by HP CWP 10/6/71-23/6/71:
232OCU 10/9/73:57 Squadron 30/10/73: 55 Squadron 20/5/74: 57 Squadron 3/6/74:
To RAF St Athan 30/10/75: SOC 24/6/76: Scrapped:

Victor B1A(K2P) XH620 55 Squadron undertaking trials with Lightning. Authors Collection

XH 646
HP Radlett for Conversion to BK1A later B1A (K2P) 19/3/65
First Flight 6/7/65 1425-1630 2.05 (H W Rayner) (3 HP Test Flights) AwC 7/9/65
RAF Marham: 55 Squadron 8/9/65: TTF 20/3/67:HP For Modifications 10/9/67-16/11/67
TTF 16/11/67: HP Radlett 13/5/68-13/6/68:TTF 13/6/68:
Flying accident 19/8/68 approx 22.00hrs collided with Canberra B (I) 6 WT325 213 Squadron over Holt Norfolk 4 killed Flt/Lt WA Galliene (Captain): F/O R S Morton (Co Pilot): Flt/Lt KJ Peacock (Nav Plot): Sdn/Ldr MT Doyle (AEO): SOC 20/8/68

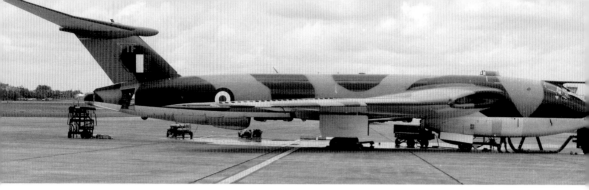

Victor B1A(K2P) XH647 TTF; note no Pods fitted. Author's Collection

XH647

HP Radlett for conversion to BK1A later B1A (K2P) 16/2/65

First Flight 1/6/65 1435-1625 1.50 (P Murphy) (1 HP Test Flight) AwC 1/6/65

RAF Marham: 55 Squadron 3/6/65: TTF 17/1/67: HP for Modifications 8/5/68-3/6/68:
TTF 3/6/68:57 Squadron 7/68-7/69: TTF 7/69-5/70: HP CWP Repair 10/2/72-19/4/72:
232 OCU 5/70-7/7/74: 214 Squadron 8/7/74:232 OCU 29/7/74: 57 Squadron 28/8/74: 232 OCU 30/9/74:

RAF Catterick 25/11/74 Crash Rescue Training RAF Fire School: SOC 26/11/74.

XH648

HP Radlett for conversion to BK1A Later B1A (K2P) 15/2/65 (1256.10hrs)

First Flight 15/5/65 0855-0915. (H W Rayner)(3 HP Test Flights) AwC 19/5/65:

RAF Honington: 55 Squadron 19/5/65(1259.40hrs):

RAF Marham 55 Squadron 25/5/65(1260.15hrs): Carried out 1st RAF Refuelling Victor Sortie from RAF Marham on 28/5/65.Captain Sdn /Ldr Alexander: 2nd Major Servicing (1000hr) 1/9/66 RAF St Athan (1756.25hrs) Rtn RAF Marham 18/11/66: 3rd Major Servicing (1000hr) 5/12/69 RAF St Athan (2763.20 hrs Rtn RAF Marham 30/1/70:4th Major Servicing (1000hr)(250hr ext) 2/10/73 RAF St Athan 3840.40hrs.Rtn RAF Marham 27/11/73:

57 Squadron 23/6/75: Total Flying Hrs 4630.35

IWM Duxford 2/6/76 Captain Sdn/Ldr A Cunnane (flying time .25) Current/Poor Condition:
Final Total on Grounding at IWM 4631.00hrs Repainted Nov 1989. Rolled out 1/4/90:

Victor B1A(K2P) XH648 IWM Duxford 1990 Heather Brooks

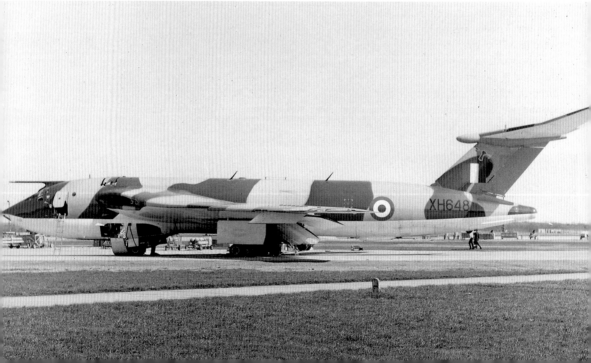

XH667
HP Radlett for conversion to BK1A later B1A (K2P) 11/2/65:
First Flight 28/4/65 1105-1300 1.55 (J W Allam) (2 HP Test Flights)
Delivered RAF Honington 55 Squadron 29/4/65
Carried out first RAF Victor tanking sortie on 7/5/65 from RAF Honington.
RAF Marham 55 Squadron 27/5/65: HP for Modifications14/3/67-26/4/67:55 Squadron
26/4/57: 214 Squadron 1/5/67: Min Tech 16/10/-18/10/68: 214 Squadron 18/10/68:Min Tech
20/8/69-23/9/69:214 Squadron 23/9/69: - 20/9/75:RAF Luqa 22/9/75
Last flight and Dumped Hal Far 23/9/75 SOC 23/9/75 Cockpit only 20/11/98

HP Victor K Mk 1 Series Tanker XA 918-941

Back in 1955 Handley Page proposed that the Victor could be a refuelling tanker aircraft owing to its large capacity bombay . This concept although rather basic was to be the starting point of what was to be the Victor Mk 1 tanker nearly 8 years later. In this version there was only one tank and the hose drum unit however the seed had been sown.

The original decision to use the B Mk1 aircraft as a tanker was taken on 22/11/62 after a study dated 1/3/62 initiated by the then VCAS   indicated that the Victor be a better choice than the Valiant due to its performance being more compatible with the Lightning F3. However the return of them to Handley Page for this conversion work would be delayed for a period of about two years to allow the B Mk 2 version to enter service at RAF Wittering it was decided that the two Cottesmore Squadrons should disband in 1964 and some of their aircraft should be delivered direct to HP Radlett to await their place on the conversion line. Before this the designated three point tanker development aircraft XA918 had been undergoing the conversion process itself from late December 1963 after it had returned from A&AEE Boscombe Down. It was decided to convert 10 aircraft from the XA series to the BK1 version and 14 from the XH series to the BK1A version. The 10 from the XA series were at that time bases at RAF Cottesmore, and Honington, With 10 Squadron some of their aircraft were placed in store at RAF Cottesmore in the care of Victor Storage Flight, these aircraft were maintained to a basic storage level before they were prepared for delivery to HP Radlett, The first aircraft delivered was XA937 as the Production Trials Installation {ProdTI] as it was known was on the 30/4/64 having come from 15 Squadron. Another 9 of this series were to follow over the next 18 months.

The work to convert these 10 aircraft was considerable as in addition to the conversion they had to be brought up to a certain modification standard as near to that of the Mk B1A aircraft as possible from the operational point of view. The bomb doors and their operating system were removed in total [Not sealed or faired over as quoted in many books and

Victor B(K)1 XA918 with 90ft HDU hose trailed. Author's Collection

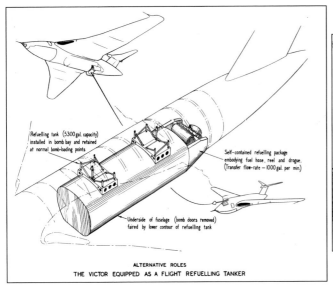

Refuelling tank (5300 gal. capacity) installed in bomb bay and retained at normal bomb-loading points

Self-contained refuelling package embodying fuel hose, reel and drogue. (Transfer flow-rate — 1000 gal. per min.)

Underside of fuselage (bomb doors removed) faired by lower contour of refuelling tank

ALTERNATIVE ROLES
THE VICTOR EQUIPPED AS A FLIGHT REFUELLING TANKER

Flight Refuelling Role 1955 version proposed for the Mk II version. HP-HPA

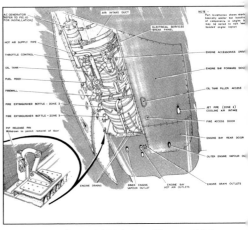

Sapphire 20701 Installation B1A, B1A(K2P), K1, K1A. Author's Collection

Victor B(K)1 XA918 and Belfast XR671 on A&AEE trials. Author's Collection

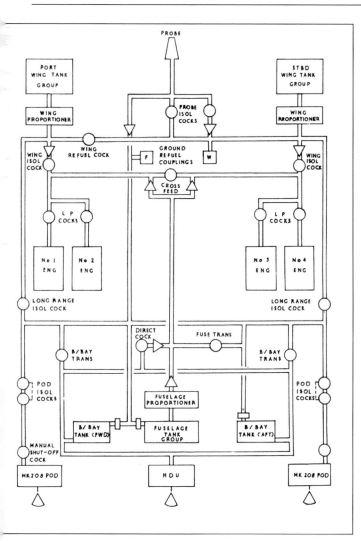

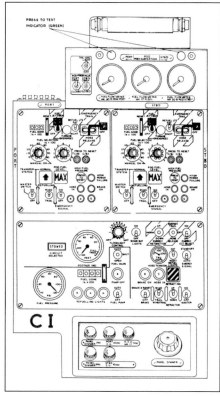

Pod and HDU Control Panel for Mk K1 and K1A Panel CI . Author's Collection

Victor Mk K1 and K1A Fuel System Simplified   Author's Collection

articles.] The bomb door gills at the front of the bomb bay were retained but changed from hydraulic to manual operation for servicing use only. The hydraulic supply system that had been used for the bomb doors was retained and modified to operate using a hydraulic jack being similar to that used on the nose undercarriage to raise and lower the Flight Refuelling Mk 17 Hose Drum Unit [HDU] that was installed at the rear of the bomb bay. In to the bomb bay were fitted two metal fuel tanks suspended from special adaptors that were attached to the stores suspension points that had been built into the Victor from the beginning. These tanks each had five large capacity fuel pumps under a curved fairing at the bottom of each tank which gave it the same shape as the now removed bomb doors together with the fairing panel that fitted over the joint between the tanks. The capacity of these tanks was 15,300lb and when installed nearly filled the bomb bay up leaving about 2 ft clearance from the top of the bomb bay tank to the bottom of the fuselage tanks in the top part of the fuselage. There was a considerable increase in the size and number of fuel pipes in that area as well as more electrically controlled ball valves. With two tanks fitted and the HDU support platform that was used to raise and lower the HDU down into the airflow space was at a premium. Two large access doors just aft of the tanks allowed extra

Panel CI Refuelling Equipment Control K1A. Authors Collection

1	HDU control panel
2	Port Mk. 20B pod control panel
3	Port wing pod temperature gauge
4	Tail nav. light switch
5	Pod pressurisation control switches
6	Starboard wing pod temperature gauge
7	Starboard Mk. 20B pod control panel

Panel CI Key. Authors Collection

space for the servicing of the HDU and access to the top of the tanks fitted in these doors were two of the under wing floodlights used for night tanking. With the HDU fairing going up and down using the old bomb door there was a need for two side easy access doors to complete the exterior of this installation. The new fully integrated fuel system offers the great advantage of permitting the transfer of all the fuel through either the pods or the HDU, or together. The engines were replaced with the Sapphire 20701 and this incorporated the engine-mounted alternators from the B1A conversion [The Auto JPT System modification was not however carried out on the airframes]

In the cabin a number of changes were incorporated, all the rear crew seats were replaced with the swivel seats,

The following equipment was removed [1] Gee, [2] STR18 HF Facilities, [3]. R1985/1986 VHF [4] Intercom.[5] Orange Putter. Leaving just the H2S and the Radio Altimeter MK 6, the Green Satin Doppler Radar with its GPI Mk 4 these were replaced by [1] Collins 618 HF SSB [2] Collins UHF/DF [3] Tacan with Air to Air and Air to Ground facility [4] Twin PTR 175 VHF/UHF R/T facilities [5] UA 60 inter comm system with 6 station boxes. As part of the tanker conversion the fuel system panel known as AT in between the pilots was changed from a sliding version as used by the bomber aircraft to one that swung up and locked down between the pilots and was much easier to use.

When unlocked and swung up it was lock up to brackets adjacent to the P12 Compass it was just under the starter button. The panel layout was changed to accommodate the bomb bay tanks and their switching and the Pod cocks. The undercarriage and flap selectors were removed from the 1st pilots panel AE to Panel A as in the B1A conversion. Rear view mirrors to allow the pilots to see the refuelling pods. A downward rear view periscope with the sighting head mounted on the underside of the nose in front of the Window Box/D Section for observing the Mk 17HDU and the refuelling activities of the wing pods. On Panel CI at the Navigator Radars station was mounted the two Mk 20B Pod Control Panels and the Control Panel for the Mk 17 HDU. On each pylon there were two under wing lights, Either side of the tail bumper wheel there were two more lights and to gether with those on the HDU doors

Victor RAF, Canberra RAAF, Lancaster G-ASSX Flying over Singapore-Malaya May 1965
Author's Collection

these were the under wing lighting to be used during night tanking. The Navigator Radar controlled these from Panel CI. Instead of the separate oxygen hose, intercom cable and separate static line system, a new combined hoses was developed incorporating all these three item in one covering with special quick release valves for the oxygen system and in corpora ting Martin Baker fasteners for the Static Lines and finally the standard intercom connectors.

On the wings fitted at Station 497 was a RAE 2000lb pylon modified for use by the Flight Refuelling Mk 20 Pods along with the necessary piping and power supplies as required. A probe was fitted above the cabin as these had not been fitted to the Mk1 aircraft with the Mk 8 universal nozzle. The aircraft were repainted in Dark Green/Medium Sea Grey upper sides and Gloss White underside.

With all the required conversion work and the embodiment of the various modification being completed. The aircraft was prepared for it Production Test Flights to the agreed schedule and level of testing. These flights were carried out by the Test Pilots and Flight test crews from HP Radlett. The number of flights required depended on the need to refly because of defects or the flight had been shortened because of weather conditions. On completion of this Production Flight Test schedule the aircraft would be cleared by the Testing Crew. The aircraft was then prepared for delivery with all out standing items cleared. The Air Ministry were then advised and details of the delivery flight date advised to HP some times the delivery was by HP Crew but on most occasions a Crew from the relevant RAF Unit would travel to HP Radlett to collect the aircraft and fly it to its new base.

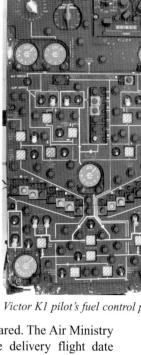

Victor K1 pilot's fuel control panel 'AT'.

Victor K1 AEO electrical control panel.

Of the 10 aircraft delivered to RAF Marham between February 1966 and August 1967 from the Company airfield at Radlett they were initially divided between 57 and 214 Squadrons in that 57 had 2 aircraft and 214 the remaining 8. Although 55 Squadron did have 1 K1 on charge at one time but this was changed with a K 1A allocated to 214 Squadron This situations was to remain virtually that way until 1975 when 55 converted to the K2 version. It was here that aircraft were split up and moved around as the remaining fleet was consolidated and certain aircraft having already been disposed of due to structural failure or having run out of fatigue life. In the end 214 Squadron operated all the remaining K1 and K1A aircraft until the last operational flight by a Mk 1 was on the 21st January 1977 and was carried out by XA937 this having been the first Operational Mk 1 three-point tanker in February 1966.

XA 918
1964
8/7(First Flight Tanker Configuration): 10.30-12.20 1.50(A J Camp)
13/7:14/7:22/7: 29/7(Handling Flights) 27/7(First Flight with Mk20B Pods): 28/8:1/9:2/9: 4/9:7/9: 8/9: 18/9: 22/9: 24/9: 29/9: 1/10: 6/10: 8/10: 10/10: 13/10: 15/10: 19/10: 20/10: (Flight Refuelling Development) 6/10: (HP Radlett to A&AEE Boscombe Down): 8/10: (A&AEE Boscombe Down to HP Radlett): (423.05hrs)
1965
25/1: 26/1: 29/1: 2/2: (Tanker Trials) 2/2: 3/2: 5/2: 9/2: 11/2: 12/2: (Tanker trials at A&AEE Boscombe Down): 12/2 (Rtn to HP Radlett): 22/3(HP Radlett to A&AEE Boscombe Down Tanker Trials en route): 24/3(2): 26/3: 27/3: 29/3 (2): 30/3 (2): (Tanker Trials at A&AEE): 30/3(Rtn to HP Radlett): 12/4 (HP Radlett to A&AEE Boscombe Down) 27/4: 28/4: 29/4:

Victor B(K)1 XA918 Mk 20B Pod with a ten-bladed Ram Air Turbine. HP-HPA

Victor BK1 XA918 with Victor B1 XA930 1966. Author's Collection

30/4: (Tanker CA Release 2 and 3 pointer A&AEE Boscombe Down): 21/5 A&AEE Boscombe Down to HP Radlett)
16/7: 21/730/7:3/8: 4/8: 6/8: 8/8: 9/8: 13/9: 15/9(2): (Tanker Trials): 21/9:(HP Radlett to A&AEE Boscombe Down) 7/10: 18/10: 28/10:3/12:6/12: 8/12: (Flight Refuelling Development at A&AEE): 8/12 (Rtn to HP Radlett) (510.25hrs)
1966
2/8:Air Test): 3/8:4/8: (HP Radlett to RAF Wyton and Night Lighting Assessment with XL161 543 Squadron and XH618 57 Squadron:(4/8): 5/8(RAF Wyton to HP Radlett):
18/8: (Fuel Jettison Test) 19/8:(Air Test): 22/8(HP Radlett to A&AEE Boscombe Down)
23/8: 24/8(Tanker Night Lighting Assessment with Vulcan XM606): 25/8:(Return to HP Radlett): 13/9(2): 16/9(2): 19/9(2)(HP Radlett to RAE Bedford for Fuel Jettison Test Landed HP Radlett:): 12/10(Flight Refuelling Test and Delivery to A&AEE Boscombe Down): 31/10: 2/11:(Flight Refuelling Trials at A&AEE)(531.25hrs)
1967
19/7:(Flight Refuelling and Performance at A&AEE Boscombe Down)(534.50hrs)
1968
26/4(2):(Fuel System Test) 27/5(Fuel Transfer Test: Empty of Bomb Bay tanks in baulked landing climb for residual fuel check): (93 HP Tanker Test Flights)(538.25hrs)
Misc Notes not all verified
Prototype 3 Point Tanker Conversion
Hose trailed at 40,000ft 8/9/64: Pods removed 21/5/65: HDU Investigation 13/9/65
P Murphy: A&AEE Boscombe Down 21/9/65 H Rayner: Fuel Jettison and Hose Oscillation 13/9/66: HDU Drogue fell off: 19/9/66:
SOC 7/70
XA 926
HP for Conversion To K1 17/9/64:
First Flight Tkr 3/3/66 1050-1135 45 min (H Rayner)(5 HP Test Flights):
Delivered RAF Marham 22/3/66: 57 Squadron 23/3/66: 28/6/66:7/66:8/66:
55 Squadron 3/6/74: 57 Squadron 17/6/74 (Oldest Mk1 Tanker):
To RAF St Athan 26/5/76 SOC 22/11/76: Extant 9/77

Victor K1 XA926 57 Squadron at RAF Abingdon for the Queens Review the RAF 1968. Author's Collection

Victor K1 XA927 214 Squadron wearing three versions of grey undersides for trials purpose in 1971. Author's Collection

XA 927
HP for Conversion to K1 17/9/64:
First Flight Tkr 12/8/66 1135-1350 2.15 Hrs (E R Thompson)(6 HP Test Flights)
Delivered RAF Marham 3/10/66: 214 Squadron 4/10/66: Grey Undersides 8/71:Repainted White undersides: Cat 3 Repair 7/8/73 Cart Spring By HSA CWP RAF Marham.
Flight trials /74
To RAF St Athan SOC 1/2/77:Extant 9/77.

XA 928
HP for Conversion to K1 10/9/64:
First Flight Tkr 12/1/66 1205-1410 2.05 Hrs (H Rayner)(8 HP Test Flights):
Delivered to RAF Marham 1/3/66: 57 Squadron 2/3/66:7/66:8/66-7/76:
(CWP Repair 5/8/70-19/1/71)
214 Squadron 9/8/76:
To RAF St Athan 15/12/76 SOC 16/12/76.

Victor K1 XA928 57 Squadron refuelling Lightning F3 XR761 5 Squadron 1966 Authors Collection

XA 930
Delivered to HP Radlett for Conversion to K1 10/5/66:
First Flight Tanker 10/3/67: 1545-1730 1.45hrs (G Moreau) (7 HP Test Flights)
Delivered to RAF Marham 31/3/67: 55 Squadron 3/4/67:214 Squadron 1/8/67:

Victor K1 XA928 57 Squadron, u/s pod on trolley under the port wing, 1971. Author's Collection

Delivered to HP Radlett 14/3/68-5/6/68(29/5/68) Fuel Transfer Test: Rtn to RAF Marham 214 Squadron 7/6/68: 7/73
CAT 3 7/73 Spar Cracks Spar3/Rib 212 (Cart Spring)
Stored RAF Marham
To RAF St Athan 9/7/74 (Flt/lt JA Brown)
SOC 17/4/75.

Victor K1 XA930 55 Squadron Air Refuelling Trials with F4M Phantom No 1 in USA. Douglas Photo

XA 932
HP for Conversion to K1 2/9/66.
First Flight Tkr. 23/6/67 1310-1330 20 min (P Murphy)(7 HP Test Flights)
Delivered to RAF Marham 10/8/67: 214 Squadron 11/8/67(22/8/67):
Foam Landing RAF Manston 8/7/68 Suspect Port U/C failure No Damage:
Cat 3 3/8/73 Cart Spring repair by HSA CWP RAF Marham Static Display RAF Marham 8517M 14/1/77(2/2/77) Cat 5 Components: STCVSS charge 77-82 Scrapped 10/86.
Removed from Dump 11/87-

Victor K1 XA932 214 Squadron 1976 Author's Collection Via Graeme Rodgers New Zealand

Victor K1 XA936 214 Squadron in Hangar at RAF Goose Bay Labrador 1973. Tony Cunnane Photo

XA 936
HP for Conversion to K1. 11/1/65:
First Flight Tkr 8/9/66 1125-1230 1.05 Hrs (M Thompson)(10 HP Test Flights) Delivered to RAF Marham 28/11/66:214 Squadron 30(29)/11/66: B Type Roundel Grey undersides/Matt finish 15/8/72:
To RAF St Athan 23/6/76: SOC 20/9/76.

XA 937
HP for conversion to K1 30/4/64: Prod TI Aircraft
First Flight Tkr 2/11/65 1020-1100 40 min (P Murphy)(7 HP Test Flights)
Delivered to MOA A&AEE Boscombe Down: 26/11/65:HP Radlett 10/1/66:
Delivered to RAF Marham from A&AEE Boscombe Down 14/2/66 Radio/ECM/Radar Compatibility Tests: Captain Flt Lt D Bywater A&AEE Test Pilot 57 Squadron 15/2/66:7/66:9/66: 214 Squadron 3/10/66(11/12/66) 12/66:HP Radlett 22/8/67-25(23)/10/67: 214 Squadron 25/10/67:
Last Operational Mk 1 Tanker Flight for RAF and 214 Squadron 27/1/77:
To RAF St Athan 7/2/77: SOC 7/2/77. Extant 9/77: P&EE Foulness 24/10/78: 3/88:8/89:1/92: 1/94 Disposed of under Tender T1025

Victor K1 XA937 214 Squadron 1967. Author's Collection

Victor K1 XA937 landing after the last operational flight of a Mk1 Victor on 27 January 1977. Author's Collection

Victor K1 XA937 214 Squadron at RAF Laarbruch January 1975 for 15 Squadron s 60th Anniversary. Author's Photo his last Mk 1 Victor Lone Ranger

XA 938
HP for Conversion to K1 30/4/64:(12/10/64)
First Flight tanker 22/7/66 1115-1225 1.10 hrs. (H Rayner)(six HP Test Flights)
Delivered to RAF Marham 27/9/66:214 Squadron 28/9/66:10/66:11/66:12/66:
Mod PE RAE Farnborough 12/9/76 (Flew in 29/9/76) SOC and to P&EE Foulness 24/10/78:
Pendine Ranges (Nr Tenby) Fuselage sectioned 2/88-7/91
Scrapped Feb/Mar94

Victor K1 XA938 214 Squadron RAF Tengah. Author's Collection

XA 939
HP for Conversion to K1 8/10/64
First Flight Tkr 24/6/66 0935-1130 1.55hrs (A J Camp). (nine HP Test Flights)
MOA A&AEE 5/7/66: Delivered to RAF Marham 18/11/66:214 Squadron 28(22)/11/66 /67:/68-73 and 12/73-3/76:
CAT 3 1/2/73-20/12/73 Spar 3/Rib 212 Cart Spring Repair by HSA CWP RAF Marham.
To RAF Catterick Fire School 29/3/76: SOC 29/3/76.

Victor K1 XA939 214 Squadron 1974. Author's Collection

Victor K1 XA941 214 Squadron Landing at RAF Luqa Malta May 1973 Author's Collection

XA 941
HP for Conversion to K1 20/12/65:
First Flight Tkr 29/9/66 1315-1455 1.40 Hrs (P Murphy) (five HP Test Flights)
Delivered to RAF Marham 16/12/66:214 Squadron 19/12/66:
CAT 3 3/6/73 Spar 3 Rib 212 Cracked: Investigation by CWP
Stored RAF Marham until 15/8/74:
To RAF St Athan 15/8/74 NEA SOC 22/11/74.

Handley Page Victor Mk BK1A-K1A XH587-651
The Valiant as a refuelling tanker was very limited not only by the aircraft's operational capability but also that of the Mk16 Hose Drum Unit (HDU). The aircraft could only refuel 1 aircraft at a time and with the need to refuel 2 Lightning's regularly as they were rather poor on range it was not really suitable. If the HDU failed then the receivers would have no alternative facility available and there was a great risk in that aircraft would have to divert to the nearest airfield that was suitable or be ditched into the sea. The need for a tanker with at least three points would help greatly and enable the process to be far more flexible. The Royal Navy on its Scimitars and Sea Vixens had used the Mk 20A-refuelling pod since the early 1960's, quite successfully. The Mk 1A Victors of the second production batch XH Series were due to be phased out of service in the medium bomber role in 1965 as the Mk 2 aircraft came in to service in the Blue Steel role. Of those remaining in service with 55, 57 Squadrons and 232OCU 23 were available for use in the tanker role conversion of these 14 were in fact selected for that purpose as three point tankers, 6 were to end up as two point tankers and 3 were relegated to the aircraft conversion role

The lucky 14 were flown to Handley Page Radlett in stages as required and temporary placed in storage prior the company starting the conversion program on them. The prototype of this three point tanker was XA918 an ex trials aircraft and had been under conversion since early 1964. The conversion program for the Mk 1A aircraft was started with XH618 which was the production Trails Installation (Prod TI) aircraft This involved the removal of the bomb bay doors and their associated systems, the removal of all the bombing equipment, the removal of the inter-comm system the VHF/UHF radios Gee,

Rebecca, the ECM system with its Vapour Cycle Cooling Pack and its associated piping The Red Steer rear warning radar was no longer required. Swivel seats replaced the rear crew seats. The Sapphire 20701 engines were retained and minor modifications carried out. Into the bomb bay went two rigid metal tanks suspended from a suspension frames that were in them selves attached to the original bomb carrier suspension points. The tanks were large enough to carry 15,300lb of fuel each, these tanks were fitted with 5 large capacity booster pumps and the output of them was connected to a gallery piping on the undersides of each tank. The output from the tanks acting as a collector tank with fuel flowing in from the wings and fuselage supplying the Hose Drum Unit the Mk 20B Pods or the engines fuel system. Fitted at the rear of the bomb bay was the Mk 17 Hose drum unit. This unit was fitted to the HDU platform that incorporated a scissor shackle suspension system that allowed the equipment with its associated fairing to be lowered into the airflow. Mk 20B pods and their associated RAE pylons were fitted to the outer wings. The associated piping and various services were fitted in the leading edge the control panels being located on Panel CI at the Navigators Position. On each pylon there were two under wing lights, Either side of the tail bumper wheel there were two more lights and to gether with those on the HDU doors these were the under wing lighting to be used during night tanking. The Navigator Radar controlled these from Panel CI. Instead of the separate oxygen hose, intercom cable and separate static line system, a new combined hoses was developed incorporating all these three item in one covering with special quick release valves for the oxygen system and in corporating Martin Baker fasteners for the Static Lines and finally the standard intercom connectors.

Changes in the cabin to the instrumentation were less than the XA series conversions the main one apart from the various avionics were the change to the fuel control panel or Panel AT, as it was known. This item had previously been a sliding panel however with the change in role it was made to hinge up and down. In the up position it was held by brackets adjacent to the P12 compass and just under the engine starting panel and when down it was much lower and easier to operate. Changes to the layout came from the introduction of the bomb bay fuel system controls and the pod cocks. The control Panels for the pods and the HDU were fitted into panel CI for use by the Navigator Radar. A downward rear view periscope with the sighting head mounted on the underside of the nose in front of the Window Box/D Section for observing the Mk 17HDU and the refuelling activities of the wing pods. Twin VHF/UHF Radio type PTR 175 were fitted as was a UA60 inter comm system, TACAN, UDF and a Collins 618T HF Radio were also fitted. There were various other modifications and updates to the aircrafts systems.

The aircraft were painted in Dark Green Medium Sea Grey upper side and White Gloss under sides before delivery the relevant operational markings being added after delivery

With all the required conversion work and the embodiment of the various modification being completed. The aircraft was prepared for it Production Test Flights to the agreed schedule and level of testing. The Test Pilots and Flight test crews from HP Radlett carried out these flights. The number of flights required depended on the need to refly because of defects or the flight had been shortened because of weather conditions. On completion of this Production Flight Test schedule the aircraft would be cleared by the Testing Crew.

The aircraft was then prepared for delivery with all out standing items cleared. The Ministry of Defence were then advised and details of the delivery flight date advised to HP some times the delivery was by HP Crew but on most occasions a crew from the relevant RAF Unit would travel to HP Radlett to collect the aircraft and fly it to its new base.

On arrival from HP Radlett the aircraft would then be taken into the hangars and under the control of the Aircraft Servicing Flight under go the Acceptance Servicing and fitting it with the Avionics and other equipment that was not supplied through Handley Page. The Squadron markings would be applied to both sides of the tail fin. There were line up markings for the pods added under the wings in the region of the pylons and for the Hose Drum Unit on the HDU Fairing and the undersides of the aft Bombay tank. All the flying controls, Hydraulics and flying controls were tested. Full engine ground runs were also carried out along with the electrical systems. The aircraft was then handed to the Squadron Crew chiefs for the Compass Swing to be carried out in conjunction with the Navigators The final task and last of all a Air Test by the Squadron QFI or Pilot Leader. The aircraft was then available for operational use in any part of the world.

Of the 14 aircraft delivered to RAF Marham between March 1966 and August 1967 from the Company airfield at Radlett they were initially divided between 57 and 55 Squadrons in that 57 had 6 aircraft 55 the remaining 8. This was to remain that way until 1975 when 55 converted to the K2 version. It was here that aircraft were split up and moved around as the remaining fleet was consolidated and certain aircraft had been already were disposed of due to structural failure or having run out of fatigue life.

Victor BK1A-K1A XH587-XH651

XH 587
HP for conversion to K1A 6/10/64
First Flight Tkr 12/4/66 1520-1645 1.25 (A J Camp) (4 HP Test Flights) AwC 24/4/66
RAF Marham 57 Squadron 29/4/66:7/66:8/66:9/66-7/73:Cat 3 1/8/73
To RAF St Athan 16/7/74 NEA SOC 17/4/75.

Victor K1A XH587 57 Squadron at RAAF Butterworth after taking part in a large refuelling exercise to the Far East in 12/69. Authors Collection

XH 588
HP for conversion to K1A 25/11/65
First Flight Tkr 10/11/66 1505-1610 1.05 (M Thompson) (7 HP Test Flights)
RAF Marham 214 Squadron 12/12/66:55 Squadron 26/1/67(1/8/67) 57 Squadron 23/6/75
Repair on site by HP CWP 21/2/67: 5/5/67Re-designated K1A)
RAF Machrihanish Fire and Rescue Training 28/7/75 SOC 30/7/75.

Victor K1A XH588 55 Squadron 1970. Author's Collection

XH 589
HP for Conversion to K1A 12/7/66:
First Flight Tkr 7/4/67 1140-1230 .50 (M Thompson)(7 HP Test Flights)
RAF Marham: 55 Squadron 28/4/67: 57 Squadron 11/3/74: 55 Squadron 25/3/74:
214 Squadron 25/6/75:Repaired on site by HSA CWP 30/11/70-24/11/72: 23/10/73-20/11/73:
RAF St Athan 6/5/76: Fire and Rescue Training:
RAF St Athan 9/7/76: SOC 10/7/76: Scrap 1978.

XH 590
HP for conversion to K1A 1/12/65
First Flight Tkr 6/12/66 1225-1400 1.35 (A J Camp) (6 HP Test Flights)
RAF Marham: 55 Squadron 12/1/67(16/1/67): 57 Squadron 25/2/74:
55 Squadron 11/3/74:Repaired on site by HSA CWP 14/9/70-19/2/71:
RAF Manston Fire School 2/7/75: SOC 3/7/75. Still not Burnt 7/87:
Scrap 9/93:

Victor K1A XH590 55 Squadron with Sea Vixen and Buccaneer. HPA

Victor K1A XH591 55 Squadron at Dubai August 1973. HPA

XH 591
HP for conversion to K1A 13/7/66
First Flight Tkr 15/4/67 1005-1140 1.35 (J W Allam)(5 HP Test Flights)
RAF Marham: 55 Squadron 1/5/67: Min Tech 17/9/68: HP Radlett -21/11/68-24/11/68:
55 Squadron 24/11/69(24/11/68): 57 Squadron 23/6/75: 214 Squadron 4/6/76:
To RAF St Athan 5/11/76 SOC 5/11/76: Scrapped 1978:

XH 614
HP for conversion to K1A 6/10/66
First Flight Tkr 21/7/67 1335-1535 2.0 (G Moreau) (8 HP Test Flights)
Delivered to RAF Marham 14/8/67: 55 Squadron 16/8/67:A&AEE Boscombe Down26/9/67-
21/12/67: 55 Squadron 2(4)/1/68: Repair on site by HP/ HSA CWP 4/1/70-1/12/70: 214
Squadron25/2/74:55 Squadron 8/4/74: Repaired on site by 71MU/HSA CWP 31/5/74-8/8/75:
214 Squadron 23/6/75:
RAF St Athan SOC 7/9/76. Scrapped 1977.

*Victor K1A XH614 and XH645 55 Squadron with K1 XA927 214 Squadron on 'E' Dispersal
RAF Akrotiri 1971* Authors Collection via Tony Cunnane

XH 616
HP for Conversion to K1A 16/8/66:
First Flight Tkr 16/5/67 1445-1605 1.20 (P Murphy)(6 HP Test Flights)
Delivered HP Radlett-RAF Marham 12/6/67 57 Squadron 14/6/67: Min Tech 25/7/67:
57 Squadron 8/67:- -15/1/76:
To RAF St Athan 19/1/76 SOC 20/1/76:(RAF Manston).

Victor K1A XH616 57 Squadron with 2 Lightning F6 with over wing tanks. HPA

XH 618

HP for conversion to K1A 14/8/64 Prod TI Aircraft:
First Flight Tkr 7/12/65 1010-1215 2.05 (J W Allam) (8 HP Test Flights)
MOA 12/1/66: Delivered 24/2/66 HP Radlett-RAF Marham (H W Rayner HP+3)
57 Squadron 2/3/66: MOA/A&AEE Boscombe Down3/5/66-21/6/66: 30/6/66-12/8/66
4/8/66 Refuelling Trials RAF Wyton: 57 Squadron 15/8/66: 9/66:
RAF Marham-HP Radlett for Mods, 19/10/67-18/12/67.
Test Flown 14/12/67: 57 Squadron 19/12/67-3/75: Flying Accident 24/3/75 collisions with
208 Squadron Buccaneer S2A XV156 over North Sea. SOC (25) 24/3/75:
Captain Flt./Lt. K Handscomb: (Survived):
Flt/Lt D.H. Crowther: Flt/Lt PJL Slatter (AEO): F/O TP Evans: F/O JA Price (Killed).

Victor K1A XH618 57Squadron 1972. Authors Collection via Alan Fisher

Victor K1XH618 57Squadron at AAEE carrying out Belfast Trials. Authors Collection via Alan Fisher

XH 619

HP Radlett for conversion to K1A   9/6/66:

First Flight Tkr 24/2/67 1545-1735 1.50 (P Murphy)(3 HP Test Flights)

Collected by RAF Marham Crew 12/4/67: 55 Squadron 20/4/67:HP Radlett 19/8/68-13/11/68 for refurbishment: 214 Squadron 8/8/73:

Awaiting Disposal 21/6/75 SOC 7/75: Cat 5 Burnt 1/77: Removed 16/1/78.

Victor K1A   XH619 and XH645 55 Squadron at RAF Tengah Singapore 16/12/69 5 Squadron Lightning's [Note the amount of fuel going into the aircraft] Authors Collection

Victor K1A XH619 214 Squadron awaiting disposal 1975 [Authors Aircraft 1973-75]

First and second pilot's position Victor B1A(K2P) XH648 at the IWM Duxford. Heather Brooks.

Navigator Radars Position. Heather Brooks

AEO Position. Heather Brooks.

Navigator Radars Position showing Pod Control Panels. Heather Brooks

Aft bomb bay tank. Heather Brooks

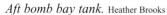

Forward bomb bay tank. Heather Brooks

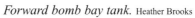

XH 621
HP Radlett for conversion to K1A 6/10/65:
First Flight Tkr 17/10/66 0955-1220 2.25 (H W Rayner) (5 HP Test Flights)
RAF Marham: 57 Squadron 30/11/66(2/12/66): Repaired on site by HSA CWP 8/10/70-9/8/71 214 Squadron 2/6/76.
To RAF St Athan 3/12/76 SOC 22/12/76 Scrapped.

Victor K1A XH621 57 Squadron 1971. Author's collection

XH 645
HP Radlett for conversion to K1A 1/12/65
First Flight Tkr 30/12/66 1230-1400 1.30 (G Moreau)(4 HP Test Flights)
RAF Marham: 55 Squadron 23/1/67-8/73: CAT 3 1/8/73 spar bolthole damage
To RAF St Athan 14/2/74 Spares Recovery SOC 9/9/74: Scrapped:

Victor K1A XH645 55 Squadron 1971 on final approach. Author's collection

XH649
HP Radlett for conversion to BK1A 5/11/64
First Flight Tkr24/5/66 0835-1045 2.10 (A J Camp)(3 HP Test Flights)
Delivered 9/6/66 RAF Marham: 57 Squadron 16(10)/6/66:9/66.
17/7/67 Min Tech: 57 Squadron 18/7/67-25/7/76.
To RAF St Athan 10/11/75 SOC 27/7/76:

Victor K1A XH649 with two Lightnings of 74 Squadron 1967. Author's collection

Victor K1A XH649 with F100 from USAF RAF Lakenheath 1967. Author's collection

XH667 and XH648 Tanking 111Squadron F3 Lightnings 8-65   Authors Collection

Victor B1A(K2P) XH667 214 Squadron 1974 Pods Fitted Authors Collection

Victor K1A XH651 55 Squadron 1971 Lightning on centre hose. Author's collection

XH 650

HP Radlett for conversion to BK1A 24/9/64:
First Flight Tkr 2/2/67 1225-1400 1.45   (P Murphy) (6 HP Test Flights)
Delivered RAF Marham 22/2/67(J W Allam and HP Crew): 55 Squadron 23/2/67
214 Squadron 22/4/74: 55 Squadron 20/5/74: Repaired on site by HSA CWP 6/74-10/7/74:
55 Squadron 12/7/74 214Squadron 23/6/75:
To RAF Manston Fire School 12/2/76: SOC 13/2/76

Victor K1A XH650 57 Squadron awaiting crew up 1974. Author's collection

XH651

HP Radlett for conversion to BK1A 9/10/64 MOA 9/1/65-30/6/65:
First Flight Tkr 21/6/66 0945-1125 1.40 (M Thompson) (6 HP Test Flights)
Delivered to RAF Marham 17(13)/7/66: 57 Squadron 13/7/66:
Cat 3-cart spring repair by HSA CWP RAF Marham 1/8/73-1974:
214 Squadron 2/6/76: To RAF St Athan 26/1/77: SOC 27/1/77.

Victor K1 XA938 RAE Farnborough 1978. Author's collection

Victor B1A(K2P) XH667 at RAF Gan 1973. Tony Cunnane